Daily Strength for Daily Living

(Volume One)

183 Devotional Meditations from the
Old Testament

Denis A. Wheadon

Authors On Line

Visit us online at www.authorsonline.co.uk

An Authors OnLine Book

ISBN 0 7552 0279 1
ISBN 978-0-755202-79-9

Authors OnLine Ltd
19 The Cinques
Gamlingay, Sandy
Bedfordshire SG19 3NU
England

This book is also available in e-book format, details of which are available at www.authorsonline.co.uk

It should be noted that frequent references will be made to the Authorised [King James] Version of the Bible through these devotional meditations. This is because the majority were originally based on this version. However, this will only occur when a greater emphasis is required than that found in the NIV, or where additional clarity is required, and the modern abbreviation – KJV – will be used.

By the Same Author

Published by Evangel Press, London

Twice A Day – *A Book of Devotions* (1976)
Once A Day – *Daily Devotions* (1978)
A New and Living Way – *A Devotional Meditation* (1979)
Daily Strength for Daily Needs – *100 Shorter Devotions* (1982)
Good Morning…The Bible Says – *Broadcast Talks* (1986)

Published by The Open Bible Trust [UK]

The Land of Spiritual Experience – A Devotional Meditation on *Deuteronomy* (1990)
A Full Reward – *Devotional Meditation on Ruth* (1991)

Published jointly by The Open Bible Trust [UK] and Grace Publications Inc [USA]

In My Father's House – *A Devotional Meditation on John's Gospel, Chapters 13-17* (1994)
Cameos in Colossians – *A Devotional Meditation on the Epistle to the Colossians* (1997)

Published jointly by The Open Bible Trust [UK] and Bible Search Publications Inc [USA]

In The Beginning – *A Study of Genesis, Chapter 1:1-5* (2001)

Published by PlaneTree Publishing Ltd

Back To Basics (2005)
A New and Living Way – *an updated and expanded version of the original published in 1979* (2005)
Grappling With Grace (2005)
In All Thy Ways – *A Christian Novel* (2006)

Republished by AuthorsOnLine Ltd

Back To Basics (2006)
A New and Living Way (2006)
Grappling With Grace (2006)
In All Thy Ways (2006)

Published by AuthorsOnLine Ltd

Daily Strength for Daily Living: Volume One – *183 Devotional Meditations from the Old Testament* (2007)
Daily Strength for Daily Living: Volume Two – *183 Devotional Meditations from the New Testament* (2007)

Introduction

Daily Strength for Daily Living comes in two volumes – *Volume One* (Old Testament) and *Volume Two* (New Testament) – and is a collection of devotional meditations taken from over fifty years of devotional ministry, many given as devotional talks over a period of twenty-two years in the Christian hotel on the south coast of England for which my wife and I were responsible until our retirement in 1993. It was my privilege to minister the Word of God morning and evening during the summer months, and in the morning only at other times. Subsequently, by popular demand, some of these talks, together with some additional radio talks, were produced in book form.

Twice A Day was published in 1976, followed by *Once A Day* in 1978. Because the demand was so great, two more books followed, *A New and Living Way* in 1979 and *Daily Strength for Daily Needs* in 1982. Then, in 1983, this ministry of the Word was extended to local radio where, for the next nine years I contributed to the "Pause Awhile" feature, a short morning talk from the Bible. Many of these were brought together in another book, *Good Morning...the Bible Says*, published in 1986, the title of which was taken from the phrase with which I began all my broadcast talks.

Sadly, all five books are now out of print, yet it would appear from frequent requests received since our retirement that there is still a demand for these talks in printed form; a demand which could not be met – until now! *Daily Strength for Daily Living, Volumes One and Two* are published by AuthorsOnLine in an attempt to meet that demand. In addition to the previously published material, there is much that, up to now, has not been published, some from the "hotel" and "radio" era, and some from the weekly *Pause for Thought* feature written every week for our local church bulletin, of which I was the editor from 1994 to 2004. In addition, some have been especially written for these two volumes.

There are several ways in which these two books can be used. I have known these talks to be used in women's meetings when members are asked to contribute short items during a member's afternoon, for example; but their original purpose was to provide a daily devotional message. Although the talks in these books are not dated, they do lend themselves to being used as daily devotional reading books if so desired. In the two books there are actually sufficient meditations to cover a whole year – even a leap year!

If the reader is considering using these books as daily devotions, it is worth noting the comment someone made concerning *Good Morning...the Bible Says*, using it for regular morning devotions. "When you get to the end you forget what you read at the beginning, so you start all over again and it comes up fresh each day!" That book only covered four months of readings; how much fresher the talks will be when, using the two volumes of *Daily Strength for Daily Living*, they are repeated after twelve months! It may be that you will never need to buy another book of daily devotional readings ever again!

Although the texts and references within the talks are taken from the popular New International Version [NIV] unless otherwise stated, any reputable modern translation can be used for reference. This is really a matter of personal choice.

It is, therefore, my prayer that you, the reader, will be richly blessed as you begin each day with the Word of God, if indeed this is the use to which you are going to put these books, and that you will meet Jesus Christ time and time again as He gives you *Daily Strength for Daily Living*.

Denis A. Wheadon
Bournemouth

Author's Note

As it appeared in *Daily Strength for Daily Needs* published in 1982, "One Hundred Devotional Meditations from the Author's Daily Ministry", the format on which these two volumes of *Daily Strength for Daily Living* is based.

The uses to which this book of Devotional Meditations may be put are many. Some suggestions are included here to enable the reader to obtain the greatest benefit from its pages according to his or her circumstances.

Originally forming part of the author's daily ministry to a company of the Lord's people meeting daily to share God's Word, each devotional thought included here may be taken as a supplementary meditation before or after the reader's regular Bible reading. On the other hand, if it encourages more regular reading of the Bible, then this can be taken as an added bonus!

From time to time the reader may be called upon to provide "a little reading" at the weekly Women's Meeting or other mid-week meeting. The short devotions in this book may be of just sufficient length to meet this requirement.

For a busy preacher seeking inspiration for a sermon, sometimes a simple thought expressed may be the very springboard from which to launch out on his period of preparation. It is possible that contained within these pages there may well be one hundred such springboards!

The pastoral visitor requiring a short additional meditation to add to his Bible reading, perhaps at the bed-side of a sick person who cannot "take in" a lengthy oration, may find this book a valuable companion to keep with him.

The busy housewife with her husband off to work and the children away to school, may find value in a few minutes' daily meditation before tackling all the usual chores around the house.

The senior citizen living alone, needing a little spiritual strength to see the day through, or even several such moments during the day as time permits, may find value in these pages, too.

Many people have expressed their gratitude to God for the help and blessing they have received from Him through the ministry of these devotions. Whatever use may be found in them by the reader, they are published here with the hope that they will reach a much wider audience through the written word, and with the simple but sincere prayer that they will provide…

DAILY STRENGTH FOR DAILY NEEDS.

Bournemouth 1981

OF PRESENT INTEREST

Author's Note

For these two volumes of *Daily Strength for Daily Living.*

It will be noted through these pages that the use of the words "I" and "you" are very sparse, but the words "we" and "us" are frequently used. This is deliberate, because I do not want to create the impression that I am telling people what to do! That is definitely not my intention. I believe it is vitally important to follow the maxim that we are in this together, that we are seeking for *daily strength for daily living* together. After all, I believe God is speaking to me through these pages just as much as He is, I hope, speaking to you.

Not one hundred devotional meditations, as in the 1982 *Daily Strength for Daily Needs*, but three-hundred-and-sixty-six devotional meditations in these two volumes of *Daily Strength for Daily Living*. Whatever use may be found in them by the reader, they are published here with the hope that they will reach a much wider audience through the written word, and with the simple and sincere prayer that they will provide…

DAILY STRENTH FOR DAILY LIVING.

Bournemouth 2007

Daily Strength for Daily Living
Volume 1 – Old Testament

1

Genesis 1:1 – In the beginning God created the heavens and the earth.

If we were given an old book entitled *The Lighting of Houses with Candles and Oil Lamps*, what do you think we would do with it? Would we throw it away because it is out of date? After all, we have had electricity for many years now! On the other hand, would we keep it for amusement because of its antiquarian value? Unfortunately, the Bible sometimes gets treated in this way, even by Christians, especially the first book, *Genesis*, which describes the creation of the universe in a very unscientific way – at least, according to modern astronomers and geologists and their account of the earth's beginnings and the solar system. What shall we do, then? Reject the whole Bible because of this unscientific description of its first chapter? Or should we keep it for amusement because of its antiquarian value? *Both would be wrong!*

We are expecting from the Bible what it cannot be expected to give. We are asking the wrong questions! The purpose of the Bible is not to tell us specifically about creation. It is to tell us specifically about the Creator. It is not the earth in the beginning but God in the beginning. The writer of *Genesis* gives us as true an account of the earth's beginnings as his limited knowledge allowed, but it was not his *primary* aim. His purpose was to record the revelation of God which he had, using the imperfect unscientific knowledge of that day. What was God to do, anyway? Wait until modern astronomers and geologists enlightened us scientifically before He revealed Himself as Creator? Of course not!

Throughout the Bible God reveals Himself to humble mankind in humble circumstances, as we are able to understand. God is not teaching us through the Bible about science or astronomy. God is teaching us through the Bible about God! So if we want to read about the universe, a good book on astronomy will help us. If we want to learn about the earth, a good book on geology will help us. If we want to learn about God, then the Bible will help us. Let us accept the Bible for what it is, God's Inspired Word concerning Himself – it is the Word of Life, vital to our every day living. So, day by day, let us seek the Lord, the Living Word, as He gives us *daily strength for daily living.*

2

Genesis 1:16 – God made two great lights…He also made the stars.

We have already said that God is not teaching us about science or astronomy in the Bible, but about Himself. We are not concerned with the *precise* mechanics of creation. No one can be *absolutely certain*, anyway, for only the Triune God was present "in the beginning". Man was not created until the sixth day! The Bible account is good enough for us, and reading through the account of the fourth day of creation, we will be blessed and encouraged by one simple little phrase. This verse tells us that God made two great lights.

All through the history of mankind God has used "great lights" to fulfil His purposes – through Bible history, people such as Abraham, Isaac, Joseph, Moses, Ruth, Esther, and so on; through Church history, people like Martin Luther, the Wesley's, C. H. Spurgeon, William Booth, Billy Graham, the list is endless! Through the years these "great lights" have shone like beacons at specific points mapped out by God in guiding His Church along. But, we may say, how can this bless and encourage us? It is doubtful if we will ever be classified as "great lights", that our names will go down in history, appear in some headline, go up in lights, feature on television, or even become famous or well known outside our family or church circle. So what real use can we be to God compared to the "great lights" of this world?

The answer is in the phrase at the end of the verse. The Bible says God *"also made the stars"*. He needs and uses "great lights", but He needs and uses the "little stars" also! He needs us and will use us if we let Him. We must not underestimate the "little stars", for the ancient travellers used to set their course, not by the sun or moon, the "two great lights", but by the stars. It was a star that led the Wise Men to the Infant Jesus. All through the history of mankind, through the history of His Church, God has used His "little stars" – the lesser lights!

There is a place in God's Plan for the "great lights", but there is also a very important place for the lesser lights, the "little stars". We can take heart and find encouragement in this fact. We may never make the headlines, our names may never go down in history, we may never become famous, but let us always remember that God *"also made the stars"*, just ordinary people to be useful for Him – people just like us!

3

Genesis 13:14 – Lift up your eyes from where you are and look.

Some people are never satisfied. Somehow they can never be content just where they are. They seem to adopt the old attitude that the grass is always greener on the other side of the fence. Indeed, their stock phrase very often is, "If only..." If only I didn't live where I do things would be so much different. But would they? This verse is a message for Christians and non-Christians alike. These are the words of God to the Old Testament character, Abraham, and He is telling him to look from the place where he is.

For the Christian, the Lord may have a work for us to do for Him, but we may be saying, "If only..." We may do well to remind ourselves of the chorus, *"Just where He needs me my Lord has placed me; just where He needs me, there would I be"*, because He may be saying to us right now what He said to Abraham all those years ago. The work He has for us to do for Him may well be right on our doorstep, in our street, in our neighbourhood. We can be sure of this, the grass is *not* greener on the other side of the fence. So let us lift up our eyes now from just where we are.

For the non-Christian who may happen to be reading this, you may be saying, "If only…" You have thought about God, you have tried to pray, you would like to be able to read the Bible, you are attracted to the Christian way of life (you probably wouldn't be reading this if you weren't!), if only your circumstances were different; if only you lived somewhere else. Let us stop saying, "If only…" and listen to the voice of God!

God may be telling us to look from the place where we are now and we may not be listening – or not wanting to listen. It is just possible that we are using the "if only" attitude to put off those things we should be doing today. It could be that we are using the same attitude to put off what we should now be doing permanently! If Abraham had adopted this attitude the Bible story may have been very different! But his attitude was the one God wanted him to adopt. It worked for him, it has worked for countless millions of people since, so let us listen once again and do as the Lord tells us, to lift up our eyes and look from the place where we are – it may surprise us what we might see!

4

Genesis 26:25 – Isaac built an altar there and called on the name of the Lord. There he pitched his tent, and there his servants dug a well.

So many of the world's problems would be solved if only men and women would turn to the Bible for their solution. What a wonderful Book for advice and guidance! If only they would take time to recognise that, as the Lord is waiting to give them *daily strength for daily living*, they should stop from time to time to see what God has to say to them. (Now translate the words "they" and "them" into "we" and "us" – or even "me" and "my"!) We really must believe in the tremendous value of God's Word. Take for instance this Bible verse. Here is the perfect pattern for family life, so necessary these days when family values seem to be falling apart at an unprecedented rate. Here are three very necessary ingredients for

successful daily living, which, if adopted, could help to halt the decline.

The family in this verse *"dug a well"*, which suggested the need to work. A happy family is one which works together. Then we are told, also, that the head of the family *"pitched his tent"*. How important to happy family life it is to have a settled home. Even those who, because of circumstances, find that they have to move *house* from time to time can still have a settled *home*. But perhaps the most important ingredient is the first one suggested in this verse, *"he built an altar"*. As a family our happiness is virtually assured if we give God His rightful place, set up the family altar, not forgetting to worship God as a family.

Circumstances may vary from family to family, but the poster no doubt many of us have seen on a church notice board through the years is still very true today, and transcends all circumstances. "The family that prays together stays together." But all three ingredients suggested in this Bible verse are necessary for successful and happy family life, and they transcend all circumstances, too – a will to work together, a settled home and the family altar. Truly good advice and guidance from a Good Book – the Bible.

5

Genesis 45:8 – It was not you who sent me here, but God.

These are the words of the Old Testament character, Joseph, spoken to his brothers when he revealed his identity to them in Egypt, after a very hard and difficult life, which began when those same brothers sold him into slavery in Egypt many years before. But Joseph was right in the centre of God's will and here in this statement acknowledged it in a very positive way. God's way is always the right way, even though it may not always be an easy way. He never makes a mistake, although He gets accused of it many a time! It was anything but easy for Joseph – he even served a prison sentence! Now he was Prime Minister of Egypt. But the way to the top had been exceedingly hard.

Many years later even Jesus prayed that there might be another way from the one He knew He had to take, although He acknowledged that His Father's way was the right and only one for Him to take. There's an important lesson here for us, too! The truth is this, Joseph only became a channel of blessing through which God could meet human need when he had been brought to the right place through trials and great difficulties. Jesus was not so much taken by men to be crucified as He was given by God for that purpose, to be a Channel of blessing to the whole of mankind. It was certainly the case with Joseph, as indeed it was with Jesus.

What is the important lesson here for us? It is this! We will only be useful for God when we are prepared to acknowledge that we are where we are today, how ever difficult and thorny the pathway may have been to get us there, or still is for that matter, because this is where God has placed us to be a channel of blessing for Him. It is not man who has put us there, but God. His way is the best way, the only right way. *"It was not you who sent me here, but God,"* Joseph said to his brothers.

Once we have allowed God to get us to the place where He wants us to be, then He can start to use us mightily for Him. It may be difficult and rough, it may even continue that way, but it is always right if God is in it. Joseph is our example; Jesus is our Supreme Example. It is up to us to live our lives to please God by following their examples.

6

Exodus 13:17 – God did not lead them on the road through the Philistine country, though that was shorter.

The children of Israel were being led out of Egypt, they were approaching the Red Sea, and once across they would be setting off on their way to the Promised Land. (Of course, at this point they were not to know about the miraculous crossing – we can only view it here with the luxury of hindsight!). Now here is an interesting fact, which forces us to look closely into the Scriptures to discover and reveal its significance. There was a much shorter route to the Promised Land than the one along which God was to lead them, but the shortest route is not always God's way.

As we said previously, how ever difficult and rough the route may be, God's way is always best and always right. Sometimes through life we are compelled to make a detour, a forced stop, to experience a period of delay. It may be an illness, an unexpected problem, a sudden change of circumstances, or even a set-back in our spiritual experience. There are so many things that might set us aside for a while.

The interesting fact revealed by this verse is that the Children of Israel could have made the journey in four or five days if they *had* gone through the Philistine country – that is, along the more direct coastal route – but God's way *took them forty years!* Why? He had much to teach them before they were to reach the Promised Land. Here, surely, is a very valuable lesson for us to learn, and one for us to remember the next time we are "set aside", or have a set-back of some kind.

God has a purpose in all things. He may have something to teach us in our detour. The delays in our spiritual journey may be there for a purpose. Instead of grumbling and complaining about it, or becoming discouraged, let us wait upon God, meditate upon His Word, and be ready to learn the lesson or lessons – there may be more than one – He wants to teach us. It may take us longer to reach our spiritual objective, but God's way is always best in the long run!

7

Exodus 14:12 – Didn't we say to you in Egypt, Leave us alone; let us serve the Egyptians? It would have been better for us to serve the Egyptians than to die in the desert!

In this exciting story of the Children of Israel and their journey, which would ultimately lead them into the Promised Land, there are many lessons for us as Christians to learn, but there are three in particular which we will consider in this and the next two devotional meditations. To help us learn these lessons well, we will draw a parallel between the life of the Children of Israel and our own spiritual life or situation. As we have already said, the Israelites have been led out of bondage in Egypt, they are now approaching the Red Sea, and once across will be out of the clutches of the Egyptians and on their way to the Promised Land, although not "through the Philistine country, though that was shorter," but by the long way round!

The parallel for us lies in the analogy we draw of the soul being led out of the bondage of sin with the promise of a new life in Christ. The Israelites began their journey in effect the moment they were led out of bondage in Egypt; the Christian begins his journey the moment he is released from sin's bondage and experiences the new birth *(John 3:3)*. Yet, in this verse, the Israelites are complaining. What they were really saying was, *"go back"*. At the first sign of difficulties – in this case, the pursuing Egyptians – discouragement came. They wanted to turn back, to give up, even believing that *"it would have been better for us to serve the Egyptians than to die in the desert!"*

There may have been many reasons for this. Maybe it was lack of faith in Moses; it may have even been lack of faith in God. They were so used to bondage, perhaps, that there was a lack of personal confidence. In that sense, they were a "damaged" people, bruised by years of bondage. Whatever the reasons, they wanted to give up and go back to their old ways.

Before we criticise them too much, let us ask ourselves a personal question: are we not like them sometimes? Or, perhaps that ought to be, most times! Discouragement comes in our spiritual lives, something goes wrong, our plans are thwarted, friends around us let us down, so many little things – and very often it is the little thing that has the most devastating effect on us. We are tempted to backslide, to give up, to go back to our old way of living. Is it a lack of faith, either personal or spiritual, or both? Is our situation so discouraging, either personal, home or church, or all three? Perhaps there is a spiritual obstacle and we want to go back.

As we shall see when we come to the next meditation, the Children of Israel did not go back, and nor must we. If the situation is very difficult at the moment, hold on, seek the Lord, the Living Word, as He gives us *daily strength for daily living*, as we continue this exciting story and learn some valuable lessons that will help and encourage us along the way.

8

Exodus 14:13 – Moses answered the people, Do not be afraid. Stand firm and you will see the deliverance the Lord will bring you today.

In our previous meditation we left the Children of Israel wanting to *"go back"*. We may feel the same at this moment in our own spiritual experience. Like the Israelites, at the first sign of discouragement, we want to give up and go back to our old way of living. But this Bible verse here is a word of encouragement, it is also a valuable lesson we must learn.

Moses was in the will of God. There was no doubt about that. His faith gave him a vision that God would find a way. The Lord would provide if they would only have faith, yet it was something that seemed to be lacking in the Israelites. How ever bleak or discouraging their circumstances might appear, God understood. He would not leave them nor forsake them. There was no need to fear the Egyptians, nor the future. This was certainly a valuable lesson they needed to learn. In a situation like this, the answer is not to go back; the answer is to *"stand firm"* – or, as the KJV translates it, to *"stand still"*.

The questions we need to ask ourselves, just at this moment, perhaps, are these. Are we completely in the will of God right now? Do we have spiritual vision? Is our faith so weak that we encourage discouragement? Sometimes there is a need for us to stand still, to review our personal situation, to take stock of our spiritual condition. This may not be very easy, but it is very necessary. Sometimes we are forced to stand still, through illness or some other circumstance, but we need not fear, neither the present nor the future, because God understands, He will find a way through our discouragements.

Once again, let us seek *daily strength for daily living* and experience from the Lord that strength He is waiting to impart to us; allow Him to strengthen our faith. In the meantime, let us not contemplate going back. For the moment let us *"stand firm"* – *"stand still"*. But remember this. We cannot stand still forever! It was not God's way for the Israelites. It is not God's way for us. This we will discover when we come to our next meditation as we continue our journey with the Israelites across the Red Sea and through the wilderness.

9

Exodus 14:15 – Then the Lord said to Moses, Why are you crying out to me? Tell the Israelites to move on.

When we left the Children of Israel, in our previous devotional meditation, standing still on the banks of the Red Sea, perhaps we were standing still, too; or perhaps, at this moment, we are forced to stand still in our spiritual journey. As we said in an earlier meditation, sometimes through life we are compelled to make a detour, a forced stop, to experience a period of delay, and it may even be caused by a setback in our spiritual experience. But, like the Israelites, we cannot stand still for ever! It was not God's way for them, and it is certainly not God's way for us.

God never fails. He did not on this occasion on the banks of the Red Sea. As this Bible verse confirms, God said, *"move on"* – or, again, as the KJV translates it, *"go forward"*. The important point is, the Israelites obeyed His command, and He saved them – gloriously! What would have happened if they had not obeyed? The answer is simple! They would have been captured, defeated, destroyed. God made the way plain, they took it, and we know the ultimate result – they arrived in the Promised Land, albeit forty years later!

The valuable lesson for us to learn is also simple. God will never fail us. He may be saying to us just now, *"move on"* – *"go forward"*. The way is made plain in His Word. Discouragements and setbacks will come, but if we are completely in the will of God, He will set the timetable for us. We must await God's command and always be ready to move when He says so. There is a need to progress daily in our spiritual like, to progress *together* in fellowship with other Christians, to *go forward* into a greater and closer experience of Almighty God, to obtain daily strength for our daily living!

The Israelites said, *"go back"* ... Moses said, *"stand still"* ... but God said, *"go forward"*. In drawing this parallel between the life of the Children of Israel and ourselves, let us apply the lessons we have learned to our personal spiritual situation. What have we learnt? It is this! *"Go back"* – NEVER! *"Stand still"* – SOMETIMES! *"Go forward"* – ALWAYS AT GOD'S COMMAND! The question we now need to ask ourselves is this: what is God's command for us at the present moment?

10

Exodus 20:21 – The people remained at a distance, while Moses approached the thick darkness where God was.

There is a little chorus that we may sometimes sing which can help us through difficult periods of our lives. *"Standing somewhere in the shadows you'll find Jesus, He's the only One who cares and understands. Standing somewhere in the shadows you will find Him, and you'll know Him by the nail prints in His hands."* We need to recognise that the Christian way of life is not always a way of brightness and light. The shadows do come, and sometimes those shadows appear as thick darkness. Even the Old Testament king, David, had this experience. "Even though I walk through the valley of the shadow...", he wrote in *Psalm 23:4*. Life is made up of good days and bad days; days when everything is bright and cheerful, and days of darkness and gloom. It happens to us all. None of us are immune.

Being a Christian most definitely does not make us immune from all the cares and problems of this life. But what we can say is this, being a Christian does make all the difference when those dark days do come, as come they will. What difference will it make, we may ask? Our verse helps us with the answer. *"Moses approached the thick darkness where God was."* As we have already seen so far, Moses had had his share of troubles, and will continue to do so. He had his dark days, yet somehow during those dark moments in his life he drew nearer to his God – who is also our God, let us never forget. This is what makes all the difference.

Centuries later this was the experience of King David as well, when he continued to write in *Psalm 23:4* that, although he was walking through the valley of the shadow, he acknowledged to God, *"I will fear no evil, for you are with me."* This is what makes all the difference. There is nothing worse than having to face a dark period alone, with no one to whom we can turn, no one who really understands, perhaps no one who cares.

For a Christian, even in the thickest darkness, God is there. All through the Bible we find people who have experienced it – Moses and David are just two we have mentioned. All through history there are people who have experienced it. To this day there are Christians who have had the same experience, and are still having the same experience. So let us take this Bible verse and substitute our own name for that of Moses, and if we are passing through a dark period just now, let us remember, the thicker the darkness the closer God will be to us … if we let Him!

11

Exodus 31:2,3 – Then the Lord said to Moses, See I have chosen Bezalel...and I have filled him with the Spirit of God.

We can all take encouragement from the truth that no one is useless to God. We all have a work to do for Him, however humble or mundane it may be. Coming to faith in Christ and earning the right to call ourselves Christian does not mean we have finally arrived; it is only the beginning – a life of faithful service lies before us. Moses kept his lines of communication open between God and himself, even in the times of thick darkness, to enable him to know what the Lord required of him through his future years of service for the Almighty. For the moment we continue to draw a parallel between the life of the Israelites and our own spiritual life as we seek *daily strength for daily living.*

As we keep our lines of communication open between God and ourselves, through prayer and meditation on His Word, and constant fellowship with His people, so He will choose or call us by name. There will be no doubt in our minds as to what He wants us to do for Him. His call is *personal* – by name; His choice is *personal to the individual* – again, by name. That is why it may vary greatly from our neighbour's calling. No two people are exactly alike in this world, and God recognises that fact; after all, He is the one who created us; so He calls us according to who we are and what we are – an individual choice.

But, we may well be saying, we are not experienced or knowledgeable enough to do what He wants us to do (so many excuses we can find!); we're too old, too young, too infirm, too immature – the list is endless. Moses had the same problem! So did a few others in the Scriptures ... and since! It is an old truth, but one that is still valid: He who calls will also equip. When God calls or chooses us *personally*, whatever the task, He will equip us *personally*, too, by the power of His Holy Spirit.

Look at this verse! We cannot help but wonder what Bezalel thought when he realised he had been chosen by God for a particular task. There was probably nothing he could say, except "yes", when he realised he had been filled with the Spirit of God for the task for which he had been chosen. Called and equipped. Now, God has not changed, so what excuse have we to give the next time He reveals to us His will, and shows us in some way what He wants us to do for Him? Here, surely, is a word of challenge as well as encouragement – and we just don't have an excuse any more, do we?

12

Deuteronomy 1:8 – See, I have given you this land. Go in and take possession of the land that the Lord swore he would give to your fathers – to Abraham, Isaac and Jacob – and to their descendants after them.

We have moved on a little in Old Testament history with this verse, but we are still drawing that parallel between the Children of Israel and the Christian. The Israelites have almost reached the Promised Land; it is forty years since they came out of bondage in Egypt;

their wanderings in the wilderness are almost over. Now God is saying to them, *"I have given you this land, go in and take possession..."* Where is the parallel? The moment we committed our lives to the Lord Jesus Christ, acknowledged Him as our Saviour, repented of our sins and sought forgiveness of those sins, and received the assurance of the Holy Spirit that we had been adopted into the Family of God, that we had become a child of God (or to put it in a nutshell, we had come to faith in Christ and now had the right to call ourselves Christian), it was as if He had set before us a wonderful spiritual land. There is the parallel!

But notice His command: *"Go in and take possession of the land..."* The Children of Israel did not expect to enter the Promised Land and only inhabit a small area, but to possess the whole, to explore and conquer every part. As Christians, we having entered the Door of Salvation, are in the Promised Land of Spiritual Experience. Our command is the same as the one given to the Children of Israel, to go in and possess it, to explore and conquer and inhabit every part. Such a wealth of spiritual gifts and blessings and experiences are awaiting us. But are we just standing at the entrance, too timid to venture forward?

It is just possible, of course, that some of us might have been standing at the entrance for a very long time. Perhaps it is many years since we came to faith in Christ, and we have failed to *"go forward"*. If the Children of Israel had failed to obey that command, they would have been destroyed on the wrong side of the Red Sea forty years before; have we so far failed to obey the same command, especially as we know we have another to obey, this one to go and take possession of the land? Let us be assured of this, all the riches of Eternal Life are ours *now* – they are set before us – are we going to settle for anything less?

13

Deuteronomy 1:22 – Then all of you came to me and said, Let us send men ahead to spy out the land and bring back a report about the route we are to take and the towns we will come to.

The Children of Israel had made a decision – it is being proclaimed by Moses to the Israelites, and is recorded in this verse – when they were faced with entering the Promised Land. Instead of actually entering, exploring, then inhabiting the land, as they had been commanded to do, they decided to delay their entry and send out a reconnaissance party instead! But, we may ask, what has this to do with us today? What bearing has this upon Christians in the twenty-first century? Quite simply this! Christians today sometimes employ delaying tactics as an excuse for not making a deeper commitment to the Lord Jesus Christ.

As we continue for the moment to draw a parallel between the life of the Children of Israel and our own spiritual life or situation, and as we think of our spiritual experience as our Promised Land, in effect we are saying, if we explore too much of this land we may become too involved. Let others go and search out, or spy out, the land. We will wait and see. But "wait and see" is not God's way in this instance; His way is "go in and take possession."

Think of all the blessings, the rich spiritual experiences, we may be missing while we're waiting. Our Promised Land is set before us; why send others ahead when God Himself has promised to go before us. Even so, there are still many Christians who need convincing, who have become so set in their ways that they will not countenance change or new experiences in any shape or form. "We are all right as we are," they say, and like the Children of Israel all those many centuries ago, they add, *"let us send men ahead to spy out the land."*

It is such a sad situation, and at the same time so very important, that it is worth looking at some more in our next devotional meditation. It may also be helpful for us to use a personal illustration to encourage us to realise the folly of disobeying God's command to go in and take possession of our Promised Land, our Land of Spiritual Experience, whilst at the same time assisting us in resisting the use of delaying tactics in our spiritual journey and thereby missing out on the tremendous blessings the Lord may be waiting to bestow on us.

14

Deuteronomy 1:22 – We will send men before us, and they shall search out the land, and bring us word by what way we must go up. [KJV]

Let us look again at the decision made by the Children of Israel to employ delaying tactics rather then obey God's command to go in and take possession of the Promised Land. As we continue for the moment to draw this parallel between the life of the Children of Israel and our own spiritual life or situation, please permit me to use a personal illustration, which may assist us in resisting our use of delaying tactics in our spiritual journey.

I recall vividly the thrill of standing with my wife on the top of a mountain in Austria many years ago. The view could only be described as breath taking. Set out before us as far as the eye could see was the land of that beautiful country. The shimmering lakes and cascading rivers, the forests and multi-coloured fields, the towns and villages with their strange shaped church spires and uniquely designed houses, the distant snow-capped mountains, the verdant valleys, a panorama of exquisite beauty and infinite variety: and yet, all this but a mere shadow of the beauty and variety of the spiritual land set before the Christian.

The joy of real experience came to my wife and myself when we left that Austrian mountain top and toured the country, visited the towns and churches, walked through the woods and fields, rowed around the lakes and picnicked beside the rivers. To have viewed the scenery from the distant mountain top, although pleasurable in itself, would have deprived us of so much greater enjoyment, and restricted our experience of that delightful country. The spiritual parallel is obvious. The joy of experience comes when we go in and possess the land. To wait and see will deprive us of so much spiritual enjoyment, and restrict our spiritual blessings.

As we said in the previous devotional meditation, there are still many Christians who need convincing, who become so set in their ways that they not only employ delaying tactics, but also adopt a somewhat rebellious attitude. What a sad state of affairs! The Children of Israel employed the same tactics and adopted the same attitude. They were the losers, not God. Must we become losers, too?

15

Deuteronomy 1:25 – Taking with them some of the fruit of the land, they brought it down to us and reported, It is a good land that the Lord our God is giving us.

As we continue to liken the Christian's spiritual experience to that of the Children of Israel with the Promised Land set before them many centuries ago, we are once again listening to the proclamation of Moses to the Israelites as he reminds them of the spies we considered in the previous two devotional meditations, and the report they gave. *"It is a good land that the Lord our God is giving us,"* he said. Only good could result from their going in to possess it. God had commanded them to go in and possess the land just as He commands Christians today to enter into a deeper spiritual commitment with and to His Son, Jesus – for us to go in and possess our Promised Land.

If we continue to rebel and employ our delaying tactics, as we have already mentioned, we may live to regret it. But, we may be saying, it is a big step to take. Of course it is! We may meet with opposition from our family and friends. Of course we might! Taking such a step will make us vulnerable to spiritual attack, and not only attack from outside the church, but also from within. That's true, too! Those who have entered this land with us – or, perhaps, to be more accurate, entered *just inside* where we may have been standing still together, possibly for a long time – they will not take too kindly to being left behind as we go forward to possess it.

Do we think God would command us to go in and posses this spiritual land, to enter into that deeper spiritual commitment, knowing that we will meet with opposition and attack, without giving us some form of protection. Of course not! No soldier is sent into battle without he is fully armed and able to resist as well as counter any attack.

We will look at this provision of divine protection in a later meditation. In the meantime, we need to look more fully at the folly of our rebellion and the regrets we will have if we fail to go in and possess the land. It was certainly the regret a lady of my acquaintance had, as we shall see in our next devotional meditation.

16

Deuteronomy 1:26 – But you were unwilling to go up; you rebelled against the command of the Lord your God.

In his proclamation, Moses lamented the fact that the Children of Israel had been unwilling to obey God and go in to possess the land set before them. They were both unwilling and rebellious, in spite of the fact that they had agreed that it was a good land the Lord was giving them. If, like them, we fail to go in and possess this land of spiritual experience set before us, continuing only to hover at the entrance, we will live to regret it. This was certainly the experience of a lady of my acquaintance.

"The greatest regret of my life," she said to me, "is that I wasted nearly fifty years of my life before entering into a full experience of Jesus Christ." She had been a member of her church since a teenager, had attended services regularly, took an active part in all church activities, but had never fully committed her life to the Lord. It was not until a visiting team of evangelists conducting a series of meetings in her village hall, preached the Gospel in such a way that she discovered a deeper meaning to her spiritual life.

The land had been before her, but she had never gone in to possess it. "I must confess," she admitted to me, "that I objected strongly to their line of preaching when I attended their first meeting. It was most provocative. I decided not to go again. But the more I thought about it, the more attracted I was, so much so that I felt compelled to go to their meeting the next night. I went to every one in the end. I made a full commitment on the last night. I'm so glad I did!"

Is there any one of us, as we read this, standing on the threshold of a great adventure, yet still with objections and reservations in our heart? Does any one of us feel the Lord calling us to a deeper commitment to Him just now, and there is rebellion against such commitment? Can it be said of any one of us, *"But you were unwilling to go up; you rebelled against the command of the Lord your God"*? Don't let us live to regret it; it's not worth it!

17

Deuteronomy 3:18 – I commanded you at that time: The Lord your God has given you this land to take possession of it. But all your able-bodied men, armed for battle, must cross over ahead of your brother Israelites.

God would not command us to go in and possess our Promised Land, to enter into a deeper spiritual commitment, knowing that we will meet with much opposition and attack, without giving us some form of divine protection. The KJV puts this verse more simply. *"The Lord your God hath given you this land to possess it: ye shall pass over armed."* That last phrase is important, because this is a *devotional* meditation (as, indeed, they all are in this book), and as such it suggests to us that we can take the phrase that we will pass over armed to remind us that we have the best protection a Christian can have – the Word of God, the Bible.

Used as God intends, the Bible can serve as our Guide Book, showing us the way through this land of spiritual experience, this spiritual adventure, just as the road map does for the motorist; it can serve as our Highway Code, enabling us to maintain the "rules of the road" as we travel; and above all, it provides us with a powerful weapon with which to defeat the enemy. The promise is that *"ye shall pass over armed"*. We neglect this powerful weapon at our peril, for the Bible also says, "the word of God is living and active. Sharper than any double-edged sword..." *(Hebrews 4:12)*. So let us make sure we use it.

I am amazed at the number of people who have confessed to me down through the years that they never read their Bible, except in church on Sunday. For some, the thought of a regular daily Bible study or meditation horrifies them. "I could never keep it up," one young man said to me. When I explained that a Christian should "feed" regularly on the Word of God just as he feeds regularly at the dining room table, or he would starve spiritually, he replied, "Oh, I let my minister do the reading for me in church. After all, that's what he gets paid for!" Regretfully, this is the attitude of many professing Christians today.

Just as the Promised Land was set before the Children of Israel all those centuries ago, and they were commanded to go in and possess it, so the Christian's Promised Land is set before us today in the form of our spiritual experience, our spiritual commitment to Jesus Christ. As we go in to possess it, unless we "pass over armed" with the powerful double-edged sword of the Word of God, we may well be defeated by the first enemy we meet. Remember, the Bible also says, "Every word of God is flawless (KJV: 'pure'); he is a shield to those who take refuge (KJV: 'put their trust') in him" *(Proverbs 30:5)*. It's up to us to be armed, then, isn't it?

18

Deuteronomy 5:32 – So be careful to do what the Lord your God has commanded you; do not turn aside to the right or to the left.

So we have ventured beyond the entrance, where we have possibly hovered for so long, and we are beginning to move forward to posses our Promised Land – at least, that is our prayer that it should be so! What do we do now? As we have already said, we must "pass over armed" with the powerful double-edged sword of the Word of God – the Bible – because it is not only a powerful weapon with which to defeat the enemy of our soul, but it is also a vital Guide Book and Highway Code. Unless we are prepared to read and meditate upon it regularly, to seek *daily strength for daily living*, we will quickly discover that we have become "lost", for we can only walk in the ways that the Lord has commanded us to do if we first know what those ways are.

Perhaps at this point in our journey there are two things we need to consider before anything else, and both are found in this verse. The first is that we must *"be careful to do what the Lord your God has commanded you."* To be able to do this, it is extremely important that we turn our entire life over to the Lord; we surrender every aspect of our being to the One who has saved us and enabled us to enter this Land of Spiritual Experience. To put it another way, to be able to obey the commands of the Lord fully we have to belong to the Lord fully, having made Him both Saviour and Lord of our life.

But now we are faced with the second thing we need to consider, and to obey the rest of His command, when He says, *"do not turn aside to the right or the left."* Easier said than done, we might say, and the only way it is possible is to realise that from now on Jesus is going to take full control of the rest of our life. There needs to be a strong determination on our part to let Him run our life for us, to let Him determine the path we should take, because the alternative is that, if we try to take control, we will deviate from the path He has mapped for us, and we will certainly become "lost" – possibly for all eternity. Now, that's a sobering thought, isn't it?

19

Deuteronomy 5:33 – Walk in all the way that the Lord your God has commanded you, so that you may live and prosper and prolong your days in the land that you will possess.

As we continue to draw this comparison between the Promised Land set before the Children of Israel many centuries ago and the Promised Land of Spiritual Experience set before the Christian today, from the moment we commit our life to the Lord Jesus Christ to the end of our earthly journey, to be able to *"walk in all the ways that the Lord your God has commanded you,"* and at the same to *"not turn aside to the right or the left,"* then the only way we will succeed is to let Jesus take full control of the rest of our life as we *"pass over armed."*

We are once again, of course, because it is so important, highly commending the importance of regular Bible study and meditation as we journey through life, to seek *daily strength for daily living.* God Himself says to us, "listen carefully and take to heart all the words I speak to you" *(Ezekiel 3:10).* The KJV packs more punch! "All my words that I shall speak unto thee receive in thine heart." Unlike an ordinary book, which contains just printed words, the Bible is a living Book from a living God, and so its words are very much alive, too. It is unique in this respect. These living words have transformed the lives of countless men and women down through the ages who have gone in to possess this Land of Spiritual Experience. It will do the same for us, if it has not already done so.

When we read it, study it, meditate upon it, because it is God's Living Word, He really speaks to us through that word. Now, the question is, if the Bible is different from any other book, should we not read it differently than any other book? And the answer, of course, is a very definite yes! To make the Bible relevant to our personal situation (which differs from person to person, incidentally), and for it to fulfil its purpose, not only should we read it as we do an ordinary book, but we must also receive it into our heart – *unlike* any ordinary book. This means putting into action what we have read; a dangerous practice indeed with some of the rubbish we read in ordinary books today!

Taking the Word of God, then, as our Guide Book and Highway Code for daily living, let us live daily according to that Word. The only effective way for us to be able to *"walk in all the way that the Lord your God commanded you"* is to receive it into our heart first. In this way we will be sure that we will live and prosper spiritually as we travel this Land of Spiritual Experience, because we will know the right way; the directions will be firmly and indelibly imprinted on our heart – and we can't find a safer place than that!

20

Deuteronomy 6:5 – Love the Lord your God with all your heart and with all your soul and with all your strength.

It is not possible to be a true Christian without an intense passionate love for God, neither is it possible to travel through this Land of Spiritual Experience without such love. We said earlier that it is extremely important for us to turn our entire life over to the Lord; to surrender every aspect of our being to the One who has saved us and enabled us to enter this Land of Spiritual Experience. It is also important for us to love Him with intense passionate love. We tend to be frightened of the phrase "passionate love" these days, because it has been sullied by so-called modern ideas. But this is the sort of love Jesus expects from every Christian.

Jesus did not say anything original on the subject, recorded in *Matthew 22:37.* He simply took this Old Testament command and gave it new meaning. As we travel this spiritual land we are required to love God with *all* our heart and with *all* our soul and with *all* our strength. If we love someone like that, what else is it but passionate love? And Jesus says this is how we should love God. It was the command to the Children of Israel as they started to go in and possess the Promised Land, and as long as they obeyed, God continued to prosper and bless them. He will do the same for us if we obey.

It is not easy to do, nor yet to understand, but it is possible, within our capacity, otherwise Jesus would not have commanded it; nor would God have instructed Moses to command it of the Israelites. We have to admit that, if He had said, "Love your sweetheart with all your heart, soul and strength," or, "Love your husband or wife...", we would understand what He meant, we would know what to do. Take heart! If we are fully committed to the Lord, fully surrendered, living our lives according to His commands, then it should not be difficult to translate our earthly feelings into heavenly feelings – to, in fact, love God with an intense passionate love in the Land of Spiritual Experience.

21

Deuteronomy 9:3 – But be assured today that the Lord your God is the one who goes across ahead of you like a devouring fire.

From time to time, as we journey through life, we come up against situations and circumstances which are new to us. Sometimes these situations can be very frightening and depressing. The recently bereaved widow who has to face the future alone; the person who must learn to live with a serious illness, or has to care for a loved one who has become permanently sick; the husband or wife who has to face a break-up of their marriage – the list is endless!

On the other hand, although possibly less distressing, there may be decisions we have to make which we know will affect our future and maybe the future of our family, too. It may involve a change of environment, a move to a new town or a new house, a change of job – a host of things that may result in a new situation. In every case we have to face the unknown future, and we cannot help but wonder! Those of us who are travelling through the Land of Spiritual Experience are not immune from these things – we have to face the same issues which affect those who are simply just journeying through life.

Here is where the Christian has an understanding, and highlights the difference between a way of life and the spiritual life, because we do not have to face the future alone, nor do we have to travel through life with no one to whom we can turn for help, for comfort, yes, and even for guidance. It is there in this Bible verse. *"Be assured today that the Lord your God is the one who goes across ahead of you"* – or as the KJV translates it, that God is the One *"which goeth over before thee."* Whenever we need Him, God is there. There is no experience beyond His understanding. There is no problem beyond His ability to solve. There is no situation beyond His desire to identify Himself with it and to see us through it.

We may feel we are facing a bleak future at this moment. Here is a word of encouragement from God's Word, which says that it is for "today" (KJV – "this day"), but we can take heart, for *every* day in the future becomes "this day" as we reach it, so here is a promise for *every* day of our lives as we travel through this spiritual land. We can be comforted to know that God is going ever before us, can't we?

22

Deuteronomy 11:11 – But the land you are crossing the Jordan to take possession of is a land of mountains and valleys that drinks rain from heaven.

We remind ourselves again that, as the Children of Israel many centuries ago were commanded to go in and possess the Promised Land set before them, so we as Christians who have entered the Door of Salvation into the Promised Land of Spiritual Experience, are subject to a similar command. With this in mind, we are now alerted to the fact in this verse that this same land which we must seek to explore and possess *"is a land of mountains and valleys."* No one is promised an easy and smooth pathway through life, and the Christian is no exception.

Does this sound ominous? Not really! There will come our mountain top experiences, there will also come the valleys, but still we must push on to explore and conquer every part of the land set before us. We must not let the valley experiences discourage us, nor must we allow the mountaintops to make us complacent. Without the valleys how could we appreciate the mountains? And without the mountain top experiences of life, how could we ever face the valleys? Our verse reminds us that we will experience both. What is more, we *need* both. God uses the varied experiences of life to build our characters and refine us for His service.

But there is more! As the hymn writer so aptly puts it, *"I do not know what lies ahead, the way I cannot see; yet One stands near to be my guide, He'll show the way to me."* As we pass through the varied experiences of life, the Christian is never left alone. One stands near to be our Guide. How do we know? Because the next verse assures us concerning this land that *the eyes of the Lord your God are continually on it."*

We will look more fully at that verse in our next devotional meditation. In the meantime, as we seek *daily strength for daily living* in God's Word, let us take encouragement from this truth that we can go in and possess the land, and can explore the land, too, with complete confidence, because the Lord is ever with us in the valleys as well as on the mountains. We are never out of His sight, and that is both encouraging and comforting, isn't it?

23

Deuteronomy 11:12 – It is a land the Lord your God cares for; the eyes of the Lord your God are continually on it from the beginning of the year to its end.

What a comforting thought it is to know that we are never left alone through life's varied experiences, because the Bible assures us concerning this land of mountains and valleys, that as we travel we are never out of God's sight in this promised Land of Spiritual Experience. There may be occasions when we feel alone, feel lost, but those are the occasions when *our* eyes are blind, not God's!

Wherever we are in this spiritual land, *the eyes of the Lord your God are continually on it.*" So we can go in and possess and explore the land with complete confidence that He is always with us in the valleys as well as on the mountains.

We can take by way of illustration an incident which happened when our son was about 2½ years old (he is well into middle age now!) so it is many years ago! My wife and I were on holiday with him by the sea. Like the fledglings falling from their nest, he wanted to "stretch his wings". So what does he do but set off along the beach at great pace, out into the big wide world away from mum and dad, without even looking back once – at first! A few hundred yards later he stopped, looked about him, and realised that he was completely lost. All around him were strangers, dozens and dozens of them! And he was *miles* away from where he had started – or so he thought.

But what was dad doing all this time? He was on the promenade keeping his eye on his runaway son. Never once did I let him out of my sight. His short-lived adventure into freedom would have ended in panic if I had not turned up at the right moment, because, you see, although my son could not see me, *I could see him all the time.* When he thought he was lost, in actual fact he had never once been lost; and as young as he was, this was a valuable lesson he learned as I joined him on the beach that day.

It is a lesson we must learn, too. We are never lost because we are never out of God's sight. Circumstances may arise which might cause us to feel lost, things we cannot understand and find very hard to accept, but God has not changed His position! And if we look around us we will see many worse off than ourselves, especially if they are not travelling through the Land of Spiritual Experience. God has His eyes on them as well, the poor and the needy, because He cares about them just as He cares about us – and He wants us to care as well, as we will see in our next devotional meditation.

24

Deuteronomy 15:11 – There will always be poor people in the land. Therefore I command you to be open-handed towards your brothers and towards the poor and needy in your land.

The idea of caring for the poor and needy of our land, and especially in the under-privileged lands of the so-called third world, is not new. It was around at the time when the Children of Israel entered the Promised Land, as evidenced in this verse. We have to admit, though, that it is not exclusively the province of the Christian to help those less fortunate than themselves. There are many non-Christian agencies doing an excellent work in this sphere. But we must recognise that it is a God-inspired responsibility for every Christian.

The Salvation Army has a phrase which sums it up perfectly – *Heart to God, Hand to Man".* Our love and devotion to God must find its expression in our love and care for people, and especially the poor and needy. Mother Teresa of Calcutta explains that loving people is a way of loving God, and, of course, she is right! As we journey through life, through the spiritual land into which we have entered, we must realise that our responsibility as Christians extends outwards from a heart of love in many different directions, rather like the spokes of a wheel. This verse not only reminds us *"there will always be poor people in the land,"* but it goes further and tells us how we should treat them. It is, in fact, a command from God. *"I command you to be open-handed towards your brothers and towards the poor and needy in your land."*

The KJV is more explicit in this matter of the open hand. Open your hand *wide*, it says. This matter of, not just opening our hand, but opening it wide to our brothers (and sisters, of course!) should suggest to us that our responsibility should be open and honest and sincere to those in need. No ulterior motives, no "what can I get out of it" attitudes, but a selfless giving of ourselves, an open heart to God and an open hand to man.

There may be those whom we know who are in need; we may be

in need ourselves; and that need may not always be born out of poverty. Hunger is not always produced by lack of bread, for frequently it can be a lack of love. Let us never forget that the quality of our love for God dictates the quality of our love for our neighbours, whether that neighbour lives in an under-privileged country across the sea or right next door just where we live. As Christians, we must not only learn to recognise need, but we must also be willing to try and meet that need in the name of the Lord in whose company we travel through this Land of Spiritual Experience. After all, God is the One whom we are serving and seeking to please in accordance with His command, so remember, *"Heart to God, Hand to Man."*

25

Deuteronomy 20:1 – When you go out to war against your enemies...do not be afraid of them, because the Lord your God...will be with you.

We live in a very frustrating world. It is doubtful that any committed Christian would disagree with that! We live in a world against which we seem to be fighting a constant battle – or should be, if we truly belong to Jesus Christ! As we look around us we see so many enemies of our soul, so many things that would turn us aside from the Lord, situations that may drag us down spiritually if we let them. Paradoxically, it is very much an uphill battle! Perhaps just at the moment we are finding the battle very hard. The more down we feel pulled the more uphill it seems! But we can take heart. God knows the battles we have to fight as we travel through our spiritual Promised Land, so we are not left alone to fight them.

We are never on our own on the battlefield, because God has promised to *always* be with us. Look at this verse! *"When"* (not *"if"*, because a Christian is always at war in the spiritual sense) *"you go out to war against your enemies...do not be afraid of them, because the Lord your God ...will be with you."* What a reassuring promise; and if God is on our side we can never lose. The hymn writer puts it this way. *"God is still on the throne, and He will remember His own; though trials may press us and burdens distress us, He never will leave us alone."* So the next time we go out to war against the enemies of our soul, or if we are feeling the battle intensely at this moment, we can be assured that the Lord our God will be with us every step of the way.

Though trials may press us and burdens distress us, He never will leave us alone. What trials? What distressing burdens? Each one of us can only answer that for ourselves. Different things affect different people. But one thing is very certain, when we go out to war, to battle, with our enemies, we do not have to be afraid of them, because the Lord has promised to be with us to give us the victory over our enemies – and it is just possible that our greatest enemy is *ourselves!* God can give us the victory over self, so that we become not self-centred but Christ-centred.

26

Deuteronomy 29:29 – The secret things belong to the Lord your God, but the things revealed belong to us and to our children for ever, that we may follow all the words of this law.

Is it not true to say that sometimes we get very frustrated, very distressed, very upset, even very angry, when we cannot understand why God allows certain things to happen, or sometimes not to happen? Such a list of things we could compile of all those things we fail to understand through our lives, as we travel through the Promised Land of Spiritual Experience, yet such a list would not help us one little bit! Everyone's list would be different, anyway.

When something happens in our lives that we cannot understand, there is a tendency to ask why it should happen to us. We may even ask what we did to deserve it. As we travel through our spiritual land we begin to wonder and question along the lines that we are a good person and we are living our life how God wants us to live it, we pray regularly, read our Bible daily, so, why? If we are not very careful, these questions could become more distressing than the tragedy or problem itself! God does not want us to travel through our spiritual land in this way.

This is why our verse is very important, because it reminds us that the secret things belong to God, and we are *not meant to know and understand everything.* We must have faith and trust the Lord to know that even if we do not always agree or cannot fully understand why, He knows best. Some disasters are man made, like the 9/11 tragedy on the Twin Towers of the World Trade Centre in New York on the 9th September 2001, whilst some are natural disasters like the Tsunami on the 26th December 2004, and yet others may be personal, like the tragic death of a loved one, especially if that loved one is a child. So let us remind ourselves that *the secret things belong to the Lord your God."* Those things we cannot understand we leave with Him.

But this verse says more. There are some things we should try and understand, because we have a two-fold responsibility to try and understand the things that *are* revealed to us, and to tell others as well. If we think careful about it, God has revealed far more to us than He has kept hidden. The verse also reminds us that those things, which God *does* reveal, belong to us and also to our children – but they will only understand if we are prepared to tell them. So let us stop getting frustrated and distressed at the things we cannot fully understand and concentrate on the things which God intends us to know and to share with others. After all, if He wanted us to know *everything* He wouldn't have had secrets in the first place, would He?

27

Deuteronomy 31:8 – The Lord himself goes before you and will be with you; he will never leave you nor forsake you. Do not be afraid; do not be discouraged.

As He set before the Children of Israel the Promised Land, with the instructions to go in and possess every part, so God has set before the Christian the Land of Spiritual Experience with similar instructions – and we have been considering this parallel for the past several devotional meditations as we have worked through the book of *Deuteronomy*. Before we move on, however, there is another important truth to consider. To be more precise, *four* important truths or promises, and they are each found in this verse. The joy of full experience comes when we go in and possess the land without reservations and hesitations, not becoming so set in our ways that we are prejudiced against any form of change, thereby depriving ourselves of so much spiritual blessing.

It is possible, at this very moment, that we may be standing at the threshold of a great adventure. As we enter deeper into this spiritual land – enter into a deeper commitment to the Lord Jesus Christ – tremendous spiritual blessing can only be the result. But we must beware! We will meet up with opposition, possibly from within the church, certainly from without, although we do not go forward unarmed in the event of these attacks. God has given us His Word; let us meditate on it regularly, seeking *daily strength for daily living.* It is our Guide Book and our Highway Code through life. It will guide us in the valleys as well as on the mountaintops.

It will "protect" us as well as providing us with a powerful "weapon" to defeat the enemy. Taking the Word of God and resolving to live daily according to its truths will not only teach us the right way to go, but it will also reveal to us something about the land through which we are travelling. We may not understand everything, may even find some things hard to accept (especially in the valley experiences), but we must never doubt that the Lord is going ever before us, and is always with us every step that we take.

We can go in and posses this spiritual land without fear because of His four-fold promise in this verse. (1) *The Lord himself goes before you..."* – so we can take each step with confidence knowing that we are safe. (2) *"The Lord...will be with you..."* – so we can rejoice at never being left alone in our travels, whether on the mountaintop or in the valley. (3) *"He will never leave you..."* (KJV – *"He will not fail thee..."*) – so we can comfort ourselves with this truth all along the way. (4) *"He will never...forsake you."* – so we can journey with confidence and comfort, rejoicing all the way to Heaven! So let God have the last word! *"Do not be afraid; do not be discouraged."*

28

Joshua 1:5 – No-one will be able to stand up against you all the days of your life. As I was with Moses, so I will be with you; I will never leave you or forsake you.

All the promises of God to His children are rich with blessing; and the wonderful thing is that He never breaks a promise. Here in this verse we have one such promise which, although made originally to Joshua following the death of Moses, applies equally to every true Christian in every age. Moses had led the Children of Israel for forty years through the wilderness whilst God prepared them for entering into the Promised Land. But Moses was not allowed to lead them into that land; this responsibility was to fall on the shoulders of Joshua. Think for a moment of the importance of this promise, not only to Joshua, but to us as twenty-first century Christians.

Joshua had taken over the responsibilities of leadership of the Israelites – an awesome task in the light of the previous experiences of Moses – and needed all the help he could get! Imagine his feelings when God said to him, *"As I was with Moses, so I will be with you;"* and as if that was not enough, the Lord went on to say, *"I will never leave you or forsake you"* – assurance indeed! Or should that be reassurance? But how does this help us in our present situation? What importance can we attach to this for us in the twenty-first century? The answer is really quite simple!

We sometimes look around and see the way the Lord is blessing others, then wonder why He is not doing the same for us. The answer to this "why?" lies not in God's attitude, but our own. He can only bless us if we let Him. If we resist His claims upon our life, how can He bless us? Yet, God's promise still holds good. He may well be saying to you and me today, "As I was with…" and we can put in any name we like of someone we know to be richly blessed "…so I will be with you." He will neither fail us, nor will He forsake us.

So as a child of God let us take our Heavenly Father at His Word and believe His promise to be true for us personally. What a difference it will make to our day! Indeed, what a difference it will make to every day of our life in the future from now to eternity! On the other hand, if you are reading this, yet you are not a child of God, heed His call, put your trust in Him and experience His promise. What a difference it will make to your day, too!

29

Joshua 1:8 – This book of the law shall not depart out of thy mouth; but thou shalt meditate therein day and night, that thou mayest observe to do according to all that is written therein: for then thou shalt make thy way prosperous, and then thou shalt have good success. [KJV]

This Book, this Bible, this inspired Word of God, this Source of *daily strength for daily living*, what a wonderful treasure it is, and it is ours! God has given it to us! All the answers to all our problems, to all the world's problems, are contained within its pages. Why are people so blind that they cannot see? Why are people so spiritually poor when here is the wellspring of riches untold? If we need blessing, guidance, advice, help, instruction, comfort, encouragement, and so much more, we can find it all in God's Word. We miss so much in this way if we treat the Bible as a closed book.

There is an old adage, which says that a book never opened is nothing more than a pile of paper! Let us think about that for a moment. Is our Bible just a pile of paper? Permit me a personal word of testimony. My Bible does not get time to be a pile of paper. It is constantly open and has been for well over half a century! I am both humbled and privileged to be able to share with others some of the great encouragement, of reassurance, of fabulous spiritual wealth, that God has given me through its open pages, and in so sharing trust that He will bless others as much as He has me through the years.

If our Bible is an open book in our life, then we can say with complete assurance that we are rich beyond measure, or to be more precise, we are prosperous. This is not being an advocate for the so-called *prosperity gospel* – most definitely not! When we talk of prosperity and success these days, it is usually the picture of a successful business person living in a palatial mansion, with a healthy bank balance to match, which comes readily to mind. But can prosperity always be judged by the amount of money credited to our account or success measured by the size and quantity of our possessions?

It is a fact that, very often some of the richest people on earth – rich in spirit, rich in heart, rich in attitude, rich in love – can claim but a few pounds or dollars or euros as their monetary wealth, whilst others may be condemned by the world as failures, yet that same world is a much richer place for their having lived in it. This is an important verse revealing an important truth, which is why we will share more than one devotional meditation on this subject. In the meantime, until we return to it in the next meditation, let us ask ourselves two challenging questions: Are we prosperous? Are we successful? But, of course, we need to think very carefully before we can truthfully answer them, don't we?

30

Joshua 1:8a – Do not let this Book of the Law depart from your mouth…

As real Christians we are *never* poor, and *never* a failure, for although we may possess very little of this world's goods or be judged as anything but successful by this world's standards, we nevertheless have the source of great riches and tremendous success within our grasp – the Holy Word of God. As we said in the previous meditation, this Book, this Bible, this inspired Word of God, this Source of *daily strength for daily living*, is a wonderful treasure, and it is ours! God has given it to us! Great riches and tremendous success can and should be ours, but once again we need to understand that this is not being an advocate for the so-called *prosperity gospel* – most definitely not! The Bible is not a magic formula to make us prosperous in this world's goods!

Here we need to be careful. The Word does not say we shall become prosperous and rich just because we *possess* a Bible. In the sense in which we are thinking of prosperity and success here, there are many people who read the Bible as a daily habit or ritual but it has very little if any impact on their lives, who study it purely as an academic exercise, and yet other who proudly carry it to and from church each Sunday, but rarely open it except when the preacher is reading it from the pulpit. They will all remain poor and needy in the eyes of the Lord.

How, then, can the Word of God make us prosperous and successful? To begin with, of course, as we have already said, our Bible must never be allowed to become a pile of paper! Then, as we open its pages, we will realise that throughout its pages, and when we come to this verse in particular, that the Word itself suggests three ways. Let us look at the first in this devotional meditation, and at the other two in the next one. *"Do not let this Book of the Law depart from your mouth..."* Never a day should go by that at some time God's Word should pass over our lips in witness, that we should take each opportunity to speak for the Lord.

Sometimes *our* words may be misinterpreted, misunderstood, misquoted, but if we quote the Bible accurately there is no argument! One of Billy Graham's frequently used phrases is, *"The Bible says..."* Let it become one of ours, also!

31

Joshua 1:8b – ... meditate on it day and night, so that you may be careful to do everything written in it. Then you will be prosperous and successful.

We may be surprised at this statement, but there are many Christians who believe that Bible meditation is more important than Bible study. As we conclude our meditation on the three ways in which the Word of God can make us prosperous and successful, so our verse continues concerning that Word that we should,

"...meditate on it day and night, so that we may be careful to do everything written in it." The surprising statement at the beginning of this devotional meditation is not intended to suggest that Bible study is not important, nor that it should be neglected. On the contrary, study of God's Word is *very* important. It should be engaged in regularly and systematically. But to sit with the Open Word, in quiet, prayerful meditation, allowing God through His Holy Spirit to speak to us, to reveal His will to us, to enjoy a deep, rich, exciting spiritual communion with our Heavenly Father through His Word, is riches beyond measure. Incidentally, it will increase and develop the value of our study, too!

But the verse says more. *"Be careful to do everything written in it."* Unless our lives, our attitudes, our actions, are patterned on the Word of God, our witness and our meditation will be futile. The in-phrase in the twenty-first century seems to be, *"Talk the talk, walk the walk."* This modern sound bite is true. We must first be willing to acknowledge the Bible as God's Holy Word to us, then be willing to obey that Word, to submit by our actions to God's will revealed in it.

So perhaps we need to make sure that our Bible is more than just a pile of paper, for it is only when it becomes an Open Book (or should that be, an *Opened* Book?) that we will receive encouragement and reassurance as an added bonus. Riches indeed! There is no need to be spiritually poor, no need to be a failure, because when we witness for the Lord, meditate on His Word, and obey His will revealed through that Word, *"then you will be prosperous and successful"* – in the right meaning of that phrase. That's how we know! Because God's Word says so!

32

Joshua 24:15 – Choose for yourselves this day whom you will serve...as for me and my household, we will serve the Lord.

Every day we are faced with making decisions. They may be simple things like what to have for breakfast, which pair of shoes to put on, or even whether to go out or stop in! Sometimes the decisions are far more important and can affect our whole future – the choice of a partner, a career, or a place to live, for example. Of course, we need to recognise that we are only able to make decisions like this because of a very special gift that God in His sovereignty has given us. It is the gift of freewill, the ability to make a choice.

Whether a person believes in God or not, this gift is still freely given. Were it not so, every human being on this planet would be a zombie! It enables us to say "no" as well as "yes". Sometimes "no" could be the right choice, anyway! This verse is a perfect example of this gift of freewill in action. It was a challenge by Joshua just prior to his death made to the Children of Israel as they were exploring and possessing the Promised Land. "Choose for yourselves this day whom you will serve." Use the freewill God has given you and make a decision, he was in effect saying.

Here they were being called upon to make a very important choice, one that would certainly affect their whole future, even beyond this life. Having issued the challenge to his people, Joshua then went on to make a positive statement concerning himself and his family. "As for me and my household, we will serve the Lord." To put it another way, having told his people that they could choose whom they were going to serve as they continued exploring and possessing the land, he also told them that he and his family had already made their choice.

But this was all so very long ago! How does it affect us in the twenty-first century? The answer is, because today our situation is exactly the same. If we have not already done so, we are actually being challenged – whether we realise it or not – by this Bible verse to make a decision now whom we will serve, and to make it today. Choose for yourselves *this day*, the verse says. After all, a decision so important as this affecting eternity cannot wait until tomorrow. One thing is certain, however, we will never make a more important decision in our life.

33

Joshua 24:15 – Choose for yourselves this day whom you will serve, whether the gods your forefathers served beyond the River, or the gods of the Amorites, in whose land you are living. But as for me and my household, we will serve the Lord.

No, it is not a mistake! Because it is so important, we are going to look at this verse again, in slightly more depth than in the previous devotional meditation. This ancient challenge made by Joshua all those years ago is a challenge that has echoed down through the centuries to us today, to *make the right spiritual choice.* We recognise that our Sovereign God allows and respects the freedom of choice He alone has granted us, even though He may sometimes disapprove of the consequences of some of our choices.

Whilst He has allowed us a free choice – *"Choose for yourselves..."*, and His Word reminds us that it is an urgent choice – *"...this day whom you will serve..."*, we are also provided with an alternative choice – *"...whether the gods your forefathers served beyond the River, or the gods of the Amorites, in whose land you are living."* But, we may ask, how does this alternative choice apply to us in the twenty-first century? What sort of alternatives do we have? What other gods do we have? When we begin to think about it carefully, we may be very surprised!

What alternatives? Practicing a religion of custom or convenience, rather than one of total commitment to the Lord is one example. Our custom, or habit, of attending church at Easter, Harvest, Christmas, but never darkening its doors at any other times in the year; the convenience of using the church for dedications or christenings, weddings, funerals, but no desire to worship God on other occasions. What other gods, with a small "g"? Anything we worship, think more of than anything or anyone else, comes first in our life, becomes a god. God commanded, "You shall have no other gods before me," *(Exodus 20:3).*

No one is saying that a television set, car, house, home comforts, money, designer clothes, and the like, are wrong. But when they come first before anything else, that makes them gods, and that makes them wrong! We can learn much from Joshua. He made a personal choice – *"But as for me and my household, we will serve the Lord."* This forceful word from a man with his mind made up, this ancient challenge from Joshua all those years ago, is a challenge to us today. It is all a matter of choice – making the right choice.

34

Ruth 1:1 – There was a famine in the land, and a man from Bethlehem in Judah, together with his wife and two sons, went to live for a while in the country of Moab.

There is a message for every one of us in every book of the Bible, and sometimes that message can come from some of the most unexpected place. That is why we are systematically working through the Bible meditating on selected verses as we seek for *daily strength for daily living.* This verse is one of those "unexpected places", for at first sight there seems very little in it to teach us a valuable lesson; but there is! The Bible says that as a result of a famine in Judah, and in Bethlehem in particular, "a man", whose name was Elimelech, took his wife and two sons to Moab, a journey of about fifty miles to the other side of the Red Sea, in what today is modern Jordan.

So what can we learn in the twenty-first century from this action which took place thousands of years ago? It is a simple lesson! We cannot help but wonder whether or not it was a mistake to move away from their homeland and live in a foreign country because *"there was a famine in the land."* Why do we suggest this? Because things began to go from bad to worse for them in the land of Moab. It would have been better if they had stayed in Bethlehem in spite of the famine. Would God really have seen them starve? It is highly unlikely!

Here, then, is the lesson for us. This action on the part of Elimelech and his family would remind us that when we take ourselves out of the will of God we cannot expect things to get better! We are told that Elimelech died in Moab, leaving his widow, Naomi, with her two sons, Mahlon and Chilion. They married two Moabite women, Orpah and Ruth. But tragedy struck again, and they also died, leaving now three widows to face the future alone. But were they alone? This beautiful story of Ruth answers that question, for it demonstrates do perfectly the personal interest and care God has in the affairs of mankind.

As through the next several devotional meditations we seek for a while in the book of *Ruth* for *daily strength for daily living*, let us do so with this important lesson firmly implanted in our mind. When we take ourselves out of the will of God we cannot expect things to get better!

35

Ruth 1:8,14 – Then Naomi said to her two daughters-in-law, Go back each of you, to your mother's home. May the Lord show kindness to you…Then Orpah kissed her mother-in-law good-bye, but Ruth clung to her.

In our continuing meditation on the book of *Ruth*, we have reached the point where Naomi decides to return to the land of her birth. She may have left her native Judah, but God was also in Moab, and she was never out of His sight, even though she grieved because she felt that the hand of the Lord had gone out against her. How wrong can we sometimes be! As F. B. Meyer so delightfully puts it, this story of Ruth "teaches us that we need never despair of our life, for in ways we know not of, God is bringing good out of evil, and sunshine from the dark and cloudy sky."

So Naomi decided to return to Judah, and in so doing gave her two daughters-in-law a choice as well as providing us with another valuable lesson. She said to the two younger women, *"Go back each of you to your mother's home. May the Lord show kindness to you."* Here was both a choice and a blessing! The Bible goes on to say that *Orpah kissed her mother-in-law good bye, but Ruth clung to her."* A touching little scene! With the choice given, the result was that one returned to her old way – or perhaps more correctly, she chose to remain in her old way – whilst the other daughter-in-law, Ruth, followed her mother-in-law into a new land, and hence into a completely new way of life.

We are reminded here, as we have already before in these devotional meditations, that the Lord gives us a choice every day, either to follow Him or return; or to put it another way, to enter a new life, into the Land of Spiritual Experience, or to remain in our natural, worldly environment. There is no compulsion, except perhaps from our own conviction, but there is certainly none from the Lord. He gives us a free choice. Ruth was richly blessed because of her decision, as our continued meditations in this book will reveal. It was an important decision.

We, too, will be richly blessed if daily we recognise that we have a choice, an important decision to make, that God is giving us that choice, and that we must always make the right one! It may be to *go in* to our Promised Land, *to possess* that land, *to explore* that land – so many different choices the Lord gives us – but let Him guide us in making the right one. We have to admit, however, that it is much easier to be like Orpah; it is not so easy to be like Ruth.

36

Ruth 1:16a – But Ruth replied, Don't urge me to leave you or to turn back from you. Where you go I will go…

Ruth had made the right choice, the right decision not to return to Moab but to remain with Naomi, her mother-in-law, as subsequent events proved. Although a Moabitess by birth, she was to embrace the Hebrew way if life, and become, in fact, an ancestor of the Lord Jesus Christ Himself *(Matthew 1:5)*. Her plea to her mother-in-law ranks as some of the most beautiful words to be found anywhere in the Bible. *"Don't urge me to leave you or turn back from you."* They are even more beautiful in the KJV. *"Intreat me not to leave thee, or to return from following after thee."* Can we fully appreciate here what it really meant for this young girl to make the decision that she did?

Ruth was not only about to follow her mother-in-law into a new land, but also into a new way of life, because she also said, *"Where you go I will go..."* Not only the separation from her own people (because, as far as we know, she had never before been out of Moab), but the loneliness of a foreign land faced her. Quite a daunting prospect! A new land, a new way of life, indeed, her decision had far-reaching effects, for the whole of her life, the whole of her being, the whole of her future was to be completely new.

As we seek for *daily strength for daily living*, is this not true for us today in a spiritual sense? God is still giving us a choice. The choice is still ours. The truth is, when we made our choice, our decision, to follow the Lord, all things became new – or, at least, they should have done. If the whole of our life, the whole of our being, the whole of our future did not become completely new, something was seriously wrong! Thinking of the analogy we used in previous meditations, when God set before us the Land of Spiritual Experience, did we go in and possess, explore and conquer it, or are we still hovering at the entrance?

Let us parallel our experience with that of Ruth's. Are we travelling new pathways through our new land? Did our decision to follow the Lord involve us in a new way of life? *"Where you go I will go..."* The words of the old chorus are particularly apt. *"Things are different now, something happened to me, since I gave my heart to Jesus. Things I loved before have gone away; things I love far more have come to stay. Things are different now."* Are they?

37

Ruth 1:16b – But Ruth replied…where you stay I will stay. Your people will be my people…

When Ruth made her decision to follow her mother-in-law, Naomi, all things became new; a new way of living, a new home, new friends, but above all, a new Power for living, which shows to us how important it is to make the right choice in the first place. *"Where you stay I will stay."* She was to have a new home, which prompts a question. Did our decision to follow the Lord result in a new spiritual home? It should have done! People are social creatures and love to gather together in all sorts of places. The public house, for example, or the social club can become like home to them. For Christians, our church should become home to us.

But more is implied. Not only a new spiritual home where we gather together to worship the Lord, important though this may be, but as the apostle Paul reminds us, "Don't you know that you yourselves are God's temple and that God's Spirit lives in you?" *(1 Corinthians 3:16)* We should maintain a new spiritual home where the Spirit of the Lord, whom we have decided to follow, can dwell at all times. *"Make in my heart a quiet place, and come and dwell therein. A little shrine of quietness, all sacred to Thyself; a little place of mystic grace, of self and sin swept bare. Come, occupy my silent place, and make Thy dwelling there!"* This prayer of John Oxenham's is particularly appropriate. Our new spiritual home must have an occupant; and our Divine Occupant will enter only if invited!

Ruth also said, *"Your people will be my people."* She was to have new friends and companions to meet, which prompts another question. Did our decision to follow the Lord include new companions and friends? It should have! Permit me a personal word of testimony! When I first really committed my life to the Lord (I had been saved and baptised several years before, but never *fully* committed) I was in the RAF at the time. My life changed in more ways than one as a result. It only took one person to say, "Hey, Wheadon's got religion!" and slowly my Air Force friends began to dwindle away. They even dubbed me with the title, "the flying parson", making it obvious that I was no longer one of them.

Was I lonely? Was I dispirited? Was I feeling out of it? Not at all! As a result of my commitment I inherited a host of new friends and companions, some of whom are still friends to this day, over fifty years later! There's a message in there somewhere, isn't there?

38

Ruth 1:16c – But Ruth replied…and your God my God.

We said in the previous devotional meditation that, when Ruth made her decision to follow her mother-in-law, Naomi, all things became new; a new way of living, a new home, new friends, but above all, a new Power for living, which shows to us how important it is to make the right choice in the first place. In that meditation we concentrated on the new home and the new friends, so now we need to look at the new Power for living. This really is *daily strength for daily living.* In these five words uttered by Ruth, her whole life was completely changed – *"and your God my God."* She was to have a new source of spiritual power, so very different from the old, and this prompts yet another question for us.

Did our decision to follow the Lord acknowledge a new power for living? It should have done! What prompted Ruth's decision? Perhaps she had seen something in Naomi's life which had attracted her to Naomi's God. A lesson here would teach us that, as professing Christians, we have the power to attract people to Christ. This is an awesome thought. Of course, we also have the power to repel them! This is an even more awesome thought! Naomi had obviously created an impression and Ruth had responded. As subsequent events proved, she made the right choice.

In acknowledging Jesus as our Lord and Saviour, we must also acknowledge the power of the Holy Spirit to enable us to live a life acceptable to Him. Without this power we will fail. Without this power we are more likely to repel people from Christ, rather than attract them to Him. So when we made our choice, our decision, to follow the Lord, all things became new – above all else, we received this new power for living, which shows how very important it was to make the right choice in the first place.

It is just a thought, but perhaps the most important question of all that we have asked so far could be the one we ask ourselves just now. Have we received, and are we daily receiving, this new Power for living? On second thoughts, maybe the truthful answer we give to ourselves before God is even more important than the question!

39

Ruth 2:11 – I've been told all about what you have done for your mother-in-law since the death of your husband – how you left your father and mother and your homeland and came to live with a people you did not know before.

Kindness and consideration of others never goes unnoticed; and if it is coupled with a strong faith, neither does it go unrewarded, not necessarily by man, but always by the Lord. Incidentally, His rewards are worth far more than man's, anyway! Such was the case with Ruth, who, although a stranger in a strange land, found favour both in the eyes of Boaz, the farmer in whose field she had gleaned corn, but more importantly, also in the eyes of the Lord God of Israel. Put simply, her kindness and consideration of Naomi did not go unnoticed nor unrewarded, neither by Boaz nor the Lord.

This verse records some of the words spoken by Boaz at this time, and they illustrate the farmer's attitude and reactions towards Ruth. Boaz was a good man, respected by the whole neighbourhood, which in itself recognised Ruth's devotion to her mother-in-law. We might even suggest that, when Boaz spoke these words to Ruth, he was voicing the feelings of the neighbourhood as well as his own. They are gracious words, acknowledging her decision to embrace a new home, a new people, a new country, but above all a new (to her) God.

Here is yet another valuable lesson for us to learn from this little book of *Ruth*; it is a lesson for us today in the twenty-first century. Let us always remember that we are strangers in a strange land. As the old spiritual song puts it, *"This world is not my home, I'm just a passin' through..."* It is so important to remember that the way we live our lives as Christians in this strange land will not go unnoticed or unrewarded, because Boaz went on to say – and we will look at it more fully in our next devotional meditation – *"May you be richly rewarded by the Lord..."* The KJV puts it more positively. *"A full reward will be given thee of the Lord God."*

We have to admit, though, that even without this added incentive, the world today could certainly do with a little more kindness and consideration of others, because the very opposite is often the case. This is why we so desperately need *daily strength for daily living*, because as twenty-first Century Christians who love their Lord, yet are strangers in a strange land, we should be setting the example by our kindness and consideration of other. So we gain this daily strength to go on living daily, setting this example, as strangers in a strange land.

40

Ruth 2:12 – May the Lord repay you for what you have done. May you be richly rewarded by the Lord, the God of Israel, under whose wings you have come to take refuge.

We began in the previous devotional meditation by saying that kindness and consideration of others never goes unnoticed, which is why the kindness and consideration Ruth showed towards her mother-in-law, Naomi, did not go unnoticed nor unrewarded, neither by Boaz nor the Lord. Here, then, were two widows, both in similar circumstances, we might say, yet in a sense they were totally different. Naomi had returned home and was living in familiar surroundings. Ruth had *adopted* her mother-in-law's homeland, and could therefore be rightly described as "a stranger in a strange land."

Being widows, there was little they could do to earn a living, so Ruth took advantage of the ancient law that allowed the poor to glean barley left over from the harvest, and gleaned enough both for herself and for Naomi. In *adopting* a new land she was also able to profit from the law of that land, which stated, "When you reap the harvest of your land, do not reap to the very edges of your field or gather the gleanings of your harvest...Leave them for the poor and the alien. I am the Lord your God" *(Leviticus 19:9,10).* The KJV uses the phrase, "the poor and stranger". Ruth was both poor and a stranger, so she was entitled to glean.

It was not by accident that Ruth began to glean in the field belonging to Boaz, for God still guides those who acknowledge Him in all things, as did this young girl. Boaz was a kinsman (relative) of Elimelech, the late husband of Naomi. He was also a godly man, a caring man, a kind man, which was why Ruth's kindness and consideration of Naomi was noticed by him. Strictly speaking, it had originally been brought to his attention by others, because he began by saying, *"I've been told all about what you have done for your mother-in-law,"* (KJV – *"It hath been fully shewed me..."*) but later he came to see for himself.

So here is yet another valuable lesson for us to learn for the twenty-first century from this ancient book. Ruth acknowledged and embraced the God of Naomi – the same God whom we worship today – and by so doing was taken under His wings where she found refuge, and so He guided her into the way, the field, where He wanted her to go. The lesson for us is that, God still guides those who acknowledge Him in all things and He will guide us daily through the Land of Spiritual Experience if we acknowledge Him daily as we travel.

41

Ruth 2:15,16 – Even if she gathers among the sheaves, don't embarrass her. Rather, pull out some stalks for her from the bundles and leave them for her to pick up, and don't rebuke her.

We have so far, in our meditations on the book of *Ruth*, been learning some valuable lessons from the actions of Ruth herself. But there is a lesson in this book to learn from the actions of Boaz. He went beyond the requirements of the law in showing kindness and consideration of Ruth. It is a kind of snowball effect! As Ruth had shown kindness and consideration towards her mother-in-law, Naomi, so here now is Boaz doing the same thing to Ruth. The important truth to notice, of course, is that the actions of both – Ruth and Boaz – were born out of their love for the same God.

Boaz's double command to his workers – or rather, the implication of these commands – is worthy of our consideration. *"Don't embarrass her...Don't rebuke her."* The law required that he leave only the corners of the field for the poor and stranger to glean *(Leviticus 19:9,10)*. By going beyond the law (not outside of the law, which is a very different thing) Boaz demonstrated a vital truth that has stood the test of time. Love for God is expressed in kindness and consideration for others, especially those less fortunate than ourselves.

Here is a truth so often overlooked by some Christians today. When Ruth went into the fields to glean corn, Boaz commanded that *"Even if she gathers among the sheaves, don't embarrass her."* Not just the corners but actually amongst the sheaves! And as if that is not generosity enough, he goes even further when he tells his workers to *"pull out some stalks for her from the bundles and leave them for her to pick up."*

Not just the corners, not just the sheaves, but now a few extras thrown in! So what can we as twenty-first century Christians learn from this? Boaz exemplifies, in his kindness and consideration of Ruth, God's love for mankind. He demonstrates also his own love for God, in that he shows by his actions what privileged people we can become, and how honoured we should feel, to be in the centre of God's will. At the risk of repetition, Christians should always recognise that love for God is expressed in kindness and consideration of others. This is a valuable lesson we all need to learn and keep uppermost in our minds

42

Ruth 2:22 – Naomi said to Ruth her daughter-in-law, It will be good for you, my daughter, to go with his girls, because in someone else's field you might be harmed.

This young girl, Ruth, although a stranger in a strange land, had found favour in the eyes of Boaz, the farmer in whose field she gleaned corn. She had also found favour in the eyes of the Lord, the God in whom she had put her trust. While she continued to glean in the fields of Boaz she reaped a rich reward; while continuing to obey the words of Boaz, when he had said to her, *"Don't go and glean in another field and don't go away from here"* (2:8), she would continue under his protection. In view of all this, Naomi felt the need to give some timely advice to her daughter-in-law.

Boaz had made a promise which required a spirit of obedience to activate it, just as the promises of God are sure only to those who believe and obey. Naomi recognised the implication of the promise and the need for Ruth to obey, and so advised her accordingly – the words are recorded in this verse. A complete reading of this short Old Testament book reveals that Ruth obeyed, and she remained faithful, and was richly blessed as a result, because the important phrase was, *"go with his girls, because in someone else's field you might be harmed."* The KJV puts it more bluntly! *That they meet thee not in any other field."*

Now, what valuable lesson can we, as twenty-first Century Christians, learn from Naomi's advice, and from this phrase in particular? Simply this! Here is a perfect example of what we can expect if we glean in the spiritual fields of the Lord; if we continue to obey His words when He invites us to come to Him and abide with Him. The promise is there, but so must the obedience be! We have to admit, there are many attractive fields in the world today where we might glean our pleasures and physical satisfactions, but the rich rewards we glean in the Lord's fields far outweigh any we might find elsewhere.

But, we may well ask, how do we know which fields are acceptable and which ones are out of bounds? Some are obvious, others less so. It is the *less so ones*, the so-called grey areas, that give the most trouble! Because this matter of obedience, and not being found in "any other field", is so important, we will look again at this verse in our next devotional meditation.

43

Ruth 2:22 – Naomi said unto Ruth her daughter-in-law, It is good, my daughter, that thou go out with his maidens, that they meet thee not in any other field. [KJV]

We ended the previous meditation asking how we can know which fields are acceptable and those that are not, as we considered the matter of obedience, of not being found in "any other field", because it is the less obvious ones, the so-called grey areas that give us the most trouble! This was a question which troubled me when I was a teenager in my church. Permit me to use this *personal* illustration here! My parents had forbidden me from attending a particular place where I could see no harm in going. After several arguments we reached stalemate! Then an opportunity presented itself in which I sought to prove my parents' decision wrong!

Once a month, all the ministers of the various churches in the town where I lived came together to form a Religious Brains Trust, where questions could be put anonymously to the panel of "experts" – a Christian version of a popular radio programme of that day. They visited each church in turn, and they were coming to my church that particular month. I would put my question to them.

"Is it wrong for me as a Christian to visit...?" and I named the place, fully convinced that there was no harm. I was even sure that they would give positive approval. My parents wouldn't have a leg to stand on! The answer, when it finally came, was totally unexpected, and in retrospect, was probably the wisest one I could possibly have received.

It went something like this: *"We believe that one day the Lord will return – the Second Coming – so the answer is entirely in your hands. We do not know when He will return, only that He will. We also know that He will return suddenly, when you least expect Him, and if you do not mind Him finding you in that place, then by all means go. If you have the slightest doubt, if you would feel even the slightest bit guilty, then it is obviously wrong for you to be there."*

What a wise answer! There was no further argument. I never did attend that particular place. In the context of this meditation from the book of *Ruth*, it would have been the wrong *field* for me. I would not have wanted the Lord to find me there! So the message of *Ruth* is a message for us today in the twenty-first century. Once again the choice is ours. If, like Ruth, we obey and remain faithful, we will be richly blessed. May it always be said of us, *"It is good...that they meet thee not in any other field."*

44

Ruth 3:5 – I will do whatever you say, Ruth answered.

Continuing this theme of obedience, we turn again to Ruth herself. She makes a promise to her mother-in-law, and the significance of it teaches us a valuable lesson for today. *"I will do whatever you say, Ruth answered,"* and this was the answer to the instructions given, which we can read for ourselves in the previous four verses of *chapter 3*. It was said of an Old Testament king that "as long as he sought the Lord, God gave him success" *(2 Chronicles 26:5)*. The KJV translates it, "God made him to prosper." Obedience to God's will and purpose always results in blessing, either in this life or the next – often in both! Such was the case of Ruth, who promised she would obey Naomi to the letter, and she meant it, for she went to Boaz and lay down at his feet – *no where else!* This was very important.

Under Hebrew law the next kinsman in line had to be given the right to purchase the land and possessions of the one who had died, and that included the widow, if there was one. Ruth was a young widow, but by her strict obedience she did not encourage Boaz to be dishonourable, so that he would be unable to acknowledge the right of a kinsman actually nearer than himself. If Ruth had not obeyed Naomi's instructions to the letter, Boaz might have weakened and failed to fulfil the law. There would have been no blessing to follow, only guilt.

There are many excellent expositions available on the book of *Ruth* if we should wish to study the law or history of this period. However, that is not the purpose of these devotional meditations, which seek to not only make the Bible relevant to our present situation, but to provide *daily strength for daily living.* So the lesson to learn from this incident is not the intricacy of Hebrew law, important though that may be, but something much more fundamental.

If we would be blessed in our daily living, if untold blessings are to be showered upon us as we go forward to explore and possess our Land of Spiritual Experience, then in obedience to the Lord's word to us (what He says in the Bible for us today; what He is – we trust – saying to us all through this book of devotional meditations) we must always be ready to say, *"I will do whatever you say."* That's plain enough, isn't it?

45

Ruth 4:14 – The women said to Naomi: "Praise be to the Lord, who this day has not left you without a kinsman-redeemer. May he become famous throughout Israel!

There are two ways of doing just about everything in this life – the right way and the wrong way! This Old Testament book of *Ruth* has been teaching us lessons in obedience, of doing things the right way. There are three main characters – Naomi, Ruth and Boaz; and in that order, beginning with Naomi, they did things the right way, they made the right choices, obeyed the laws of God, and untold rich blessings followed, as witnessed in this verse. If we read the whole of the book of *Ruth* we will find that Naomi obeyed the laws of God in her advice to Ruth; by her strict obedience to Naomi, Ruth did not encourage Boaz to be dishonourable; in obedience to God's law Boaz fulfilled that law.

We will, of course, have to read the whole of the book of *Ruth* to understand what we mean about this chain of obedience! If any one of the three had failed there would have been no blessing for the others. Each depended on the other, often without realising it. The lesson for us is simply this, not only must we be obedient to the Lord's will for us personally, by doing things the right way, and thereby being blessed ourselves, but we must also realise that we are responsible for each other. It is a sobering thought, but our disobedience could result in denying blessing to another – maybe several others!

Indeed, there were others who witnessed the untold blessings that followed obedience, who rejoiced with Naomi as she rejoiced. Ruth's blessing of a son, the subject of the women's praise to the Lord in this verse, was Naomi's blessing too, and without a doubt Boaz would be blessed – what father is not blessed when he is presented with a son? Without knowing at this point in time, Ruth was to find a place in the genealogy of the Davidic line by which the Lord Jesus Christ came. Had she not obeyed, this important link would have been broken.

This really sums up all the lessons we have learned from the book of *Ruth* through the past several devotional meditations. Our obedience brings blessings from the Lord both to us and others, but our disobedience could result in blessing being denied to someone else. Ruth's blessing of a son, which is what caused the women of Israel to rejoice with the words they expressed to Naomi, was in fact Naomi's blessings as well as a blessing to Boaz – and ultimately through Jesus Christ to the world. Who knows just how our blessings may bless others! But those blessings must begin with our obedience!

46

1 Samuel 3:1 – In those days the word of the Lord was rare; there were not many visions.

The days referred to in this verse were those at the time of Eli the priest and Samuel, many thousands of years ago, but God's Word is a living oracle, relevant just as much for us today as when it was first written. The KJV translation of this verse gives us a much more tender and poignant expression. *"The word of the Lord was precious in those days."* Because of the relevance of this ancient Scripture to us in the twenty-first century, it would not be wrong to restate this verse, and say, "The Word of the Lord is precious in *these* days." Something that is precious is irreplaceable, of great value (not necessarily costing a lot of money) and enhances our lives and gives added dimension to living.

No doubt we all have in our possession items that are extremely precious. In monetary terms they may be worthless, yet they are irreplaceable, of great value to us, and they enrich our lives to possess them. To others they would mean nothing. Now, many people possess a Bible. It may be the old Family Bible complete with metal clasps that has been handed down through the generations; it may be the Sunday school prize that has sat on the shelf unopened for years; it may be a Book that is read occasionally, perhaps at Easter and Christmas, and then read more as a duty than a pleasure.

Then there are those who study it regularly as an academic exercise, expounding on it as history, or philosophy, or literary appreciation, or a host of other subjects. Sometimes public pronouncements from people of such ilk can be very misleading, such as denying important fundamental truths as the resurrection, the virgin birth, even the deity of Christ. Through the centuries so-called scholars have tried to cast doubt on the authenticity and reliability of the Bible. They have all failed, and will fail, while there are those who are prepared to defend the Bible, to whom the word of the Lord is precious.

To the unbeliever and the academic alone the Bible is just a book. To the born again believer the Bible is God's Word, and is precious. It is irreplaceable by any other book, how ever good that book might be. It is of great value, not particularly in financial terms, but in terms of enriching and enhancing our lives. It is a Book which gives an added dimension to living, and provides *daily strength for daily living.* But only the born again believer who knows personally the Author, can truthfully say the Word of the Lord is really precious.

Can we, personally, say that, not only is the Word of God precious to us these days, but also that we know the Author? Now, there's a question for us to ponder!

47

1 Samuel 16:7 – The Lord does not look at the things man looks at. Man looks at the outward appearance, but the Lord looks at the heart.

So often we look on this verse as a challenge, in that we are reminded how the Lord looks on our hearts, not on the outward appearance as man does, so it behoves us to be sure of our inner spiritual experience. A mere façade of pious spirituality is not acceptable to God. But there is a rich blessing to be found in this verse if we approach it from the opposite direction! Not only do we see a challenge here, but there is also encouragement and comfort – and that is certainly a rich blessing.

When we are criticised, even persecuted, because people around us, even sometimes those nearest and dearest to us, do not understand why we do or say certain things, then here we can find encouragement and comfort. We can realise that they are looking on the outward appearance without fully appreciating the true motive behind our actions and words, whereas, God knows, He cares, and He understands, because He is looking on our heart. He knows we are seeking to do only His will, and that may well meet with opposition from others.

So the next time we feel "let down" or discouraged because those around us, or even close to us, just do not understand and even oppose us, let us remember that *"the Lord does not look at the things man looks at. Man looks at the outward appearance, but the Lord looks at the heart."* He is the One we must seek always to please. Here is a word of challenge, of course, because what He sees in our heart must be acceptable to Him, but it is also a word of encouragement and comfort from a God who cares and understand, from One who loves us, and from One who does *not* look on the outward appearance – a rich blessing, indeed!

48

2 Samuel 24:24 – But the king replied to Araunah, No, I insist on paying you for it. I will not sacrifice to the Lord my God burnt offerings that cost me nothing.

Reading the verses immediately before this verse, we learn that King David had been instructed to build an altar on the land of a man called Araunah and offer a burnt sacrifice to God, as was the custom in Old Testament times following an act of disobedience which resulted in dishonour to God because of the mistake. The circumstances of David's mistake is not important to this devotional meditation, but his reaction is!

Araunah felt honoured that the king should visit his land to build an altar, and offered David every facility to make the task easier, even to supplying the animal to sacrifice and the wood to burn. If he had been asked, he probably would have built the altar itself for David. How easy it could have been for the king. But David realised that in worship and service to God, that which costs nothing is valued in the same way – nothing! It was in these circumstances that David made this statement. *"I will not sacrifice to the Lord my God burnt offerings that cost me nothing."*

What, then, is the lesson for us to learn from this ancient incident? We would suggest two. The first is that the altar reminds us that when we fail God, as we all do from time to time – something we must admit to if we are honest – then He is always ready and willing to forgive the sinner who comes to Him sincerely in repentance seeking for His forgiveness. Such seeking is not easy but costly, for we have to admit that we are wrong, we have made a mistake, and that is never easy! Secondly, having sought and received forgiveness, service for God must follow. This, too, can be costly in that we are required to give of our time, our talents, our treasure.

To put it another way, to spend hours in God's service we would normally spend on our own pursuits; use our abilities in God's service that we would normally use to gratify our own desires; give money for God's service which would normally be wasted on possibly selfish activities. Too costly? Let us remember, service that costs us nothing is worth nothing. If we can identify with David in our personal circumstances right now and react like him, in the words of this verse, then we will have learned a very valuable lesson indeed, giving us more *daily strength for daily living*!

49

1 Kings 20:28 – The man of God came up and told the king of Israel, This is what the Lord says: Because the Arameans think the Lord is a god of the hills and not a god of the valleys, I will deliver this vast army into your hands, and you will know that I am the Lord.

This seems a strange thing to say, especially when it is not a true statement, that *"the Lord is a god of the hills and not a god of the valleys."* But, we may be saying, if it is in the Bible it *must* be true – if we accept the truthfulness of the Bible, that is. Of course we accept the Bible in its entirety. Every word is true. But so often we are like the Arameans (or Syrians, as they are better known today), and get things wrong! It was them who were wrong, not the Bible, when they thought the Lord was a god of the hills but not of the valleys. What a mistake! And they were to pay for their mistake!

The Syrians were preparing to do battle with the Israelites at a place called Aphek; the Syrian army outnumbered the Israeli army;

but the Bible says "the man of God" came to the king of Israel and gave the assurance contained in this verse. *(As an aside, it is strange how history tends to repeat itself! Syria, Israel, middle-east unrest, is as familiar to us today as it was in Old Testament times!)* But how does this verse help us today? By realising our mistake, if indeed we do think like the Syrians of old. We have already looked at this in a previous meditation, when we were reminded that in the Promised Land there are both hills and valleys.

When everything is going well, in the hilltop experiences of life, we have a great sense of God's presence. We rejoice in the fact that He is near and we can feel that nearness. The Lord is indeed a God of the hills. But when we pass through the valley-like experiences, when everything seems dark and the whole world appears to be against us, then we feel God is afar off – or worse, like the Syrians, we say He is not in the valley with us. There lies our mistake! Let us not make the same mistake as the Syrians, or we may suffer for it as they did. Instead, let us take comfort and encouragement from the abundance of Scripture which reminds us that we are never out of His sight, that He is with us always until the end of the world, that we are never alone. Whether we are on the hilltop or down in the valley, God is always at hand.

The hymn-writer puts it so beautifully. *"No, never alone, No, never alone, He promised never to leave me, never to leave me alone."* Let us make sure we learn from the mistake of the Syrians. God has promised never to leave us alone, whether we are on the hilltop or down in the valley, wherever we are in the Land of Spiritual Experience – and that is a promise worth having!

50

2 Kings 2:14 – Where now is the Lord, the God of Elijah?

These are the words of Elisha, but notice this, when Elijah's mantle fell on him at the beginning of his ministry, his cry was not for his predecessor, Elijah, as one would expect, but for Elijah's God. Now this is very important, because it presents us with a tremendous lesson in this devotional meditation, providing us with the *daily strength for daily living* that we seek. It is a word of challenge and a word of encouragement, as we can so often find in just one verse.

First of all, the challenge! If we are to fulfil the spiritual tasks set before us, as we go in to possess, explore and conquer the Land of Spiritual Experience we have considered many times before in these meditations, we have to realise that we must not depend upon *people* for our spiritual strength, how ever good those people might be, how ever helpful or encouraging they may be to us, how ever supportive they have been to us through the years. Our dependence must be entirely upon God. There is the challenge.

Yet, as we have said, so often there appears in a single verse or phrase of Scripture more than one nugget of truth, and in this verse there is a word of encouragement as well as a word of challenge. Not only is the challenge given to us to place our trust and dependence upon God alone, but we are encouraged by the fact that although our circumstances may change, our fellow-servants may be called to higher service just as Elijah was (how futile it would have been to depend entirely upon them for spiritual strength!), God Himself does not change.

The question we may well ask ourselves is, do we need spiritual strength just now? If we do, then let us be assured that the strength we need is always available. As Elisha called upon the God of Elijah, so can we, for the God of Elijah is our God also. He alone will give us the strength we need for every task. He alone will give us *daily strength for daily living.*

51

2 Kings 5:12 – Are not Abana and Pharpar, the rivers of Damascus, better than any of the waters of Israel? Couldn't I wash in them and be cleansed? So he turned and went off in a rage.

The story of Naaman is a familiar one. He was a man who seemed to have just about everything. Wealth, position, power, family, rank

– everything, that is, that this world had to offer – "but he had leprosy" *(2 Kings 5:1)*. He did not have health! A man, in spite of everything, who had a problem, a need, but a man who was unwilling to accept the solution, the cure. This verse tells us that *"he turned and went off in a rage."*

Whilst the story of Naaman is a familiar one, and there is much we could say concerning the faithfulness of the little maid, the significance of Elisha sending his servant rather than coming out himself, the seeking of cleansing with wealth being so futile – so many different truths by which we might profit spiritually – the message here that may be of the greatest help in giving us *daily strength for daily living* is a very simple one, and it is based on Naaman's reaction to Elisha's instructions.

There are many today who have great needs, soul-sickness, seeking satisfaction in life, searching for an inner peace, which always seems to escape them. Many today are seeking a cure for their sin-sick soul. Yet the solution and cure is so very simple – Jesus, the Saviour of the World, from Whom flows freely the Water of Life, of salvation, is alive and is here now. *But many turn away in a rage.* They seek the solution in the rivers of pleasure, they look for a cure in the rivers of wealth, they try to find that inner peace in the rivers of knowledge and education. But Jesus is the only way.

No doubt Abana and Pharper were much cleaner than Jordan, but Jordan was the only way of cleansing. No doubt Abana and Pharper were much more attractive than muddy Jordan, but there was no other way for Naaman. Worldly pleasure, education, knowledge, wealth, all may seem more attractive to the world's eyes for soul-satisfaction, for soul-cure, than Jesus, but Jesus is the only way to inner peace, to eternal life, to a deep sense of soul satisfaction. We are not saying pleasure, education, knowledge and wealth are wrong, but these things alone will not cleanse a sin-sick soul. Only Jesus can do that.

Naaman turned and went off in a rage. If we would find *daily strength for daily living*, we must be sure we never do!

52

2 Kings 7:9 – Then they said to each other, We're not doing right. This is a day of good news and we are keeping it to ourselves… Let us go at once and report this to the royal palace.

These are the words of four very sick men, taken from the story about four lepers who lay dying. But, we may be asking, why do we need to know about these sick men in this devotional meditation? The answer is, because this story of the four lepers presents us with a challenge today, even though we hear very little about leprosy these days as in Bible times. The city of Samaria had been besieged for so long by the Syrians that conditions in the city were desperate. Just outside the gates lived these four lepers. Beyond them was the Syrian camp. And this is where the story becomes interesting!

One night, due to a divine intervention, the Syrian forces fled the camp, the siege was over, but no one knew – except the four lepers who had come seeking food. Immediately they made their discovery of a deserted camp they began to eat and drink in plenty with no thought of the starving people in the city just a short distance away. Unless there was someone to tell them there was plenty of food for the taking in the Syrian camp they would die, and the lepers up to this point had not even given it a thought. Then they came to their senses!

This verse records for us that *"they said to each other, We're not doing right. This is a day of good news and we are keeping it to ourselves...Let us go at once and report this..."* So they did just that and the city was saved. But where is the challenge to us, we may ask? Just beyond our door – where we live, where we worship – there are multitudes of people who are dying in their sins, starving to death for lack of the Bread and Water of Life. This is a day of good news, not just *this* day as we read this meditation, but *every* day for a Christian is a day of good news.

We know there is more than sufficient "spiritual food" to "feed" all who come to the Saviour, but people need to be told. *"We're not doing right...*" if "*...we are keeping it to ourselves.*" As Christians we would be failing in our responsibility if we did not tell them. This would make us no better than those lepers. So let their example, when they finally came to their senses, be a challenge to us, and like them, let us go and tell those in spiritual need.

Because there is such a spiritual hunger today in the world of the twenty-first century, with all its consumerism and commercialism, it may help us to look again at this verse in our next devotional meditation, coupling it with some verses in the New Testament, thereby continuing the challenge to us to tell others about Jesus in this increasingly commercial world which tends to drown out the "good news" we need to go and tell.

53

2 Kings 7:9 – We're not doing right. This is a day of good news and we are keeping it to ourselves...Let us go at once and report...

We looked at the story of the four lepers in our previous devotional meditation, in which this verse appears. We also said that there is so much spiritual hunger today in this world of consumerism and commercialism, that we would look at this verse again and couple it with some verses from the New Testament, to continue the challenge to us as Christians to tell others about Jesus in this increasingly commercial world which tends to drown out the "good news" we need to go and tell. In *Luke 2:10,11* we are told that an angel appeared to shepherds one night and said, "Do not be afraid. I bring you good news of great joy that will be for all the people. Today...a Saviour has been born to you; he is Christ the Lord."

Here is a phrase – "*good news*" – which, appearing as it does in these two verses, presents us with a stark contrast. Indeed, it faces us with an important choice, to either withhold the *good news*, to suppress it, as in the Old Testament verse, or to joyfully share it with others, as in the New Testament verse. Whilst it is usually only at Christmas time when our thoughts turn especially to the coming of the Christ-child at Bethlehem, this is a truth that is relevant and important *every* day of the year. And why did He come? As the apostle John tells us, Jesus came that we may have life, and that we may have it to the full *(John 10:10)*.

Jesus did not remain a Babe. He became a Man, died and rose again, to give all who truly repent and believe the gift of eternal life. He is not a dead prophet, but a risen, living Saviour and Lord – our Saviour and Lord, if we believe. One day, as promised, He is coming again to take us to be with Himself for ever. Now that is surely what we can call really GOOD NEWS. So here is the challenge to us continuing; what are we going to do for the rest of our lives? Are we going to withhold this good news, suppress it, keep it to ourselves? Or will we realise that this is not God's will for us, and come to the understanding that, *"We're not doing right. This is a day of good news and we are keeping it to ourselves...Let us go at once and report..."*? If we do, then we can spend the rest of our lives joyfully sharing the good news with others.

There are many in this world today who are just waiting for someone to say, "I bring you good news of great joy that will be for all the people. Today...a Saviour has been born to you; he is Christ the Lord." At Christmas time, of course, this message tends to get drowned out especially with consumerism and commercialism, but things are really no different *every* day of the year. So let us face the challenge and spread the "good news" *every* day.

54

1 Chronicles 16:28,29 – Ascribe to the Lord...ascribe to the Lord glory...ascribe to the Lord the glory due to his name.

The word "ascribe" in these verses could just as easily be translated as "attribute" or "give", which is the word used in the KJV, anyway. Three times we are urged to give to the Lord, yet it has nothing to do with money – the concept so often uppermost in our minds when we talk about giving. So what are we being required to give here? As the verse continues the word "glory" is added, and if the question "why?" is still in our mind, the phrase, *"due to his name"*, answers it! In other words, we are being urged to recognise the Lord for who He is and thereby give the glory due to Him.

How can we do this? The answer is in that final phrase. We ascribe, or give, to the Lord the glory due to His *name*. As always, the Bible gives us all the answers we need. *Proverbs 18:10* – "The name of the Lord is a strong tower; the righteous run to it and are safe." We give glory to Him for His PROTECTION. All true Christians can testify to the protection God gives them day by day. *Song of Solomon 1:3 [KJV]* – "Thy name is as ointment poured forth." Just as ointment can be used to sooth and heal physically, so we give God glory for His SOOTHING and HEALING power in our spiritual lives.

Acts 10:43 – "Everyone who believes in [Jesus] receives forgiveness of sins through his name." So we give to the Lord glory for our SALVATION; we recognise Him for what He is, the Saviour of the World. *John 14:13* – Jesus said, "I will do whatever you ask in my name." This reminds us that we give Him glory for His PROVISION for our every need (not always our wants, of course!) And so we could go on, and on, for the Bible is full of reasons why we should *"ascribe to the Lord the glory due to his name."*

But we have looked at sufficient reasons to show how right it is to give Him glory, and how He has the right to expect it from us, because day by day we enjoy His protection, experience His soothing and healing power, thank Him for our salvation and appreciate His daily provision.

So as we give to the Lord *daily* glory for His *protection, soothing, healing, salvation, provision,* so the Lord will give to us *daily strength for daily living.*

55

2 Chronicles 7:14 – If my people, who are called by my name, will humble themselves and pray and seek my face and turn from their wicked ways, then will I hear from heaven and will forgive their sin and will heal their land.

There are still those who would tell us that the Bible is out of date, that it is not relevant today, and therefore there is little point in reading it. Quite apart from all the prophecies that have been fulfilled, and are still being fulfilled at this present time, there are many other verses which, because the Bible is God's Word to us in every age, are not only relevant but also vital to our present situation. This verse is one that is very important to us all right now in the twenty-first century. Although we may be looking particularly at the United Kingdom (once known as Great Britain) in this meditation, the situation facing this country can be replicated in many other major countries in the world today.

Britain was once known as a Christian country, but during the past few years there has been a steady decline in moral and spiritual standards. Since entering the new millennium the deterioration seems to have escalated dramatically. There is no need to enumerate all the sad and tragic events which have tended to push the word "Great" out of Great Britain. A glance at any daily newspaper will tell us all we need to know in this respect. All who love our country must surely be concerned about the direction in which we seem to be heading, even the direction it seems in which the Government is leading us, and wonder what can be done to stop the rot, to halt the decline.

It is so easy to criticise politicians and statesmen and those in authority; it is so easy to blame this group or that group; but the answer is not to try and apportion blame. We need to get our priorities right. So, what is the answer? Is there an answer? Whilst this verse was originally directed to the Children of Israel (and still is, for that matter!), it can now equally be directed at our own country, whichever country we live in at the moment. As we look around and sorrow at what we see, let us read this verse slowly and prayerfully.

It is just possible that this could be the answer to all our problems. It is certainly worth serious consideration. If we are struggling for the spiritual strength to daily combat the frightening decline we see around us, take heart, because this verse is one of many in the Bible that will give us *daily strength for daily living.*

56

2 Chronicles 14:2,3 – Asa did what was good and right in the eyes of the Lord his God. He removed the foreign altars and the high places, smashed the sacred stones and cut down the Asherah poles.

There is an interesting incident, which we mentioned very briefly in one of our earlier devotional meditations, concerning the third king of Judah, which contains many valuable lessons for us in the twenty-first century to help us gain *daily strength for daily living.* The king's name was Asa, and this verse tells us that he *"did what was good and right in the eyes of the Lord his God."* But this was only the start, as we will discover in this and the next few meditations.

As we begin to look at the spiritual aspects of this Old Testament incident, which has to do with altars of strange gods, images, and the building of fenced cities in Judah, we may well ask, what lessons from these ancient days can we learn that will help us today? The answer is, many! So we begin by asking, what were the "good and right" things Asa did which received the approval of God? This verse tells us! He "removed" … "smashed" … "cut down" all those things of which God disapproved. Asa is known as the king who set out to rid his land of idolatry.

Of course, we may be saying this is not relevant, because in this modern age we do not worship idols. We have no little images in our house, no wooden figures, neither on the sideboard nor set up on a pole! We have nothing that resembles a god. But is this true?

An idol or god does not have any particular shape. Anything that comes before God our Heavenly Father becomes an idol; can become our god. It may be square, with a glass screen and knobs; it may be a large object in our garage with a wheel on each corner; it might even be in the form of paper, green, blue, brown, purple, with the Monarch's portrait or other image on it! So here may be the first lesson the Lord wants to teach us.

What God may well be saying to us right now is that we must always be prepared to remove, smash and cut down anything that is displeasing to God in our life. The moment He reveals to us through His Spirit things that would hinder our relationship with the Lord, we must be prepared to obey. It may even mean removing, smashing and cutting down barriers we never knew existed until He reveals them to us! Now, there's a thought!

57

2 Chronicles 14:2,3 – Asa did that which was good and right in the eyes of the Lord his God: For he took away the altars of the strange gods, and the high places, and brake down the images, and cut down the groves. [KJV]

As we continue to look at the spiritual aspects of this interesting incident in the life of Asa, the third king of Judah, we ended our previous devotional meditation by saying that, like Asa, we must always be prepared to remove, smash and cut down anything that is displeasing to God in our life, if that is what He is saying to us right now. It may even mean removing, smashing and cutting down barriers we never knew existed until He reveals them to us! Permit me to use a personal illustration of that thought!

Many years ago I was involved with a week long Christian Convention, where people were blessed and healed, mentally, physically and spiritually. During that week a delegate handed to me three full packets of cigarettes. "Please destroy them for me, Mr. Wheadon," she asked. And, of course, I was happy to oblige!

Apparently, during one of the convention sessions, a young man had given his heart to the Lord and had become soundly converted. Without any prompting from those around him, he took from his pocket the three packets of cigarettes, which were ultimately handed to me.

To use the KJV phrases, *"he took away...brake down...cut down."* In handing over those cigarettes he had broken down the old. No one had told him about smoking; the Holy Spirit had revealed to him the need to break from the dirty habit! If his body was to be the Temple of the Living God, as the Bible declares, then this young man was not going to desecrate that Temple with poisonous tobacco smoke! Those sixty cigarettes could have become a barrier between God and himself. By breaking down the old and starting with the new, his relationship with the Lord was complete.

So many things in our lives, our homes, our churches, may need to be broken down, to be taken away. There is no need to list them in detail here! Each one of us, if we are honest with ourselves, will know if there is a need to break down the old, won't we?

58

2 Chronicles 14:4,6 – He commanded Judah to seek the Lord, the God of their fathers, and to obey his laws and commands...He built up...

As we continue to look at the spiritual aspects of this interesting incident in the life of Asa, the third king of Judah, we ended our previous devotional meditation by saying that many things in our lives, our homes, our churches, may need to be broken down, to be taken away, and that each one of us, if we are honest with ourselves, will know if there is a need to break down the old. But, of course, having broken down the old we need to begin to *"build up"*. Now, here is another valuable lesson for us. Notice, in this verse, Asa only began to build up *after* he had encouraged the people to *"seek the Lord, the God of their fathers, and to obey his laws and commands."*

If we would gain *daily strength for daily living* from the Lord, then daily we must seek His will in our lives; ask for His help and guidance; and where it is necessary to build up in the place where we have broken down the old, we do so only under His direction. Of course, this means we must be really honest with ourselves. We need to be sure in our own hearts that there is nothing which would hinder the work of the Holy Spirit, either in our lives as individuals, or in our church as a company of believers.

Only in this way can it be said of us, as it was said of Asa, he *"did what was good and right in the eyes of the Lord his God."* So far, then, we have been looking at what Asa did to receive this acclaim from God, and hopefully learning valuable lessons for ourselves, but the "interesting incident" has not quite come to an end! So, in our next devotional meditation we will look at the results of his obedience to God, and reflect on the fact that we can only achieve similar results in our lives if we exercise similar obedience.

59

2 Chronicles 14:7 – So they built and prospered.

As we conclude our look at the spiritual aspects of this interesting incident in the life of Asa, the third king of Judah, we ended our previous devotional meditation by promising that we will look in this meditation at the results of Asa's obedience, reflecting on the fact that that we can only achieve similar results in our lives if we exercise similar obedience. What, then, were the results of his obedience? The answer is in this verse. *So they built and prospered."* Not just built, we notice, but he prospered as well. But here we have to be careful!

There is a tendency to think of money, of worldly wealth, when we talk of prosperity; and some even preach what has become known as the "prosperity gospel", which is *not* taught in Scripture! But let us remember that we are looking at this Old Testament incident along spiritual lines. *Daily Strength for Daily Living* is a book of *devotional* meditations. There is no harm in us as Christians confessing that we are very rich people if, by so doing, we are not referring to money but praising God for the wealth of spiritual blessings He has given us. If we have the Lord as our Saviour, enjoy the power of the Holy Spirit, and live daily in the presence and will of our Heavenly Father – what greater prosperity can we have than this?

Those of us who daily try to serve the Lord, obeying His will, seeking always to please Him, can testify to the fact that as we build a sound spiritual life so we will prosper in the things of the Spirit. It is one thing just to build for the sake of building; it is quite another to build and prosper in the things that really matter. So what is the Lord saying to us here? It is simply this! If we are doing what is good and right in the eyes of the Lord, as we constantly and consistently break down all those things that would hinder His Spirit, and daily seek only His will for us, then as we build up so we will prosper in the things of the Spirit.

How much today, in the twenty-first century, do we really need *spiritual* prosperity in our lives, in our homes and in our churches? The Word of God assures us that we can have it, for as long as we seek the Lord and His will for us, He will make us to prosper. The Bible says so, and that is surely good enough for us!

60

2 Chronicles 28:1,5—Ahaz…did not do what was right in the eyes of the Lord…The Lord his God handed him over to the king of Aram. The Arameans defeated him and took many of his people as prisoners and brought them to Damascus.

If we were looking for a study in contrasts, we could do no better than compare the lives of these two kings of Judah – Asa, whom we have been considering in the past few devotional meditations, and Ahaz, described in this verse. The contrast lies in the bold statements concerning each king. *"Asa did what was good and right in the eyes of the Lord his God … Ahaz did not do what was right in the eyes of the Lord."* There is, however, a tremendous lesson for us to learn in relation to our responsibilities from the story of these two kings, and especially now from Ahaz.

Asa, as we know, prospered and built, and so his people prospered with him. Not so with Ahaz! The result of what we are told about him in the first part of this verse is recorded in the second part. *"The Lord his God handed him over to the king of Aram [Syria]. The Arameans [Syrians] defeated him and took away many of his people as prisoners and brought them to Damascus."* What a contrast! But what a lesson we can learn in this study of contrasts! When we fail to obey the Lord in everything, and do wrong in His sight, whilst we will suffer personally as a result, so might others as a result of our actions. As Christians we have a responsibility to and for others also.

We may not be carried away captive into Syria, but our sufferings can be just as devastating. Look what happened to Ahaz! Look what happened to his people! By our disobedience we may be the cause of others being led astray; by our failure to acknowledge God's will we may be responsible for many being carried away captive into sin. Christians have a responsibility not only for their own spiritual walk with the Lord, but for the spiritual walk of others, also, that in no way should we cause the downfall of others.

Think of what the outcome was for the people of Asa, who prospered and built, then think of what the outcome for the people of Ahaz could have been if the first part of this verse had read, *"Ahaz did what was right..."* Now, how do we appear "in the eyes of the Lord"? Like Asa, and unlike Ahaz, may it always be said of us, "they did right in the eyes of the Lord." It is the only safe way, after all, and it is a responsibility we have to accept!

61

Ezra 5:11 – We are the servants of the God of heaven and earth.

The history of the Children of Israel moves on, and with it, so do our devotional meditations! We have now come to a point in their history where we discover that the walls and the city of Jerusalem are in a state of disrepair, and perhaps the most serious of all, the temple was in ruins. This was the result of the nation being taken away captive into Babylon. Now they had returned (or, at least, some of them had) and they had set about rebuilding the walls, the city and the temple. But they were being challenged! And it is in the reply they gave to this challenge where we find a valuable lesson to give us our *daily strength for daily living.*

It is to be found in the reply the Jewish elders gave when they were asked on whose authority they were building the temple in Jerusalem. There are two very significant things in their reply to give us this valuable lesson. Not only did they credit God with the full authority, but they also acknowledged their own position in relation to Him – servants! It is a case of, those who honour God, He will honour them, even if they are servants; or, more especially, if they are self-confessed servants. Here, then is the significance.

A true servant is one who has surrendered all his rights and privileges to his master. Today we hear so much concerning people's rights; the demand for this or that privilege; the claims of our own authority. Hardly a day goes by that we fail to hear someone quoting "human rights legislation"; or demanding compensation for some breach of his or her human rights. We seem to live in a "compensation culture" these days! How often we hear of people who are afraid to make an important decision for fear of being sued for compensation if it turns out to be a wrong one!

But this should not be so for us if we are true Christians. We surrender our rights to the Lord Jesus; we seek not to please ourselves, to demand privileges for ourselves above others, to claim personal authority above that of our Lord – as true Christians we seek only to please Christ by obeying our Master in all things. We need to realise that the measure of our spiritual experience is governed by our reply to the question, "who authorised you?" The elders replied, *"We are the servants of the God of heaven and earth."* When challenged on anything spiritual in our life, what reply do we give?

62

Ezra 7:14 – The Law of your God, which is in your hand.

This verse contains a rather strange phrase. It came in a letter received by Ezra from the King of Persia. But, we may ask, what is so strange about it? Referring to the Word of God, if the king had said, "which is in your head", or even, "which is in your heart", these would be natural expressions, but to say, *"which is in your hand"* is a little unusual. Ezra was a knowledgeable man, having spent much time in the study of God's law, and was required to pronounce frequently upon his studies. We might say that, having devoted himself to such study, Ezra probably had more head knowledge of God's Word than anyone else in Israel at that time.

But there is more! The fervent way in which he pronounced upon that Word would suggest that he believed fervently in what he had learned from his studies; or, to put it another way, he possessed much heart knowledge. As it says elsewhere in the Old Testament, to do with a command of the Lord received by the prophet Ezekiel, but obviously a command also obeyed by Ezra, "Listen carefully and take to heart all the words I speak to you" *(Ezekiel 3:10)*. It is made much plainer in the KJV. "All my words that I shall speak unto thee receive in thine heart, and hear with thine ears." Head knowledge and heart knowledge.

Yet Ezra was an extremely practical man. Reading through the book that bears his name, we quickly realise that he was a man of action, that he put into practice the Word of God which he had studied and in which he believed. He was prepared to *do* what the Lord required of him as revealed through God's Word. So perhaps this verse is now beginning to appear less strange than we at first thought, and is providing us with a perfect example of what God requires of us in this modern age, this twenty-first century.

There are many people who are prepared to study the Bible today, even though not all of them will believe it, sadly. No doubt there are a large number who do believe in it, yet are not particularly moved by it. But the Bible also says we should be *doers* of the Word of God as well as hearers. So the lesson we can learn from Ezra (and Ezekiel, for that matter) is that we should not only be prepared to study the Bible – *head knowledge* – and believe sincerely in what we have studied – *heart knowledge* – but we are also required to act upon, to put into practice, that which we have studied and in what we believe – *hand knowledge* – so that it may be said of us, as it was to Ezra, that what we do for Him is according to *"the Law of your God, which is in your hand."* Now, that is what we call *practical* Christianity.

63

Nehemiah 8:10 – The joy of the Lord is your strength.

As Christians it is our responsibility to work hard for the Lord. We are often being reminded that we are saved to serve! Let us thank God for every Fellowship that encourages an "every-member-ministry". After all, there is much to do for Him, and if we are honest, there never seems to be enough hours in a day to get through all we want to do! I often used to say to my wife that I wish we could have forty-eight hour days, but she always reminded me just as often that I would probably not be satisfied even then. Twenty-four hours are what we are given, no more and no less. I guess she was right!

Incidentally, just as an aside, I thought there would be plenty of time come retirement – how wrong I was! A recent imaginary conversation with the Lord went something like this! *"Dear Lord, You know I have so much I want to accomplish for you in my retirement, yet there is so little time in which to do it. Please will you give me forty-eight hour days?"* The reply seemed to come back, *"If I gave you forty-eight hours, you would soon be asking for seventy-two! I have given you twenty-four, use them wisely for Me, and I will bless you!"* It seems my wife was right in the first place!

Even so, there may be times when we look back upon all that we have completed in His name and wonder where we managed to get the strength from, let alone the time; why we were not more tired, in fact. Our bodies may have become a little weary, but spiritually we somehow seem to have become stronger. How can this be? The answer is probably in this verse – *"the joy of the Lord is your strength"*. Of course, we must be careful not to become weary in well doing, but that is another issue. Experience somehow teaches us that the harder we work for the Lord the more joy we receive, and in turn find added strength – and time – to do even more!

Therefore, if we acknowledge that God, in His infinite wisdom, has given us only twenty-four hours in each day, and if we accept our Christian responsibilities faithfully and use those hours wisely for Him, then we will never run out of strength and will gather great joy as we go along! But, not only is this a responsibility, this verse is also a promise, and we can take it as such. Thinking about it, we can suppose it would be true to say that, whilst the joy of the Lord is our strength, the strength of the Lord is our joy, too. Now, there's a promise for us! One well worth thinking about! So what can we do for the Lord today?

64

Esther 8:8 – No document written in the king's name and sealed with his ring can be revoked.

The Bible, this Book from which we obtain *daily strength for daily living*, is incomparable amongst all books. Even though it is sometimes described as "the world's worst read best seller", it still is the best seller, and we might be surprised to learn that more people are beginning to read it in the twenty-first century than read it in the previous one, according to reports from Bible Societies. So, what makes the Bible so unique?

As Christians, we believe that *all* Scripture is God-breathed – that is, given by inspiration of God *(2 Timothy 3:16),* even though at least forty different authors from various social backgrounds wrote the Bible over a period of several thousands of years, yet, in a sense, there is only one Author. There is a complete unity of Scripture. There is no other book like it. Or to put it another way, the Scriptures are *unique* because the Author is God Himself!

Human authors may have held their pens, but it was the Lord who penned the words! The Living God produced the Living Word, in effect!

This has serious implications for us, as a spiritual parallel of this verse reveals. There are three (a three-point sermon!) important points. (1) The Bible is God's Holy and Infallible Word – *"the writing which is written in the king's name"*. (2) The Bible has the seal of royal authority – *"sealed with the king's ring"* – thus making it valid. The Word of God has such a "Seal" in the life, death and resurrection of Jesus Christ. Our Sovereign God set His divine seal of approval on the sacrifice of His Son at Calvary by raising Him from the dead. Jesus alone makes the Bible a valid document, authentic in every way. (3) Because this royal "Seal" is also a divine "Seal" it takes away man's authority to alter it in any way by addition or subtraction – *"may no man reverse"*.

This is one of the reasons why there are so many problems in the Church today, especially in Britain, because leading Churchmen try to undermine the authority of Scripture by casting doubt on some of its fundamental doctrines. They try to change the words to support their own pet theories. This is how false cults arise. It is good to have something about which we can be so certain in an uncertain world; to have something so positive in a negative world; to have something so secure in a world of so much insecurity.

What a different world it would be if we could all acknowledge this truth. And just what is this truth? That we must accept and obey God's Word *exactly* as it is – after all, this is what makes the Bible such a *unique* Book in the first place!

65

Job 2:13 – Then they sat on the ground with him for seven days and seven nights. No-one said a word to him, because they saw how great his suffering was.

As Christians who are seeking *daily strength for daily living*, we need always to bear in mind that our responsibilities are first of all towards God, then towards other people, before ourselves. As the Sunday school chorus puts it, *"J-O-Y, surely that must mean, Jesus first, yourself last, and others in between."* Very often our consideration of others reflects our true consideration of God. There are so many people around who are in need of a little sympathetic understanding, of a little kindly consideration, and it is our responsibility as Christians to give it.

But, we may say, we are not very good at talking, we find it hard to speak to someone in trouble or in need, we don't know what to say. Do we not sometimes use this as an excuse for doing nothing? Not my problem, we console ourselves! Take a look at our verse. This Old Testament character, Job, was in serious trouble. So serious, in fact, that his three friends who came to visit him didn't know what to say – *so they said nothing*, but stayed with him just to show that they really cared.

There is a delightful little story told about Queen Victoria, staying at her home, Osborne House on the Isle of Wight, an island just five miles off the South Coast of the United Kingdom, who, upon hearing of the death of one of her estate workers, ordered her carriage and set off to visit his widow. She entered the humble cottage and stayed for some time, whilst the neighbours formed a small crowd outside. When the queen left, the neighbours asked the grieving widow what the monarch had said to her. She replied, to everyone's amazement, "Nothing!" When pressed for an explanation she said, simply, "She just sat beside me, held my hand, and we wept together!" The queen herself was in mourning, having only recently been bereaved of her beloved Prince Albert.

If we take our Christian responsibilities seriously, if we really care about others, if we really want to show consideration for those in need, *we will do something*. Very often a handshake, a smile, or by just being there in a time of need, can mean more than any words spoken; and even if we are unable to actually be present, we could write a letter, maybe make a telephone call, and we can all pray for them *and let them know we are praying.* It is not always necessary to ***say*** we care, but it is necessary to ***show*** that we do!

66

Job 22:21 – Submit to God and be at peace with him.

Here in this verse we have a worthwhile piece of advice, although the KJV translation has much more impact! *"Acquaint now thyself with him, and be at peace."* There is another Old Testament verse, which says something similar. "Be still, and know that I am God" *(Psalm 46:10)*. The wonderful thing is that Almighty God has revealed Himself to mankind through His Word – the Bible. He is not an obscure Deity hidden away in some distant corner of the universe, but a loving Heavenly Father who desires that we who are His children should come to know Him, to become acquainted personally with Him.

This is why the word *"acquaint"* in the KJV has more impact, and can mean much more to us, than the word *"submit"* in the NIV. There are three things this verse is telling us: that the experience of becoming acquainted with God is something for the *present*, something that is *personal*, and something that will bring us *peace*. So often we are tempted to put off to tomorrow what we should do today. We promise ourselves that one day we will make a deep commitment to God, will really get to know Him, become personally acquainted with Him. But God requires that this should be a PRESENT experience – *"Acquaint NOW thyself with him..."*

It is so easy to recognise the need in others. Here is an experience for our neighbours, our friends, our loved ones, anyone but ourselves. This is not God's way. His desire is that this should be a PERSONAL experience – *"Acquaint now THYSELF with him..."* Jesus once said, "Peace I leave with you; my peace I give you" *(John 14:27)*. This sense of inner peace is a direct result of knowing God, of personal commitment to Him, of becoming acquainted with Him personally. We cannot have one without the other. What blessings await us. What blessings we could miss.

God's desire is that we should enjoy a PEACEFUL experience – *"Acquaint now thyself with him, and BE AT PEACE."* Let our prayer and desire be in the words of yet another Bible verse, "I want to know Christ" *(Philippians 3:10)*. This is what seeking for *daily strength for daily living* is all about, because all these Bible verses are worthwhile pieces of advice. Of course, it is up to us to take them and profit by them, isn't it?

67

Job 23:8 – I go forward, but he is not there; and backward, but I cannot perceive him… [KJV]

No doubt, if we are honest with ourselves, we have at some time come to a point in our life where we found it impossible to pray. It may have come on more than one occasion! Although we still believed in God, and continued to acknowledge Jesus as our Saviour, we found it difficult to communicate with our Heavenly Father. It was as if there was a barrier between God and ourselves which, try as we might, we could not break it down. It can be a very frightening experience, especially if it has happened more than once.

Sometimes there is a logical explanation. It may be the result of some bitter experience; it can happen with a bereavement – although there are those who have testified to the fact that, when a loved one was taken to be with the Lord, it brought them nearer to their Heavenly Father, not farther away from Him. Then, again, someone, from whom we least expected it, letting us down rather badly, could have caused it. On the other hand we might not have found a logical reason; it just happened!

Of course, we may be amongst those fortunate people to whom such an experience has never come. There is a word of caution here for those of us who have never had such an experience from those of us who have! We know how very distressing it can be, even frightening, and we probably thought it could never happen to us. But it can, and it did, and it might happen to any one of us, for none of us are immune. So none of us can become too complacent.

As we introduce the experience of Job in this and the next few devotional meditations, it is important to realise that to reach a point where we cannot seem to find God, where somehow we just cannot seem to get through to Him, is not of itself sinful. Jesus Himself passed through such an experience on the Cross, when He cried out, "My God, my God, why have you forsaken me?" *(Matthew 27:46)*. But had God really forsaken Him? Of course not. God had turned His back on the sin Jesus bore for us. He did not turn His back on His Son!

Job's experience of looking all around and not finding God – *"I go forward, but he is not there; and backward, but I cannot perceive him* – can become our experience, may have been our experience, may well become our experience again, but there are too many valuable lessons in this experience of Job's to pack into one meditation, which is why we will return to it in the next. In the meantime, let us be assured that, God is still close by, He has not forsaken us.

68

Job 23:8,9 – If I go to the east, he is not there; if I go to the west, I do not find him. When he is at work in the north, I do not see him; when he turns to the south, I catch no glimpse of him.

There may come a time in the future, perhaps we can recall a time in the past, or maybe we are here and now in the present, passing through an experience, which makes us cry out to God, "Where are You, Lord?" We may have at some time come to a point in our life where we found it impossible to pray; this may be our experience right now; it may be a future experience. Like Job, we look to the east, the west, the north, and the south, but we cannot find God – our prayers seem to hit a barrier. There is no way through! They seem to bounce off the ceiling!

To put it another way, wherever we look, whatever we do, wherever we go, however much we try, we cannot seem to communicate with the Lord. We feel cut off. We feel lost. We feel alone. What, then, can we do? One thing is certain, though, *we must never give up!* Jesus didn't, Job didn't, others who have passed this way didn't, nor must we! We must always remember that God does not cut Himself off from us. He does not construct the barrier and shut out His children. When we cannot pray, when communication appears impossible, when God seems no longer to be there, *this originates from us.*

Whatever the reason or cause, it is we ourselves who have cut the lines of communication, erected the barriers, and shut God out. Not deliberately, of course, but nevertheless, the result is the same. We cry out, "Where are You, Lord?" It is a distressing situation in which to be. Permit me a personal intrusion, because I want to share a word of encouragement based on my own experience. I still remember a time – it is many years ago now – when, like Job, I looked all around and failed to find God. The frightening thing was, I was actively engaged in Christian ministry at the time, extremely busy working for the Lord, when I suddenly appeared to be alone, deserted by Him!

The detailed circumstances are not important here, suffice to say that I continued to be like Job, and trusted in the God I could no longer find or with whom I could no longer communicate. It was a hard and difficult time, but praise His Name, He eventually brought me through; and if He could do it for me, He can do it for anyone who trusts in Him through similar circumstances. Job's faith was such that, as he passed through his distressing situation where his search for God seemed to be in vain, *he did not give up!* We may lose sight of God, but God never loses sight of us. We may even reach a point where we feel God no longer cares or understands – I did! – but be assured from His Word that there is never a moment in time when God ceases to love us, as we shall see when we conclude our contemplations from the book of *Job* in the next devotional meditation.

69

Job 23:10 – But he knows the way that I take; when he has tested me, I shall comer forth as gold.

As we conclude our contemplations from the book of *Job*, we realise that his faith was such, that even as he passed through this distressing situation where his search for God seemed to be in vain, he could say, as this verse records, *"But he knows the way that I take."* As we said in the previous meditation, we may lose sight of God, but God never loses sight of us. We may even reach a point where we feel God no longer cares or understands, although we can have the assurance from His Word that there is never a moment in time when God ceases to love us.

Perhaps it might be helpful to recall the illustration (used back in *Meditation No.23)* when our then 2½-year-old son became "lost" on the beach whilst on holiday, although in fact he had never been lost at all, because I could see him *all the time* from the promenade. We can be assured that when we feel lost spiritually, and running along the beach of life – could it be that we are running away? – God is there on the promenade keeping His eye on us. How ever far we run, how ever distressing the situation might be, we can be assured that *"he knows the way that I take"*. He cares and understands all the time. The moment will come when He joins us on the beach! Then we will fully realise that we have never been lost from His sight at all.

But there is one other lesson we can learn from Job. This verse continues, *"when he has tested me, I shall come forth as gold."* Every experience in life can be for our profit if we let it. Even a bitter experience of spiritual loneliness can actually strengthen us if we are prepared to allow such an experience to teach us. A refiner of gold skims off the dross from the molten metal to reveal the pure gold underneath. It shines in contrast to the dull impurities on the surface. There may be impurities in our spiritual lives, which must be removed before we can be of use to our Heavenly Father. It may have been those impurities that produced the barrier in the first place which cut us off from God. If the refiner is asked how he knows when the gold is fully refined, he would reply, "When I can see my face reflected on the surface of the pure gold."

Such an experience, then, can make us better Christians, if we let it. The important thing to remember is that God is always there, God always understands, God always cares, God never ceases to love us. If we feel the opposite of these things, either now or in the future, let us just hold on, never give up, and keep our faith. Then, when we come forth as shining gold, not only will we be blessed ourselves by such an experience, but we will be able to bring blessing to others also. After all, there is nothing greater than personal experience for sharing blessing with others.

Dare we suggest that, if we were able to ask God how He knows when we are fully refined, He would say to us, "When I can see my face reflected in you!"

70

Psalm 1:2 – His delight is in the law of the Lord, and on his law he meditates day and night.

A verse like this immediately poses a question – who is it that delights in God's Word and who meditates on it constantly? The answer is in the verse immediately before it – it is the person who is blessed. So the first important truth this verse tells us is that regular and constant Bible meditation brings great blessing – gives us *daily strength for daily living* – indeed, it is this blessing of the Lord which gives us such joy, such delight, in His Word.

But this verse tells us more, and here we have to be careful, because the word *meditation* can mean different things to different people. Here we are talking about *Bible* meditation. There are several different ways of using the Bible. There is the academic approach, where the Bible is treated as an ancient textbook, and very often scholars will try to cast doubt upon the truth of it. They seem to forget that before anything else the Bible is a *spiritual* Book, it is God's Word to His people, even though it does contain history, philosophy, geography, and many other things scholars like to get their academic teeth into!

Then there is pure Bible study, where the student takes the Word of God and studies it as a spiritual textbook, endeavouring to discover what God's Word has to say to him or her personally about the important issues of life, both here and in the hereafter. Profitable Bible study requires a notebook and pen to permanently record those discoveries. Many people use the Bible simply as a book they love to read, enjoying the stories, the poetic language, especially of the KJV – reading for pure literary pleasure.

But there is another way suggested by this verse, and the two volumes of *Daily Strength for Daily Living* are the product of that way – Bible meditation. Life is so busy – even more so, it seems, in the twenty-first century – so hectic, rushing by so quickly, that it is necessary from time to time for us to stop, to be still before God and to listen for His voice. Bible meditation is simply taking the Word of God, sitting quietly with it open before us, reading and listening – for as we meditate (that is, think seriously) on the words we read, God *will* speak to us through its pages. This will bring us great blessing, resulting in giving us tremendous joy, tremendous delight, which brings us back to where we started!

71

Psalm 8:4 – What is man that you are mindful of him?

Here is an amazing fact! God can speak to us and reveal tremendous truths from reading books other than just the Bible, and not necessarily *Christian* books. An example of this can be found in a book written by a scientist, who described in great detail the universe in which we live. The book revealed facts concerning the grandeur of the universe, yet set against the background of the vastness of the created cosmos, it emphasised the smallness of humankind's place in it.

We look upon our world – the earth – as a big planet, yet our nearest star – the sun – is thousands of times bigger. We look upon the sun, then, as a giant star, yet in cosmic terms it is but a *dwarf* star, a minute star in a tiny solar system. We look upon our solar system with the other planets circling around the sun – Mercury, Venus, Mars, Jupiter, Saturn, Uranus, Neptune, Pluto, as well as our own Earth – yet it is but a speck within a universe so colossal, so vast, that measurements of distance become meaningless. As the author of the book says of such vastness, it is mind-boggling!

Whilst we think of the greatness of the universe, and then recognise that God is even greater than all this, this short verse of only nine words could be described as mind-boggling, too! *"What is man that you are mindful of him?"* Measured against the vastness of God's created universe, and given that we are so sinful and rebellious, is it any wonder that the mind boggles when we realise that this great God loves us, cares about us, wants only the best for us, is, in fact, mindful of us? He gave His Son to die for us that we who believe might have eternal life.

Jesus who is alive *now*, has promised to return to Earth to take us to be with Himself for ever. The Holy Spirit of God is available to the whole of mankind to enable us to live a righteous life in a sinful world until we reach our eternal reward. This is not pie in the sky but down to earth fact! Or as someone once said, *"This is not pie in the sky till we die, but meat on the plate while we wait!"* This is how much God loves and cares about us. The greatness of God is not measured by the vast universe He has created, but by the fact that He is mindful of us as individuals – and that really is mind-boggling!

72

Psalm 14:1,4 – The fool says in his heart, There is no God…Will evildoers never learn?

In our previous devotional meditation we commented about a book written by a scientist in which he described in great detail the universe in which we live. It made interesting reading as fact upon fact revealed the grandeur of the universe – *cosmic consciousness*, the author called it. We also said in our previous meditation that God can speak to us and reveal tremendous truths from reading books other than just the Bible, and not necessarily *Christian* books. This scientific book was one example, which even the author himself actually described as mind-boggling.

He stated, for example, that if we could drive to the sun – the nearest star to earth – at a steady fifty-five miles an hour non-stop, it would take one hundred and ninety-three years to get there, such is the great distance from our planet. Yet, the next nearest star, *Alpha Centauri*, is so far away, that travelling at the same speed it would take us *fifty-two million years to reach it!* And even then we would have travelled only a very short distance into space! The universe is so colossal, so vast, that measurements of distance become meaningless, and indeed the mind boggles! So what truth can God reveal to us through all this vastness?

As we look at the wonderful beauty and order of creation on our own planet, then beyond it to the perfect symmetry and order of the vast universe, we cannot accept that it all happened just by chance; behind the beauty, the order, the perfect symmetry, there must be an all-controlling, intelligent Force – and this is where God is able to speak to us through this verse. *"The fool says in his heart, There is no God..."* Man has gained much knowledge concerning the creation of the universe – he may gain even more in the future with the launch of the massive Hubble telescope some years ago and the constant launching into space these days of bigger and bigger scientific satellites – but who, except a fool, can fail to acknowledge the hand of a controlling and caring God behind such creation?

The second part of this verse, *"Will evildoers never learn?"* is translated in the KJV as, *"Have all the workers of iniquity no knowledge?"* Man has always tried to take the credit for his own knowledge, but without God there would be no knowledge. So let us be wise, acknowledge God in our hearts, marvel at His wonderful creation, and praise His Name that He is still in control in spite of what man may say or do – those evildoers who will never learn! The choice is really ours, individually, to be wise or remain a fool!

73

Psalm 20:7 – Some trust in chariots and some in horses, but we trust in the name of the Lord our God.

It is quite surprising the number of professing Christians these days who put their trust and hopes in material things, who pin their faith and their future on the things they can see around them, rather than on a Person, the Founder of our Faith, the Lord Jesus Christ. But, we may be saying, surely this is understandable, just look at the sort of world we live in. Yet, can we really use this argument as an excuse? If we are honest with ourselves, the answer has to be "no!" Especially so when we realise that this is not a new experience, confined to the twenty-first century. Even in David's day the situation was similar, as he reminds us here in this verse. *"Some trust in chariots and some in horses..."* and we can replace the words "chariots" and "horses" with their modern equivalents, and the Old Testament situation is immediately transported into the twenty-first century!

There has always been a natural tendency for us to trust the things we can see; but material things are temporal. Only the things of God are eternal, and these we cannot see. Even in a highly materialistic world, such as the one we live in today, it is still only the eternal things, the spiritual things, which are of lasting benefit to us. As one writer once put it, *"Only one life, it will soon be past; only what's done for Christ will last."* The world is driven by materialism; mankind in general is carried along by it, like a tidal wave; should Christians, then, be seen riding the crest of that wave? The answer, of course, is a definite "no!"

Therefore, our testimony as Christians must be similar to that of David's. Whilst we acknowledge and recognise that there are those around us who trust only the material things of life – and they are the poorer for that, not the richer, incidentally – those of us who own the name of Christ and acknowledge Him as Saviour and Lord, must at all times *"trust in the name of the Lord our God."* Our complete trust for everything, past, present and future, must be fully found in Him, and no other! That is something, of course, which applies in every age. So now we are left with a soul-searching question – where do we put our trust today?

74

Psalm 23:1 – The Lord is my shepherd, I shall lack nothing.

Known as the Shepherd's Psalm, *Psalm 23* is almost as familiar outside the Christian community as it is within it. Perhaps that is why there is a wealth of *daily strength for daily living* in each of its verses. What, then, is the essential message of *Psalm 23* for us today? Put simply, it is that the Lord cares for us all individually at every stage of our journey through life. David, the writer of this Psalm, began his working life as a shepherd boy and ended it as a king. Life for him had many and varied experiences; in fact, through his writings, we get the distinct impression that he looked on life as more of a pilgrimage than anything else.

In this particular Psalm the first words – recorded in this verse – begin with an important statement, *"The Lord is my shepherd..."* In the last verse, David wrote, "and I will dwell in the house of the Lord for ever." In between these two verses he describes all the varied experiences through which he was to pass – identical experiences through which we, as Christians, will pass today as we journey to the house of the Lord ourselves – as we journey to heaven! As we shall see in this and the next six devotional meditations, no matter what stage of the journey we may have reached, nor what our need might be at each stage, the Good Shepherd cares for us individually all along the way.

But there is a condition attached! There always is with something really worthwhile! Unless we start our journey acknowledging the Lord as our Shepherd, then not only will we fail to end up dwelling in His house for ever at the end of that journey, but we will also have taken ourselves outside of His protection and guidance as we travel that journey through life. There is another verse in the Bible, which says, "You were like sheep going astray, but now you have returned to the Shepherd and Overseer of your souls" *(1 Peter 2:25)*.

This would suggest to us that the Lord is not simply our Shepherd, but the Shepherd of our *soul*, thereby reminding us of the importance that God places upon His care for His people, upon us; that, as a shepherd cares for his sheep so God cares for us, who are like sheep going astray. As we look at these verses of the Shepherd's Psalm in these devotional meditations, let the essential message impress itself upon our heart. The Lord cares for us individually, whatever stage of life's journey we may have reached or whatever our need might be right now, because He is the Shepherd of our soul.

75

Psalm 23:2 – He makes me lie down in green pastures, he leads me beside quiet waters.

The essential message of *Psalm 23* for us today is that the Lord cares for us all individually at every stage of our journey through life. The parallel between the eastern shepherd of Bible days and the Lord is, therefore, relevant for us today in the twenty-first century. In our previous devotional meditation we reminded ourselves that the Lord is the Shepherd of our *soul*, which is why God places great importance upon His care for His people through every stage of our journey through life. This verse demonstrates this perfectly. *"He makes me lie down in green pastures, he leads me beside quiet waters."*

As the heat intensified towards the middle of each day in those eastern fields, the flock would become weary. So the shepherd would make them lie down in pastures of tender green grass, making sure it was beside quiet waters. The KJV translates it as "still waters". Sheep cannot drink from running water. A shepherd who really cared for his sheep would know that. Our journey through life is not always easy. As Christians we find our spirit becoming tired and weary, in need of spiritual refreshment.

If we can say, *"The Lord is my Shepherd..."* then as our circumstances make it necessary, so our experience will be that He will make us lie down in green pastures, and He will lead us beside quiet, or still, waters. Someone once wrote that spiritual refreshment comes when we "lie down in the green pastures of Scripture and allow ourselves to be lead beside the quiet waters of prayer." So the message for us as we seek for our *daily strength for daily living* is this – if we have acknowledged the Lord as the Shepherd of our soul, and we are aiming to journey through life to the house of the Lord, where we hope to dwell for ever, then we must not neglect our regular Bible reading and times of prayer.

We might take it a stage further and suggest that, without this *daily strength for daily living*, without this daily spiritual rest and refreshment, we may never make it to that final heavenly abode!

76

Psalm 23:3 – He restores my soul. He guides me in paths of righteousness for his name's sake.

The essential message of *Psalm 23* for us today is that the Lord cares for us all individually at every stage of our journey through life. The parallel between the eastern shepherd of Bible days and the Lord is, therefore, relevant for us today in the twenty-first century. Unlike the modern shepherd, who may care for his sheep, and who would possibly hesitate to actually say he loved them each one, there was a tender intimacy between the eastern shepherd of the Bible and his sheep. Not only did he care for them, but he really loved them individually – probably even had a name for each one, and used their names!

There is that delightful parable Jesus told (recorded in *Matthew 18:11-14*), which illustrates perfectly this love and care. There was a shepherd who had one hundred sheep, but when he counted them at the end of the day he discovered that one was missing. So leaving the ninety-nine safely in the fold, he searched hard and long until he found the one sheep that was missing. It had strayed from the pathway, but the shepherd loved and cared so much that he would not leave it to wander alone. As pilgrims along the road of life, travelling the Land of Spiritual Experience we mentioned in earlier devotional meditations, we may stray from the pathway.

What could cause us to stray, we may ask? It could be through some act of disobedience. It could be through neglect of the Bible and prayer – or, as we said in the previous meditation, we have neglected to lie down in the green pastures of Scripture or have failed to allow ourselves to be lead beside the quiet waters of prayer. It could be so many different things which have caused us to stray. But if we can say, *"The Lord is my Shepherd..."* then we will also be able to say, *"He restores my soul. He guides me in paths of righteousness for his name's sake."* The Shepherd of our soul cares for us all along life's pathway; He searches for us when we go astray.

Like the eastern shepherd, He searches until He finds us; and because He is the Shepherd of our soul, He will restore that soul and lead us back on to the right pathway. The message from this verse for each one of us is simply this – if we have wandered from the pathway (and we may just at this moment feel spiritually lost and alone), then we must allow the Good Shepherd to not only find us but to bring us back as well.

77

Psalm 23:4a – Even though I walk through the valley of the shadow of death, I will fear no evil, for you are with me.

The essential message of *Psalm 23* for us today is that the Lord cares for us all individually at every stage of our journey through life. As we continue to draw the parallel between the eastern shepherd of the Bible and the Lord – the Good Shepherd – the writer of this Psalm, David, a shepherd-boy who became a king, no doubt, as he penned the words of this verse, was thinking of the dark ravines and towering cliffs through which he would often lead his sheep, where the light would be blotted out and dark shadows would be everywhere. In a place like that sheep could so easily be lost, wild animals may lurk eager to destroy; a frightening place and a frightening experience.

By themselves the timid sheep would be terrified. But they were never alone. The shepherd who loved them and cared for them was always with them, and they were able to pass through these valleys without fear. On our pilgrimage, our journey through life, our traverse through the Land of Spiritual Experience, we too are called upon to pass through dark valleys from time to time. Our Promised Land is full of hills and valleys. Being a Christian does not exempt nor immune us from the valley experiences. Someone once described life as "a vale of tears, sorrow and frustration, of trials, tribulations and disappointments."

We are not sure it is quite as bad as that! But notice, the Bible says we are passing *through* the valley, which can be a comfort. But the valleys do come. The little home with the curtains drawn, a home of sickness or bereavement; the railways disaster, the aeroplane crash, the road accident; a letter or telegram bearing earth-shattering news; the telephone call, the tragedies and sorrows conjured up by the television news of disaster. Whichever way we look we see and hear evidence of the valley of the shadow. But if we can say, *"The Lord is my Shepherd..."* and mean it, then when our valley experiences come, we will also be able to say, *"Even though I walk through the valley of the shadow of death, I will fear no evil, for you are with me."*

If we have proved the Good Shepherd's love and care through the brighter moments of our journey through life, then we will experience His sustaining grace and comforting arms as we journey along the dark pathway. The Shepherd of our soul is beside us; if we trust Him we will not be afraid, and He will see us safely through. After all, the Bible does say, "Even though I walk *through...*" doesn't it?

78

Psalm 23:4b – Your rod and your staff, they comfort me.

The essential message of *Psalm 23* for us today is that the Lord cares for us all individually at every stage of our journey through life. So far, in the last few devotional meditations, we have said that God places great importance upon His care for us because He is more than just our Shepherd, He is the Shepherd of our *soul.* Life is like a journey, and we have reminded ourselves that God's care extends to providing spiritual refreshment all along the way as we "lie down in the green pastures of Scripture and allow ourselves to be lead beside the quiet waters of prayer." We have been assured that if we wander from the pathway, whatever the reason (and there could be many), God loves and cares for us so much that He will search for us.

Just as the eastern shepherd searched for one sheep that had gone astray, although there were ninety-nine safely in the fold, God will search until He finds us, then gently lead us back into the safety of the right way. In our previous meditation we realised that we are all called to pass through the valley of the shadow from time to time, but if we acknowledge that the Lord is our Shepherd, then with this Shepherd of our soul beside us, and with our trust in Him, we will not be afraid on the dark pathway, and He will see us safely through. In this verse we are reminded that the shepherd always carried a rod and a staff with him.

The rod was a heavy club which he used to slay any wild animals that would attack the sheep. The staff was a crook which would be used to restrain the sheep from wandering. We might say that the rod was used to protect from *outward* attack, and the staff to protect from *inward* wanderings. This is significant, because if we can say, *"The Lord is my Shepherd..."* then we will also be able to say from first hand experience, *"Your rod and your staff, they comfort me."* We will know that we have the Lord's protection from the *outward* attacks of the devil – who is still a mighty force to be reckoned with in this world – and we will also know that we have the Lord's protection from all the *inward* wanderings of self.

What wanderings, we may ask? All those things which could cause us to wander from the pathway and make it necessary for the Shepherd of our soul to come searching for us, to bring us back into the right way. We have to admit that our Good Shepherd thinks of everything, doesn't He?

79

Psalm 23:5 – You prepare a table before me in the presence of my enemies. You anoint my head with oil; my cup overflows.

The essential message of *Psalm 23* for us today is that the Lord cares for us all individually at every stage of our journey through life. The parallel we have been drawing between the eastern shepherd of the Bible and the Lord, continues to be relevant, because there would come those occasions when a sheep was wounded, in spite of the love and care shown by the shepherd. More often than not it would have been from an attack by its natural enemy, a wild animal, having wandered out of the shepherd's care. Out of a heart of love, the shepherd would pour soothing oil into the wounds of the injured animal. Even though they might be surrounded at the time by wild animals, he would take time to comfort the sheep with extra food.

The love and care shown by the shepherd would be in abundant measure. Perhaps now we can begin to see the relevance of the continuing parallel! Such a description of loving care is one to be cherished, for it illustrates so perfectly the Good Shepherd's love and care for His children – for us! It is possible that our life at this moment is wounded; that some experience or circumstance has caused us to suffer; we may even feel right now that we are surrounded by enemies in the form of others who just don't understand us, don't *want* to understand us, or are even hostile to us – people we thought were our friends! Spiritual and emotional wounds can go far deeper than physical ones.

But if we can truthfully say, *"The Lord is my Shepherd..."* then the experience will follow, and we will be able to say also, *"You prepare a table before me in the presence of my enemies. You anoint my head with oil; my cup overflows."* Once again the essential message of this Shepherd's Psalm is demonstrated. The Lord is waiting to bless us, to refresh us, to heal us, to sustain us, for He is a God who cares for us all individually at every stage of our journey through life, every step we take through the Land of Spiritual Experience – through the bad times as well as the good – but we can only know the Lord's anointing, the Lord's refreshment in special times of need, the Lord's showers of blessing, if we are prepared to turn to Him and acknowledge Him as the Shepherd of our soul.

80

Psalm 23:6 – Surely goodness and love will follow me all the days of my life, and I will dwell in the house of the Lord for ever.

The essential message of *Psalm 23* for us today is that the Lord cares for us all individually at every stage of our journey through life. But if we are able to truthfully say, *"The Lord is my Shepherd..."* (as in the first verse of this Psalm), then through the many and varied experiences of life we will have the assurance that He will be with us (as described in the intervening verses of the Psalm) and at the end of our journey we will dwell in His house for ever (as in the last verse of this Psalm). Unless we begin that journey with the Lord we cannot expect to end it with Him. So the parallel between the eastern shepherd of the Bible and the Lord continues to be relevant for us all in the twenty-first century.

So let us look at the end of our journey through the eyes of the shepherd. On their final journey home, the shepherd leading his sheep would look ahead, scanning the road, so that there would be no fear, no danger, for the sheep. He would lead them safely back to the fold, and they would know it as they followed with trust and confidence. As those of us who, at the beginning of our journey, acknowledged the Lord as our Good Shepherd, and day by day follow Him with trust and confidence, whatever circumstances may have arisen, whatever experiences we may have pass through, we shall not want, we shall not fear, and we will arrive safely home.

The Lord who cares for us *now*, who cared for us at the start of our journey, and has cared for us every second, every minute, every hour, every day, every year to the present, will continue to care right to the very end of our journey...and beyond! This verse says, *"Surely goodness and love will follow me all the days of my life, and I will dwell in the house of the Lord for ever."* It is a wonderful promise and a comforting fact for the future, but it all depends upon the answer to a most important question – indeed, all that we have considered in this and the past six devotional meditations depends upon that same important question – *is the Lord really our Shepherd?*

81

Psalm 25:1 – To you, O Lord, I lift up my soul.

We really do have to admit that we live in a very frustrating world, in many ways an apparently God-forsaken world, one which makes tremendous demands upon us as Christians. Our spiritual self is, in a sense, fighting a constant battle with the world and those things that would draw us away from God. We often hear the phrase "Spiritual Warfare" used these days. We realise, of course, that there has always been opposition between the things of God and the things of the devil; we might say, a constant fight since the beginning of time. A battle it may be, but a *losing* battle it need not be if, like the Psalmist in this verse, we learn the secret of victory, which is to constantly lift up our soul, our whole spiritual self, to God.

Let us begin by lifting up our soul in GRATITUDE to God, thanking Him for what He has done for us in the past, is now doing for us in the present, and has promised to do for us in the future. Regularly let us lift up our soul to God in PRAYER. No matter how grateful we are to the Lord, this will not benefit us greatly unless we keep in constant contact with the Source of spiritual power to overcome the world. So gratitude and prayer must go hand-in-hand. But there is more!

One of the greatest enemies of our soul is hatred. We have only to read a newspaper or watch a television newscast to realise that most of the evil things that happen in this world have their roots in hatred! There is so much hatred in the world of the twenty-first century. When there is love in our heart there is no room for hate. They are two emotions that cannot dwell together. If we are to be victorious, we must counteract any hatred by lifting up our soul to God in LOVE. Gratitude, prayer, love are but three things – there are many more, and we can each compile our own list of emotions in which want to lift up our soul to God.

The important thing, of course, if day by day we are to live a victorious Christian life, is for us to be prepared to LIFT UP our soul to God above the frustrations and cares of this earthly life. A chorus Christians sometimes sing contain lines that might help us. *"Turn your eyes upon Jesus, look full in His wonderful face, and the things of earth will grow strangely dim, in the light of His glory and grace."* Only in this way is our constant victory assured. Why don't we try it sometime?

82

Psalm 27:1 – The Lord is my light and my salvation – whom shall I fear? The Lord is the stronghold of my life – of whom shall I be afraid?

There are several places in the Bible where we read that Jesus is the Light of the World – perhaps the most familiar verse is *John 8:12* – and that He came into this world to dispel the darkness of sin. All through the Bible sin is depicted by darkness and righteousness by light. Jesus Christ is the Supreme Universal Light. We also read that He is the Saviour of the World – and, again, perhaps the most familiar verse is *1 John 4:14* – offering salvation to all who will come to Him in repentance seeking forgiveness of their sins and acknowledging Him as their personal Saviour and Lord. Just as He is the Supreme Universal Light, so He is the Supreme Universal Saviour.

Then we read, too, that Jesus promised a tremendous spiritual strength. In the KJV the phrase in this verse, *"The Lord is the stronghold of my life,"* is translated as, "The Lord is the *strength* of my life." So to all who believe in the person and work of the Holy Spirit, and experience a daily infilling of His power, this promise assures us of the provision, amongst other things, of a stronghold for our life *(John 16:5-16)*; that the Holy Spirit is available to the whole world. People all over the world can testify to experiencing this great Power. So to Supreme Universal Light and Supreme Universal Saviour, we can now add Supreme Universal Power.

Now here is a surprising statement – the fact that we believe Jesus to be the Light, Saviour and Strength (Stronghold) of this World *will not help or benefit us one little bit!* Even the devil believes that! This belief in itself will not dispel the darkness of sin in our life, will not save us from our sins, nor provide a strength (stronghold) for our life, either. An abstract belief is not enough. So where does that leave us? How can we receive *daily strength for daily living* from such a belief? The answer is in this verse. Notice carefully what it says! It is only when, like the Psalmist, we are prepared to acknowledge the Lord as MY Light and MY Saviour and the Strength (Stronghold) of MY life that we will receive all that we need to live a life acceptable to Him. It is only when we make the abstract personal. It is only then that it will help and benefit us.

Our belief in Him must not only be universal – that indeed He is the Light, Saviour and Power of the whole world – but above all it must always be personal. If we are feeling at this moment that the Holy Spirit is stirring us to spiritual awareness; if we are feeling that Jesus, through that same Spirit, is drawing us to Himself; if we believe that God is calling us into a closer relationship with His Son; then remember that, like the Psalmist, our response must always be personal. The Lord is MY Light, MY Saviour, MY Strength – the Psalmist's experience must become ours, a truly *personal* experience.

83

Psalm 31:14,15 – But I trust in you, O Lord; I say, You are my God. My times are in your hands.

There are three specific things referred to in the Bible that *abide* – that is, things that will last for ever – and they are each to be found in this verse. This is a word of testimony, too. David, the shepherd-boy who became king, is here stating his beliefs and experience. It should be the experience of every Christian as well. The Bible also says, "And now these three remain: faith, hope and love" *(1 Corinthians 13:13)*. Every day every true Christian can draw *daily strength for daily living* by saying with the Psalmist, *"I trust in you, O Lord."* There may be times when we cannot understand why God allows certain things to happen, we may even question Him, but we must never doubt Him. One thing we need to be absolutely sure about, and that is that His way is always the right way, no matter how difficult it is for us to accept, and so we go on trusting Him day by day. This is *absolute faith.* This is the faith God requires of us daily.

The true Christian is also able to say with the Psalmist, *"My times are in your hand."* The past, present and future are in His hands, so we have a sure and certain hope. As the Christian song-writer expressed it, *"I'm in His hands, whate'er the future holds, I'm in His hands. The days I cannot see have all been planned for me; His way is best, you see, I'm in His hands."* There are those who would tell us that there is no hope for this world – the doom merchants! But the Bible says that Christians have *absolute hope,* and a constant hope, too, for it is one of those things that will abide – will last for ever.

The third thing this verse refers to is love, for we are able to say with the Psalmist, *"I say, You are my God."* Notice, it does not say *a* God or even *the* God, but *my* God – as we said in our previous devotional meditation, the Psalmist's experience must become ours, a truly *personal* experience. One of the shortest sentences in the Bible simply says, "God is love" *(1 John 4:16)*. It may be short but it says a lot! All through the Bible there is evidence of God's love for His children. We who acknowledge Him as *my* God are His children. He is a God who cares, who understands, who wants only the best – this is *absolute love.*

So as we put it all together, we realise this verse is giving us *daily strength for daily living* because it is revealing to us absolute faith, hope and love, three things that will abide, which is something worth knowing in this unstable world.

84

Psalm 31:15 – My times are in thy hand. [KJV]

As Christians our hymnbook can very often become a companion to our Bible – not a substitute, but a supplement. This is why it is appropriate to look at this verse again, but this time using the Bible and the hymnbook side by side. Is it not true that sometimes we are fearful of the *future*? The world situation, the situation in our own country, even our own town or village, makes us afraid of what lies ahead of us. The Bible says, *"My times are in thy hand."* So we need not fear. Our hymnbook says (and we quoted it in the previous meditation), *"I'm in His hands; I'm in His hands; Whate'er the future holds, I'm in His hands. The days I cannot see have all been planned for me, His way is best; You see, I'm in His hands."*

But what of the *present*, we may ask? Minute by minute, the future becomes the present, and passes into the past; and we have to live in the present with all its problems and difficulties. This may be true, but the Bible does say, "your strength will equal your days" *(Deuteronomy 33:25)*. God's promise as we go forth each day is that He will give us sufficient strength to face that day; so let us stand on His promises. *"Standing on the promises of Christ our King, Through eternal ages let His praises ring: Glory in the highest, I will shout and sing, Standing on the promises of God."* The Bible says, *"My times are in thy hand"* – and that includes *now!*

There may be those of us who are concerned about the *past*. Memories, regrets, joys, sorrows, we cannot forget them. Perhaps not, but there is no need to fear them. There is no condemnation for the true Christian, because, if we can truthfully say, *What a wonderful change in my life has been wrought, Since Jesus came into my heart. I have light in my soul for which long I have sought, Since Jesus came into my heart"* – then we need not be fearful of the past. Because we know that, *"My times are in thy hand,"* we can also say, *"I'm possessed of a hope that is steadfast and sure, Since Jesus came into my heart. And no dark clouds of doubt now my pathway obscure, Since Jesus came into my heart."*

Jesus is a Friend in the storms of life, a Friend at all times, both past, present and future, a Friend who sticks closer than a brother *(Proverbs 18:24)*, not a distant God, an impersonal Deity, but a personal Saviour, a loving Heavenly Father. So here is a wonderful word of encouragement and comfort for us. If we can say, *"I've found a Friend, O such a Friend! He loved me e're I knew Him; He drew me with the cords of love, And thus He bound me to Him. And round my heart still closely twine Those ties which nought can sever; For I am His, and He is mine, for ever and for ever .I've found a Friend, O such a Friend! All power to Him is given To guard me on my outward course And bring me safe to Heaven"* – then we can also say from experience, *"My times are in thy hand."* And that is encouragement and comfort indeed.

85

Psalm 34:3 – Glorify the Lord with me: let us exalt his name together.

It is good when we can do things together. When God made man, He commented that it was not good for man to be alone, so He made a woman as his companion. That really has been the pattern down through the ages. Men and women are described as "social animals" – not a very complimentary description, but true nevertheless! We are not created to be alone, although circumstances sometimes force us into such a situation. So how can we find *daily strength for daily living* in this verse? As so often happens, we can look at a verse of Scripture, and because the Bible is God's *Living* Word, it can reveal many different things to us from that one verse. *"Glorify the Lord with me: let us exalt his name together."* How can we do this?

Christian fellowship is the practice of "togetherness". God designed it that way, because so often a solitary pleasure can be greatly increased when it is shared with others. We should not stay alone to praise and glorify the Lord, but join with others of like-mind; take every opportunity to worship together. This is why becoming a member of a local church is so important. But this verse says more to us than just exhorting us to go out and join others in our praise and worship, it is also reminding us that there may be those who are unable to get out, the infirm, the elderly, the housebound – what about them? How can they obey this Scriptural injunction? The answer is, only if we who are strong and healthy can give them an opportunity to do so.

So, in this verse, we have both an exhortation and a challenge. Wherever we live, it is almost certain that we will never be very far from a lonely person, someone who is not able to join us in our worship. What great joy we could bring to them by a personal visit; for us to join *them* in our worship. Visiting a lonely person in the name of the Lord is in itself an act of worship. We do not have to confine our worship to a Sunday, for every day is a time to glorify the Lord. What a thrill it will give the lonely when we call and say,

"Glorify the Lord with me: let us exalt his name together." Let us take this verse as an exhortation, but never let us forget that it is also a challenge!

86

Psalm 34:8 – Taste and see that the Lord is good.

Having someone try to describe for us something of which we have had no experience can be a most frustrating experience in itself! It may be the exquisite taste of some exotic fruit they have enjoyed, or a special dish they have recently relished. How ever good their description might be, it could never compare with actually tasting that food for ourselves. On the other hand, if we have already tasted those things they are describing, we know exactly what they are talking about and can share in the pleasure and delight with them.

Of course, this could apply to almost anything. A piece of music, a colourful picture, a charming and picturesque place visited, a good book – the list is endless – and the descriptions may be absolutely perfect, but they are nothing compared with the real thing, the *personal* experience. Now, this is what this verse is saying to us. *"Taste and see that the Lord is good."* We could literally spend hours telling someone how good the Lord really is; of the tremendous blessings He gives us day by day; of the thrill of knowing we belong to Him, that we are children of God; of the comfort and peace we have of knowing he has forgiven our sins and that we have received the gift of eternal life.

Similarly, we could spend all day telling someone of all the good things God has done for us through the years and what He means to us right now. They may even believe every word we say, that they believe God really does exist and that He is a good God. They may even believe that He is a God who cares and loves them; that He understands them and is concerned about them. But believing is one thing and experiencing is another. This is where we, who are Christians, face a challenge and at the same time are presented with a mission.

So what is the challenge for us? Perhaps it is for us not to say anything more about God being good. We have already witnessed to that fact, so now let us go on to encourage them to *taste and see that the Lord is good* for themselves, to not just believe it, but to experience it for themselves! Maybe, for those of us who *have* tasted, this could be our mission in life, helping others to share the experience.

87

Psalm 37:3-5,7 – Trust in the Lord...Delight yourself in the Lord...Commit your way to the Lord... Be still before the Lord...

This verse is actually a "composite verse", actually made up of several phrases from *Psalm 37*, and tells us four things that we should do to make life easier and more enjoyable. This is what *Daily Strength for Daily Living* is all about! Anything that can enhance our daily living can't be bad! First, then, we should TRUST IN THE LORD. It is God who has created us, who loves us, who cares about us, who desires only the best for us, so we can have absolute trust in Him. The Bible also reminds us that if we trust we will not be afraid.

We need not fear the past, the present, nor the future, which will naturally result in the second thing this composite verse tells us, to DELIGHT YOURSELF IN THE LORD. Being a Christian is not, as some people think, a miserable affair. Someone once said to me, "I wouldn't like to be a Christian. You can't do this and you can't do that. There's no fun in it!" My reply was simple. "Don't you believe it! All those things I supposedly can't do I don't want to do, anyway. As a Christian I find there are so many things I can do which give me so much joy and pleasure, I wouldn't change my way of life for anything."

To put it another way, I have great delight in the Lord – He thrills my soul – because Christians do not travel through life alone. They constantly obey the third thing this composite verse says: COMMIT YOUR WAY TO THE LORD. It is so much easier and comforting to have a good guide with us when in a strange place.

There is no stranger place than the world in which we live! It is a source of comfort to know that we can commit our way to the Lord, that He will guide us safely through life, and He will make our journey that much easier – notice, we said *easier*, not easy!

And finally, our composite verse tells us to BE STILL BEFORE THE LORD. (The KJV uses the phrase, "Rest in the Lord.") Having put our trust in Him, found great joy and happiness by delighting ourselves in Him, and allowing Him to guide us daily through life, we can then rest in Him, be still before Him. No need to get up-tight, frustrated, depressed, fearful – so many unpleasant words we could use – just rest and relax in the Lord daily, gaining *daily strength for daily living*. What a difference it will make to our life!

88

Psalm 40:1-3 – He turned to me and heard my cry. He lifted me out of the slimy pit, out of the mud and mire; he set my feet on a rock and gave me a firm place to stand. He put a new song in my mouth, a hymn of praise to our God.

When the Psalmist gave his testimony, for that is what he is doing in these verses, telling what the Lord had done for him in his life, he should have been relating the experience of all true Christians everywhere. These verses outline four things which should always be present in that experience. It is good for us from time to time, if we are going to gain *daily strength for daily living*, to take stock of our own spiritual experience and standing before the Lord. These three verses will help us do just that!

There must have come a time in our Christian life when we realised our own sinfulness, our need of a Saviour, and cried out to God for salvation – and HE TURNED TO ME AND HEARD MY CRY. And then what did He do? Our testimony should continue with the tremendous confession that HE LIFTED ME OUT OF THE SLIMY PIT of degradation, OUT OF THE MUD AND MIRE of our sin. But that was only the beginning. The well-known hymn, *"Rock of ages cleft for me, let me hide myself in Thee"*, serves to remind us that Jesus Christ is the Rock of our Salvation, that only upon Him can we find a firm foundation upon which to build a strong spiritual life. So our testimony should always include the experience that HE SET MY FEET ON A ROCK – Himself!

Driving through a strange town or city can be quite daunting, so we are always grateful for a little guidance, either from a good map or a well-meaning person. The Bible provides us as Christians with a perfect Guide Book through life. Constant prayer keeps us as Christians in contact with its Author – the Lord. So we can testify to the fact that He has ESTABLISHED MY GOINGS. At least, that is how the KJV translates this verse! Strangely, the NIV translates it as something completely opposite! He *"gave me a firm place to stand."* Either way, standing or going, the Lord and His Word is still our Guide.

Christians love to sing. Every year there seems to be a plethora of new songs and hymns coming into use. The reason, of course, is because as true Christian's our testimony includes a realisation that HE PUT A NEW SONG IN MY MOUTH, A HYMN OF PRAISE TO OUR GOD. So, putting it all together, we should now know what should be included in our experience and in the experience of all true Christians everywhere. Yes, it is good for us from time to time to take stock of that experience!

89

Psalm 46:10 – Be still, and know that I am God.

There seems to be so much pressure crowding in upon us these days, so many demands seem to be made upon our time, so many calls upon our talents and skills, that, if we are really honest, both with ourselves as well as with other people, we are forced to admit that life becomes almost unbearable at times. "How can we continue to cope?" we ask ourselves. Yet this is the pace of life today – we live in a fast moving busy world set to become even faster and busier now we are in the twenty-first century – and unless we recognise our problems now and do something about them, the results could be quite disastrous. Indeed, we will not be able to cope!

But there is a solution! In the Psalm from which this verse is taken we are reminded that God is both our refuge and our strength, and that He is an ever-present help in time of trouble. This is a great comfort, yet we so often try to go it alone in our own strength, then wonder why we fail. So let us gain some *daily strength for daily living* by learning a valuable lesson from this verse, which is particularly poignant, for it tells us to *"Be still, and know that I am God."* Our Heavenly Father is aware of the pressures upon us and makes provision for it, not by taking those pressures away, but by providing a way for us to cope with them.

We need to recognise the importance of regular personal Bible reading and meditation – a regular and systematic exercising of "the incredible privilege of prayer" – privately as well as corporately. We need to find a few moments each day to "be still" before Him, to really come to know God as a personal and loving Heavenly Father who cares about us each one. Here, then, is the secret to coping! If we can find a few moments each day to "be still" before God, to gain *daily strength for daily living*, we will be surprised just how different our problems and pressures will appear … or maybe they will even disappear!

90

Psalm 47:6,7 – Sing praises to God, sing praises; sing praises to our King, sing praises. For God is the King of all the earth; sing to him a psalm of praise.

How people love to sing! All over the country at this moment someone somewhere will be singing, some in groups, some on their own. In some cases it will be pop-songs, for others it may be a choral concert or opera, and of course there will be hymn singing. So perhaps we can rephrase our opening sentence and say, how Christians love to sing! This is not unique to the twenty-first century, as this verse reminds us. God's people have been singing praises to Him since Bible times. So what can this verse teach us that will help us receive *daily strength for daily living*? The simple answer is, when we sing it should always be with purpose and understanding.

Singing with purpose involves acknowledging who God is. *"Sing praises to God, sing praises..."* reveals the purpose of our singing, to praise the Mighty God of the Universe, the Creator, Governor and Preserver of the World in which we live, the Saviour of Mankind – we could go on extolling His being. But there is more! The verse continues, *"Sing praises to our King, sing praises. For God is the King of all the earth..."* In acknowledging Him as King of all the earth, even of those who do not acknowledge Him as such, we demonstrate our recognition of Him as our Supreme Sovereign Head in full control, not only of the universe, but also in our own lives.

Now, there's a thought! As Christians, in our singing with purpose, we must recognise that we are His loyal subjects, in complete control, even more subject to Him than to any earthly monarch. We sometimes sing, *"Our God reigns,"* – a modern song which has become popular – and so He must, in our lives, all the time.

However, we have to turn to the KJV translation of the phrase, *"sing to him a psalm of praise,"* to learn our second lesson! "Sing ye praises with understanding." (As an aside, I have to admit that I cannot fathom the NIV translation of this phrase!) We wonder what goes through the minds of a football cup final crowd when they sing, *"Abide with me"*, or the group in the public house singing, *"The old rugged cross"*. The words of our hymns and sacred songs were written out of spiritual experience and understanding. Should we not sing them in the same way? So when we sing praises to God, let us make sure we are singing with purpose, acknowledging Him as King, and to understand exactly what it is we are singing.

91

Psalm 66:16 – Come and listen, all you who fear God; let me tell you what he has done for me.

With a Bible verse like this, it is a perfect opportunity for me to give my personal testimony, to tell others what the Lord has done for me in my life, but that is not the purpose of this devotional meditation! What the writer of this verse has done is to set us all a good example, to remind us that we all have a responsibility in this life to share the spiritual experiences we have with others, and for us all to encourage each other to be open and honest about our faith.

Those of us who have acknowledged Jesus Christ as our Saviour, know our sins have been forgiven, and have the complete assurance of salvation, in the words of this verse, *"let me tell you what he has done for me."* If we have discovered the additional dimension to living, know personally the power of the Holy Spirit in our life enabling us to overcome all sorts of seemingly impossible problems, then in the KJV translation of this phrase, "I will declare what he hath done for my soul." On the other hand, of course, if we have no real experience of Jesus Christ, no experience of the Holy Spirit, no experience of the transforming power of God the Father, then we have nothing to declare!

That is a very sad situation indeed, because we are missing out on so much in life and in the life to come. Perhaps, after all, there is a place in this devotional meditation for my personal testimony, so please permit me to take the opportunity! Well over half a century ago Jesus Christ came into my life – at my invitation, I might add, because He will never force Himself upon anyone – and He has been my constant Companion through life ever since. From that moment when I repented of my sins, sought for and received forgiveness for those sins, and acknowledged Jesus Christ as my Saviour, I have been richly blessed beyond measure. I have enjoyed that added dimension to life, which gives a thrilling purpose to living, and entered into experiences which would have been impossible without the Lord. Even now I am experiencing *daily strength for daily living* from His Word, and I am not ashamed to declare that I am a born again believer – a Christian.

So, as this verse has encouraged me to "declare what he hath done for my soul," it is my prayer that it will encourage others to say also, *Come and listen...let me tell you what he has done for me."* Why not start today, with the very next person we meet!

92

Psalm 68:11 – The Lord announced the word, and great was the company of those who proclaimed it.

As Christians we will never know this side of eternity just how much good, spiritually, we have accomplished during our lifetime. But one thing is certain, that which we have accomplished has been the Lord's doing, not our own! Indeed, as this verse reminds us, it is the Lord who has given us His Word, who has *"announced the word."* And, here is a challenging thought, He has given it to a particular people for a particular purpose: He has given it to us who are Christians for that particular purpose, as this verse reveals.

In a sense there are two Words; there is first the *Incarnate Word*, that is, Jesus Christ Himself. The Bible says, "In the beginning was the Word, and the Word was with God, and the Word was God…The Word became flesh and lived for a while among us" *(John 1:1,14)*. The second is the *Written Word*, the Bible itself, which tells us that, "All Scripture is God-breathed" *(2 Timothy 3:16)*. The KJV uses the phrase, "All Scripture is given by inspiration of God," which is really the same thing! Yet, in another sense, there is only *One Word*, for the Incarnate and Written Words are inseparable. We would not have the Bible without Christ (not even the Old Testament, which points towards, and prepares the way for, His coming from the beginning of time), and without the Bible we would know virtually nothing about Christ.

But this verse says more than just, *"the Lord announced the word,"* but goes on to say, *"great was the company of those who proclaimed it."* The KJV uses the word "publish" instead of "proclaim". Our responsibility, then, as Christians is to publish the

Word. How do we do this? First of all, by the testimony of a changed life. Someone once said, when Christ comes into the heart the devil goes out. Now that should make a difference! The Word is published through the lives of transformed Christians. Then, of course, there is the spoken word. We are to *tell* others about the Word. The Bible tells us of the early Christians, "Those who had been scattered preached the word wherever they went" *(Acts 8:4)*. This must be our example for today.

Some publish or proclaim the Word by writing books, some are privileged to broadcast on the radio or television – indeed, there is even at this very moment a great company of people publishing and proclaiming the Word somewhere in the world. So this verse reminds us that, whilst it is the Lord who has given us His Word, it is our responsibility as Christians to be amongst that great company, doing what that great company are doing…publishing or proclaiming the Word.

93

Psalm 68:19 – Praise be to the Lord, to God our Saviour, who daily bears our burdens.

The greatness of the God whom we worship is not measured by the vast universe He has created, but by the fact that He is mindful of us as individuals. This great God, who is even greater than the universe itself, is a God who loves us, cares for us, and wants only the best for us. We do not worship a God who is remote, a distant Deity dwelling on a distant star! We do not pray and sing praises to a God who is unconcerned about mankind, who is so *great* that He has no feelings for the *insignificant* – men and women and young people who inhabit the earth.

No, our God cares and loves us as His dear children, He is *"God our Saviour"*, providing a way of salvation to enable us to have the precious gift of eternal life. He is, indeed, the God of our salvation. But this verse adds another dimension to this great God of the universe, and demonstrates again that He is a God who loves and cares for us as individuals. *Praise to the Lord, to God our Saviour, who daily bears our burdens."* It's that last phrase which is important! The God whom we worship not only provides a way of salvation, not only gives us the precious gift of eternal life, has not only promised to come again to earth to take us to be with Himself for ever *(John 14)*, but in the meantime has promised to bear our burdens day by day.

As our great Burden-bearer, He longs to be involved in every area of our lives. He has promised never to leave us, or to forsake us, never to allow us to bear our burdens alone, for by acknowledging Him as our Saviour He will *daily* bear our burdens if we but place those things that concern us most at His feet, hand those concerns over to Him *and leave them there*. There is always the temptation to bring our burdens to the Lord, spend time asking Him to take them from us, then take them with us when we leave!

There is one thing more we should notice. We are seeking for *daily strength for daily living*, and the emphasis is on the word "daily". So it is with this verse. God has promised to bear our burdens *daily*, not just once in a while or even once a year. We who have acknowledged this great God of the universe as our personal Saviour, have the assurance that day by day we are not left alone to struggle, for He is daily bearing our burdens – truly a *Great* God in every respect, even greater than the great universe He has created.

94

Psalm 73:22-24 – I was senseless and ignorant; I was a brute beast before you. Yet I am always with you; you hold me by my right hand. You guide me with your counsel, and afterwards you will take me into glory.

It is good that the Christian should be reminded from time to time of the whole concept of his or her spiritual experience, both past, present and future. It is equally good that the non-Christian should be reminded of what it really means to be a Christian (that is, if a non-Christian happens to be reading this book! If not, then perhaps it would be good for us who profess the name of Christ to go and tell them!). In these verses we have such a reminder. As true Christians we can look back to the past when we were spiritually senseless and ignorant, were brute beasts, and as such needed a Saviour. So we remember the moment we acknowledged our sinfulness, came to faith in Christ, and were born again. In other words, remember the time we actually became a Christian.

Now, as a result, in the present, we have a constant companionship with our Saviour. We are always with Him, and He with us, because Jesus is not a dead prophet but a risen *living* Saviour. What a wonderful assurance, what a marvellous experience: *"I am always with you; you hold me by my right hand."* That which we have committed unto Him, our life, our soul, our all, He is now keeping daily, with the promise that one day in the future He will take us into glory. What a promise to the Christian! Without the past there would be no present; without the continued present there would be no future – this, then, is the whole concept of our true Christian experience. It really is a wonderful assurance and a marvellous experience.

But it is only for the Christian. What, then, is the message for the non-Christian who may happen to be reading this? Or, as we have said, what is the message for us who profess the name of Christ to go and tell them? It is simply this: *see what you're missing!*

95

Psalm 74:16 – The day is yours, and yours also the night.

What this verse is really saying is that time belongs to God. If the day belongs to Him, and the night belongs to Him as well, then there isn't really anything left, is there? So when we say that we haven't got time to pray, to read the Bible, to worship God, to serve the Lord, are we not robbing God of what is rightfully His anyway – time? We have twenty-four hours each day, seven days each week, fifty-two weeks each year, and all that time belongs to God! He gives it to us for our benefit. Whether we do benefit from it or not depends entirely upon how we use it.

It is a strange thing, but we hear a lot especially these days in Christian circles about tithing our income, but very little if anything about tithing our time. Special stewardship meetings are held, even special people appointed to promote stewardship, in an attempt to guide and regulate the giving of our money to the Lord's work; but what about the giving of our time? We tithe our income because we recognise that a tenth of our wealth, according to the Bible, belongs to the Lord. Supposing we tithe our time and give a tenth of that, even though the total belongs to God, what then? It is quite a thought, isn't it?

One of the greatest problems for a Christian today is the pace of life, the pressure of time, robbing us of those essential moments which we should devote exclusively to God. To say we have no time for God is no excuse, for this verse reminds us that, *"The day is yours, and yours also the night."* What a difference it would make to our day if we could take time to be quiet before God, to pray, to meditate on His Word, to worship Him, to come to Him and obtain *daily strength for daily living.* Perhaps there is value in a book such as this one, helping us to begin each day giving God back a little of His time, although only very briefly, if indeed that is the purpose to which the reader is going to put this book. It is certainly not a tenth, which is the meaning of the word "tithe", but it is better than no time at all!

How we use God's time is actually in our own hands; He allows us to use it as we will; if we use it wisely it will benefit us greatly, which is why God gave us time in the first place! By all means let us give our money to the Lord, but let us not forget to give our time as well – it will make such a difference to our day. It is just a though, but why not start *today!*

96

Psalm 87:7 – All my fountains are in you.

Up in the Cotswold Hills, a very popular holiday area in the United Kingdom, there is a little spring which bubbles and gurgles into a little stream, which in turn runs merrily down the hillside. It is a very little stream, children can and do play in it without fear of being drowned, and it serves no useful purpose except to provide a pretty view for those who may want to picnic beside the rippling water, or an equally pretty setting for the camera enthusiasts desiring a picturesque background for their photographs. At the other end of this stream, however, there are many large bridges spanning it, ocean going liners and cargo boats have, in the past, sailed along it, large river craft still ply its waters, and it is still a useful waterway even though it no longer serves the United Kingdom with one of its principal sea ports.

This "stream", which at its mouth is six miles across, has in its history been (and still is to a large extent) a very useful river, a vital waterway for trade and industry, a playground to bring delight and pleasure to thousands: the annual Boat Race between Oxford and Cambridge, two great universities in the United Kingdom, for example, or the Henley Regatta, and the many pleasure boats through the Oxfordshire countryside, as well as through the capital itself, London. But the great River Thames had to have a source…a delightful little spring way up in the Cotswold Hills!

So far, this devotional meditation has taken on the form more of a geography lesson, rather than providing something to give us *daily strength for daily living.* But there is a purpose! We will find a clue in this verse. The Psalmist acknowledged that, *"All my fountains are in you,"* or as the KJV puts it, "All my streams are in thee." This verse, then, reminds us that as Christians the source of all spiritual usefulness, our spiritual joy, our very spiritual experience itself, must begin somewhere. That "somewhere" is in God, for it is to Him that the Psalmist is referring.

If we are to live as God would have us live, then like the Psalmist, we must acknowledge Him as being the Source of all that we are and all that we can become. As the hymn writer so adequately sums it up, *"My God, the spring of all my joys, the life of my delights, the glory of my brightest days, and comfort of my nights."* Now, that's a geography lesson worth learning!

97

Psalm 92:13 – Planted in the house of the Lord, they will flourish in the courts of our God.

Sometimes the Bible appears to have a strange way of expressing a very important truth. This verse is one example. It is a verse which reminds us of our commitment to the Lord in this life and how it will affect us in our future life – or, to put it another way, having accepted God's gift of eternal life, the way we live that life this side of the grave will determine how we continue that life on the other side of the grave in eternity! Now, it is an established fact that anything that is planted, if it is to survive, must have roots that go deep, otherwise the slightest storm will destroy it, whether that "thing" is a tree, a bush or a small plant.

This is an important feature of the Christian way of life. Unless we are deeply rooted and grounded in the Lord, unless our spiritual roots go deep in our commitment to Him, then the storms of life will destroy us, will destroy our faith: whether we are so-called "big" Christians with "big" responsibilities, or only so-called "small" Christians with "lesser" responsibilities. (Incidentally, the importance of our work is not of interest to God; the way in which we discharge our responsibilities are the things which really count with Him! A "small" responsibility in man's sight can really be a "big" responsibility in the sight of God.)

The promise of God's Word is that those who are *"planted in the house of the Lord, they will flourish in the courts of our God."* The important word here is "flourish". It is a word which means, "to grow abundantly, to thrive prosperously," and are very apt descriptions of a true Christian. We are, of course, talking of *spiritual* prosperity, not material prosperity, which is not a Biblical concept! The deeper we are rooted in Him the more abundantly we grow spiritually. The more firmly planted in this life the more prosperously we will thrive in the next. We cannot divorce one life from the other. In a sense it is the same life, anyway – eternal life both sides of the grave!

This is God's way, and His way is always best, always right.

What we are and what we have become mentally and spiritually in this life by God's grace will not be wasted in the next. So, perhaps this verse is not as strange as it first appeared. What it is simply saying to us is, let us be sure that we are deeply *"planted in the house of the Lord"* (that is, in this great world which He has created), then we will be sure to *"flourish in the courts of our God"* (that is, in eternity, the place He has gone to prepare for us on the other side of the grave). When we really come to think about it, this is not a frightening though but a very comforting one.

98

Psalm 103:11 – For as high as the heavens are above the earth, so great is his love for those who fear him.

It is not often that I mark my Bible other than underline a verse or phrase that has helped or blessed me. But in the margin beside two verses in *Psalm 103* I have placed a mark to remind me of the tremendous blessing received from these two verses. In this and the next devotional meditation I invite you to share this blessing with me; and perhaps you might want to mark your Bible in a similar way!

This verse prompts the first mark in our Bible. *"For as high as the heavens are above the earth, so great is his love for those who fear him."* Just how high is heaven above the earth? No one knows! What does it matter? The astronauts (or was it the cosmonauts?) travelling through space said they had not seen God on their travels! Did they really expect to? The Psalmist here is not giving us a lesson in astronomy. He is illustrating God's great mercy towards each one of us who have come to faith in Jesus Christ.

God loves us so dearly, that He is extending His mercy towards us just as far as it is possible to extend it, and so the Psalmist uses the heavens as the farthest vertical point known to him – heaven, where God dwells! The mercy of God extends from heaven itself right down to us here on earth. There is no distance too far! There is no restriction on that mercy towards *"those who fear him."* When we sing the hymn, *"How Great Thou Art"*, how much greater can God be than to show such love and mercy towards us? We can certainly mean what we sing!

Although the Saviour would not physically come to earth until many years after the Psalmist penned these words, we can be sure that God, who is Sovereign and knows the beginning from the end, would have the sacrifice of His Son in mind; that God's love and mercy towards us is in Christ. Indeed, it is because of His love and mercy He gave us Jesus as our Saviour. So I was prompted to place my first mark. Perhaps you might like to do the same!

In the margin of my Bible I placed a vertical line to remind me of God's love and mercy extended right down from heaven to me.

99

Psalm 103:12 –As far as the east is from the west, so far has he removed our transgressions from us.

It is not often that I mark my Bible other than underline a verse or phrase that has helped or blessed me. But in the margin beside two verses in *Psalm 103* I have placed a mark to remind me of the tremendous blessing received from these two verses. In the previous devotional meditation I invited you to share this blessing with me, with the suggestion that perhaps you might want to mark your Bible in a similar way!

This verse prompts the second mark in our Bible. *"As far as the east is from the west, so far has he removed our transgressions from us."* Just how much farther from the east can one get than the west? This is nothing to do with conflicts between east and west, which have been going on for hundreds of years anyway, nor has it to do with diplomatic relations (or lack of them!) between the so-called Eastern World and the Western World. Just as in the previous verse, considered in our previous meditation, the Psalmist was not giving us a lesson on astronomy, so in this verse we are not being given a lesson on geography!

Because of God's love and mercy stretching right down to us, our Heavenly Father has removed our transgressions, our sins, from us just as far as it is possible to remove them. He is, of course, referring to *"those who fear him"* – those who have claimed forgiveness for their sins, having repented of those sins in the first place; or, to put it another way, those who have come to faith in Christ. Who is this God whose love and mercy is so great that He is prepared to remove our transgressions so far away from us? "I, even I, am he who blots your transgressions, for my own sake, and remembers your sins no more" *(Isaiah 43:25)*. He is our Heavenly Father, the Father of our Lord Jesus Christ, about whom Isaiah also writes, "He was pierced for our transgressions...for the transgression of my people he was stricken" *(Isaiah 53:5,8).*

In the margin of my Bible I placed a horizontal line to remind me of how far God had removed my transgressions from me.

These two lines, which intersect each other, form a cross! For me, not just *a* cross, but *the* Cross, reminding me of the tremendous blessing received from these two verses; but more so it reminds me of God's love and mercy towards me in Christ. Perhaps you may desire to mark the margin of your Bible at this point with the Cross to remind you of this tremendous blessing, of sins forgiven and removed because of God's love and mercy towards you. But we should always remember this, unless this is a true *experience* in our life, there is no point in defacing the margin, for it will be nothing more than just a mark!

100

Psalm 107:8 – Let them give thanks to the Lord for his unfailing love and his wonderful deeds for men.

One of the tremendous blessings that can come with regular Bible meditation is when we come across a passage of Scripture that gets us really excited. Whenever we read the Bible it must bring us great blessing, of course, and never cease to thrill us – because it is God's Word to us – but just once in a while we could get extremely excited about something the Lord wants to reveal to us. This happens to me many times, but there was one occasion when I was particularly thrilled, an experience that remains fresh in my memory to this day, and this I want to share with you here.

Some years ago I was sat reading my Bible for no other reason than to experience the sheer joy of reading God's Word. Sometimes I would read it with the purpose of preparing a devotional meditation, asking God to reveal to me what He would want me to share with His people. At other times, I would take the Bible with notebook in hand, and set to work on serious study. But on the occasion about which I am relating here I was just reading the Bible for pure pleasure. Reading from *Psalm 107*, I came to this verse. *"Let them give thanks to the Lord for his unfailing love and his wonderful deeds for men."*

At this point there was nothing particularly outstanding about the verse until, as I continued reading, I came to *verse 15*, and began to read, *"Let them give thanks..."* Just a moment! I've read that before! Oh yes, *verse 8*! Continue reading! Imagine how I felt when I came to *verse 21* and began to read the same words again. How strange! Three times that verse is repeated. I wonder if it comes again? Sure enough, as I continued through the Psalm, it came again in *verse 31*. Four times! Then the question came into my mind which caused all the excitement. What is so very important in this passage of Scripture that the Psalmist has to exhort us four times to give thanks to the Lord for His unfailing love? What are the wonderful deeds for men which warrant their mention four times in the one Psalm?

In my excitement I remember praying, "Lord, show me, please!" Where should I look? I read the whole of the Psalm again. I read the four verses very carefully just in case there was a slight variation and the answer to my questions would be given. But no, all four were *exactly* the same. I instinctively knew I would discover the answer because I was so sure the Lord was waiting to reveal it to me. It did not just come – handed to me on a plate, so to speak – I had to seek diligently. Here is a side lesson we can all learn. If a thing is worth having it is worth working for!

Before we return to look at *how* the Lord revealed what He wanted me to know from His Word in the next devotional meditation, and also *what* He wanted me to know in the next few meditations, let us realise from what we have looked at in this meditation that, if we are to glean *daily strength for daily living* from regular meditation on His Word, and experience extreme excitement from that Word, there will be times when we will have to seek diligently until we find!

101

Psalm 107:8 – Oh that men would praise the Lord for his goodness, and for his wonderful works to the children of men! [KJV]

In our previous devotional meditation we promised to return in this meditation to find out *how* the Lord revealed what He wanted me to know from His Word, then prepare the way for looking in the next four meditations at *what* He wanted me to know. Please continue to permit me to relate the personal experience that illustrates the situation, which caused me all the excitement in the first place! As I continued to ask the Lord to reveal to me why this verse appeared *four times* in the one Psalm – and as it was some years ago when I was sat reading my Bible for no other reason than to experience the sheer joy of reading God's Word, it was the KJV from which I was reading – the words of Jesus came to me.

"Ask, and it shall be given you; seek and ye shall find; knock, and it shall be opened unto you: For everyone that asketh receiveth; and he that seeketh findeth; and to him that knocketh it shall be opened" *(Matthew 7:7,8 KJV).* I continued to ask, I continued to seek, and I suppose, in a spiritual sense, I was knocking as well! *Then the answer came!* It was as if the Lord was telling me to look at the four verses *immediately before* the four I had been reading. Even after all the years that have intervened since this experience, the tremendous excitement I felt at that time is still fresh in my memory. Once again it demonstrates that we are dealing here with a *Living* Word the Author of which is still *alive!*

Whilst I did not set out with the original intention of preparing these devotional meditations from *Psalm 107*, which form the subject of the next four meditations, nevertheless, in sharing my discovery with you now, I trust you will experience some of the excitement that came to me all those years ago, and is still with me to this day. This, then, is *how* the Lord revealed to me what He wanted me to know. What a wonderful Book the Bible really is, for in revealing to me *what* He wanted me to know, He disclosed the Christian's Spiritual Journey, mapped out so clearly. *"Oh that men would praise the Lord for his goodness, and for his wonderful works to the children of men!"* [KJV] These words have taken on new meaning for me, and I trust they will for you, too, as in the next four meditations we go on an exciting journey together!

102

Psalm 107:14 – He brought them out of darkness and the deepest gloom and broke away their chains.

In revealing to me what He wanted me to know, by prompting me to look at the four verses *immediately before* the four that had attracted my attention, God disclosed the Christian's Spiritual Journey, mapped out so clearly. *"Let them give thanks to the Lord for his unfailing love and his wonderful deeds for men."* Or, as the KJV translates *Psalm 107: 15,8,21,31,* "Oh that men would praise the Lord for his goodness, and for his wonderful works to the children of men!" These words have taken on new meaning for me, and I trust they will for you, too, as in this and the next three meditations we go on this exciting journey together!

Let us look at *verse 14* together: *"He brought them out of darkness and the deepest gloom and broke away their chains."* Here is the beginning of our Spiritual Journey. The moment we committed ourselves to the Lord Jesus, claimed Him as our personal Saviour, sought forgiveness for our sins, He brought us out of the darkness of those sins, dispelled the deepest gloom that surrounded us, and broke away the chains that bound us. Sin is always identified with darkness in the Bible just as righteousness is akin to light.

For some of us it may have been a long time ago when the Lord brought us out of darkness. There may be others who have only been travelling the Christian pathway a short while. But we all had to begin; we all had to be born again; we all had to come to faith in Christ; we all had to be brought out of the darkness of sin; we all had to share in the experience of the hymn writer, Charles Wesley, expressed in his hymn, *"Long my imprisoned spirit lay Fast bound in sin and nature's night; Thine eye diffused a quickening ray; I woke; the dungeon flamed with light. My chains fell off, my heart was free, I rose, went forth, and followed Thee."*

Not one of us can expect to travel the Christian pathway unless we begin in the right way. This spiritual journey starts the moment we are brought out of darkness, when our feet are firmly placed on the road that will ultimately bring us to heaven; and let no one tell us that there is another way! Jesus is the *only* Way. The Bible says so. Jesus is the only One who can bring us out of the darkness of sin and dispel the deepest gloom that surrounded us. Jesus is the only Saviour who can break the chains of sin that bind us and set our feet on the right road. "Salvation is found in no-one else, for there is no other name under heaven given to men by which we must be saved" *(Acts 4:12)*. That name is Jesus.

"Let them give thanks to the Lord for his unfailing love and his wonderful deeds for men." Why? Firstly, then because HE SAVES US!

103

Psalm 107:7 – He led them by a straight way.

In revealing to me what He wanted me to know, by prompting me to look at the four verses *immediately before* the four that had attracted my attention, God disclosed the Christian's Spiritual Journey, mapped out so clearly. *"Let them give thanks to the Lord for his unfailing love and his wonderful deeds for men."* Or, as the KJV translates *Psalm 107: 15,8,21,31,* "Oh that men would praise the Lord for his goodness, and for his wonderful works to the children of men!" These words have taken on new meaning for me, and I trust they will for you, too, as in this and the next two meditations we continue on this exciting journey together!

Now let us look at *verse 7* together: *"He led them by the straight way."* Isn't that wonderful? Having brought us out of the darkness of sin and set us on our Spiritual Journey, the Lord now leads us by "a straight way" – or as the KJV translates it, "by the right way." We are not left to find our own way, nor are we just given a set of directions to follow alone. The One who saves us is there to guide us, too. As we were saying earlier, as we meditated on our journey through the Land of Spiritual Experience in *Deuteronomy*, the Lord not only goes *before* us as we go in to explore and possess the land, but He also goes *with* us as our Companion.

No doubt we have all experienced the well-meaning person who is willing to direct us when asked the way. We arrive on the edge of a strange town, but we are not sure of the route we should take to enable us to arrive at our destination, so we ask that well-meaning person who happens to be passing by. Then it begins! The directions become more complicated and confusing as the seconds tick by, until in the end we are more lost than we were before we asked! How much easier it would have been if it were possible for the well-meaning person to have climbed into the car with us and *shown* us the way. There would be no confusion, for the well-meaning person would have become our well-meaning *guide.*

Now, this is exactly what Jesus does for us. He is our Companion and our Guide. He travels *with* us as well as going on *before* us. While He is with us we will never be lost! While we are allowing Him to show us the way we will never take the wrong turning! The route of our Spiritual Journey will be assured, as long as we keep Him as our Companion and Guide, all the way to heaven, our eternal home.

"Let them give thanks to the Lord for his unfailing love and his wonderful deeds for men." Why? Secondly, then because HE GUIDES US!

104

Psalm 107:20 – He sent forth his word and healed them; he rescued them.

In revealing to me what He wanted me to know, by prompting me to look at the four verses *immediately before* the four that had attracted my attention, God disclosed the Christian's Spiritual Journey, mapped out so clearly. *"Let them give thanks to the Lord for his unfailing love and his wonderful deeds for men."* Or, as the KJV translates *Psalm 107: 15,8,21,31,* "Oh that men would praise the Lord for his goodness, and for his wonderful works to the children of men!" These words have taken on new meaning for me, and I trust they will for you, too, as in this and the next meditation we continue on this exciting journey together!

Now let us look at *verse 20* together: *"He sent forth his word and healed them; he rescued them."* This same wonderful Lord who brings us out of darkness and guides us safely along the right way all the way to heaven, our eternal home, blesses us abundantly all along that way. He has sent us His Word – how much we should treasure this precious Book. In it we find guidance and strength, comfort and joy, instructions and advice – it gives us *daily strength for daily living* – all we need, in fact, to bring us untold blessings as we travel life's pathway.

Please permit me another word of personal witness! I can only say from my own experience that I receive so much blessing from reading my Bible that I wonder sometimes just how I could manage through life without it. Not only have I been blessed by being able to share God's Word with other people in so many different ways down through the years – for well over half a century as I write this – but I am doubly rewarded as God blesses me personally through His Word when actually sharing it with others! I have to *receive from* Him before I can *share for* Him!

But look again! This verse also says He *"healed them; he rescued them."* Not only has the Lord brought us out of the darkness of sin – a *past* experience – but all along the way, through the power of His Holy Spirit in-filling us day by day, He is healing our bodies, our minds, our souls, and rescuing us from the power of the devil – a *present* experience. Let us make no mistake about it, the devil is still a power to be reckoned with today! But, praise God, He can heal us, rescue us, constantly bless us; yes, He *can* do it, He *is* doing it, and He will *go on* doing it all the way to heaven, our eternal home.

"Let them give thanks to the Lord for his unfailing love and his wonderful deeds for men." Why? Thirdly, then because HE BLESSES US!

105

Psalm 107:30 – He guided them to their desired haven.

In revealing to me what He wanted me to know, by prompting me to look at the four verses *immediately before* the four that had attracted my attention, God disclosed the Christian's Spiritual Journey, mapped out so clearly. *"Let them give thanks to the Lord for his unfailing love and his wonderful deeds for men."* Or, as the KJV translates *Psalm 107: 15,8,21,31,* "Oh that men would praise the Lord for his goodness, and for his wonderful works to the children of men!" These words have taken on new meaning for me, and I trust they will for you, too, as in this fourth meditation we continue on this exciting journey together! (I hesitate to use the word "conclude" here, because this is a journey that will still continue even *after* we have reached our desired haven – our Heavenly Home!)

Finally, let us look at *verse 30* together: *"He guided them to their desired haven."* Now isn't that thrilling? No wonder I experienced a sense of excitement when I fist read this – it completes the journey so perfectly! The God who brought us out of the darkness of sin now brings us into the place He has gone to prepare for us, guiding and blessing us all the way along until we reach our Heavenly Home. We recall the words of Jesus when He said, "Do not let your hearts be troubled. Trust in God; trust also in me. In my Father's house are many rooms…I am going there to prepare a place for you. And if I go and prepare a place for you, I will come back and take you to be with me that you also may be where I am" *(John 14:1-3).*

How happy and content we should be to know that the One who is now guiding and blessing us along life's way will be there with us when we reach eternity! What greater reward can we ask for than to be with Jesus for ever at the end of our earthly journey? We are assured from His Word, once we have committed our lives fully to Him, allowing Him to bring us out of darkness, and have welcomed Him as our Guide and Companion, enjoying untold blessings as we travel "by the right way", then He will reward us for being faithful to Him by bringing us into our "desired haven."

"Let them give thanks to the Lord for his unfailing love and his wonderful deeds for men." Why? Finally, then because HE REWARDS US!

Now we know why this verse appears four times. They direct us to the four verses *preceding* them, which assure us that we are never alone at any time on our Spiritual Journey through life. The Lord is with us when we begin (indeed, He is with us even *before* we begin!), with us all the way, with us when we come to the end, and with us constantly when the journey is over. Yet, in a sense, the journey will never be over, because we will continue on together enjoying this wonderful companionship with our Lord for all eternity. Yes, *we will* "give thanks to the Lord for his unfailing love and his wonderful deeds" *to us!*

106

Psalm 113:3 – From the rising of the sun to the place where it sets the name of the Lord is to be praised.

If more people were prepared to obey the frequent exhortation of the Bible, to be found more frequently in the *Psalms* than anywhere else, there would be less grumbling, even less complaining, and the world would be a much happier place. Dare we say it – the Church would be a happier place, too? What is this exhortation? It is made up of only three words! *Praise the Lord!* Of course, we have to understand that it is not enough to simply *say* "praise the Lord"; we must praise the Lord from a full and sincere heart, *then* say it. There is a difference. True and sincere praise begins from within, from the heart, before it travels to the lips!

This verse tells us just *when* the Lord's name should be praised. At first reading it would appear that during the day is the only appropriate time, between the rising of the sun and its setting again later in the day. Of course, if we follow this line of thinking, then someone is bound to ask, "What if it's cloudy and we don't actually see the sun rise; what then?" We have to say that both of these ideas are very far from the truth. What this verse is really saying, and here is a word of enlightenment as well as encouragement, is that there is never a moment when it is inappropriate to praise the Lord.

If we think about it for a moment, when we read that, *"From the rising of the sun to the place where it sets the name of the Lord is to be praised,"* we realise that somewhere in the world every minute of the twenty-four hour day the sun is rising and setting at the same time! Wherever it is rising, just a little further east it is setting; wherever it is setting, just a little further west it is rising – it is a continuing process. Our praising of the Lord should be a continuing process, too! If our hearts are full of praise twenty-four hours a day, seven days a week, fifty-two weeks a year, there is no room for grumbling or complaining – there's no time left!

As we pause and take stock of our situation, whatever and wherever it might be, we will find there is so much for which we can praise the Lord. Praise Him for what we have, for what we are, and even for where we are. So let us stop our grumbling, stop our complaining, stop getting depressed, and while the sun continues to rise and set anywhere in the world, where we are let us go on praising the Lord. It may surprise us how changed the world will be – but it must first start with us!

107

Psalm 116:1—I love the Lord, because… [KJV]

We are using the KJV translation here, because it lends itself to this devotional meditation better than the NIV, which would read, "I love the Lord, *for…*" It is not always the long passages of Scripture which bring the greatest blessings, nor yet even a single verse. Sometimes a simple sentence or phrase, and on occasions only part of a sentence, can bless beyond measure. Here is one such example. *"I love the Lord, because…"* is not even a grammatically correct sentence (it would have been the same in the NIV), it isn't even a *whole* sentence, but what tremendous blessing it can give if we are prepared to stop and give our own *personal* reasons as to why we *personally* love the Lord.

The Psalmist has compiled his list, as a continuation on beyond this verse would reveal. As we meditate upon God's Word the Holy Spirit will help us to compile ours! Let me explain what I mean, and at the same time once again illustrate why I believe it is so important that we should regularly read and study the Bible, not forgetting the value of meditating on the Word. *I love the Lord, because* He first loved me and gave Himself for me. *I love the Lord, because* He has given me eternal life. *I love the Lord, because* He gives me His companionship day by day, for He is alive, He is no dead prophet! *I love the Lord, because* He has gone to prepare a place for me in heaven (the Bible says so!). *I love the Lord, because* He is coming back again, as He has promised, to take me to be with Himself for ever (the Bible tells me that as well!).

And so we could go on, for the list is endless! If we would glean *daily strength for daily living*, as we meditate daily on His Word, our life will take on a new meaning, there will develop an added dimension to our daily living, as we stop and take stock of our spiritual situation; when we are prepared to give our own personal reasons, not only to the Lord, but to ourselves as well. It may be helpful for us to spend a few moments sometime today, then perhaps continue to do it every day, taking this verse (or part-verse), begin by saying, *I love the Lord, because...* then try giving our reasons "why" – and if for any one of us this is a new idea, when the blessings start to flow, we may wonder why we left it so long!

108

Psalm 116:14,18 – I will fulfil my vows to the Lord in the presence of all his people.

This verse says three important things to us concerning our spiritual commitment, concerning the promises we make governing our life. The first is that our initial consideration must be to the Lord. Our spiritual commitment must first be to God Himself and no other.

The second is that the promises we have made are always in the present – *now!* This is drawn out more forcefully in the KJV translation of this verse: "I will pay my vows unto the Lord now…" What it is really saying is, yesterday's achievements, promises and commitments are not sufficient in themselves for today. We must commit our life afresh to the Lord *every* day.

The third is that our spiritual commitment is not a secret thing, for the Word of God says we should not hide our light under a bowl, but place it on a candlestick for all to see *(Matthew 5:14)*. In other words, a candle hidden under a bucket or bowl is useless, it helps no one, but on a candlestick it makes useful illumination and benefits everyone. No matter what the consequences, we must never be ashamed to let everyone know where we stand spiritually. As the hymn writer, Isaac Watts, so beautifully penned it, *"I'm not ashamed to own my Lord, Or to defend His cause, Maintain the honour of His Word, the glory of His cross."*

There is a story told of a teacher who asked her class if anyone went to church. At first, no one raised their hand. One boy went every week, but he wasn't sure he wanted the rest of his class to know. There were some people who might laugh at him. Then another boy raised his hand. Others followed, and soon the first boy was surprised to see that over half his class attended church regularly. So he raised his hand, a little ashamed that he hadn't had the nerve to raise it earlier. The lesson we can learn from this story is that we must not be ashamed of our faith. What God has done for us is a miracle, and we should want the whole world to know; to take every opportunity to let others know what we believe. Pay our vows to the Lord in front of other people, because we never know how much good it may do for others.

Therefore, our spiritual commitment must be made TO THE RIGHT PERSON (the Lord), AT THE RIGHT TIME (now), and IN THE RIGHT PLACE (in the presence of all His people). Three very important obligations worthy of serious consideration – at least the Psalmist thought it important enough to repeat the words four verses later in the same psalm!

109

Psalm 118:24 – This is the day the Lord has made; let us rejoice and be glad in it.

Which day? Sunday? Weekday? Today? True, there is much to rejoice over on the Lord's Day – the first day of the week when we celebrate Christ's resurrection, and because of this we know our sins forgiven, having accepted Christ as our *personal* Saviour; we experience, too, the joy of salvation and the blessings of the Holy Spirit. We also have the assurance that Jesus has gone to prepare a place for each of us, as He promised, in *John 14*, saying that He will come again to receive us unto Himself. These are the promises and blessings to all true believers.

Yes, there is much to rejoice about as God's people share in worship in many churches throughout the world, meet around the Lord's Table and observe the Lord's Supper, or hear the Lord's name uplifted in the faithful preaching of the Gospel, and as people are brought into the kingdom of God. But we do not confine our rejoicing to the Lord's Day, for Christianity is not a one-day-a-week affair; it is a way of life, and that means seven days a week, because the Christian life is meant to be lived every day. We may begin the week in the Lord's House, but we have to go on rejoicing all the rest of the week, remembering that *every day* is the day which the Lord has made.

Please permit me a personal illustration. I remember visiting a saintly old soul in hospital some years ago. She was obviously nearing the end of a very hard life, having lost two sons in the Second World War, nursed a sick husband for many years until he died, and was never able to boast of possessing much of this world's treasures. What she did possess, however, was beyond price. She had a radiant faith in her Risen Lord. It expressed itself in her very being. At the time of my visit she was being given oxygen, one lung having collapsed and the other was severely congested. She whispered something to me, which I missed the first time. I leaned closer, and she whispered again, "Praise the Lord!" Within a few hours she had gone to be with her Lord.

There is never a moment in any day when we cannot rejoice and be glad over something. The next time we feel like grumbling, let us remember, whatever day it happens to be, that "this is the day the Lord has made: let us rejoice and be glad in it." Such an attitude will make quite a difference to life – especially to *our* life!

110

Psalm 119:11 – I have hidden your word in my heart that I might not sin against you.

To neglect the Word of God for a Christian is just as detrimental to health as neglecting good nourishing food – both our spiritual and physical health will suffer. Perhaps this is why the Psalmist reminds us in this verse of the importance of hiding God's Word in our heart. It is the physical heart, as any doctor will tell us, which keeps us alive. Although the brain is looked upon as possibly being the most vital organ in the human body, if the heart stops supplying it with blood, then even the brain will die. A strong heart, then, promotes a strong healthy body.

In the spiritual realm, hiding the Word in our heart will ensure a strong healthy spiritual heart, which in turn will promote a strong healthy spiritual life. If the devil can weaken our heart with sin – it is sin, after all, that separates us from God – then he will, for he knows that sin is like a disease; it will destroy spiritual life as effectively as physical disease destroys the body in the physical realm. In any case, it is the power of God's Word in us that keeps us from sin. Of course, we should be aware that God's Word hidden in our heart is not the same as God's Word being retained in our memory. It is not a process of recollection but a process of commitment – a commitment of love.

The heart is the seat of love – "Love the Lord your God with all your heart" *(Matthew 22:37).* The heart is the seat of praise – "I will praise you, O Lord, with all my heart" *(Psalm 9:1).* The heart is the seat of service – "Serve the Lord with all your heart" *(1 Samuel 12:20).* The heart is the seat of trust – "Trust in the Lord with all your heart" *(Proverbs 3:5).* We could go on and on listing the value of the heart to God, each revealing the need to keep our heart healthy and free from sin for the Lord's sake. God's Word is the only real power we have available for our heart that is greater than the power of sin.

How, then, can we ensure a strong and healthy spiritual heart and life? The Psalmist gives us the answer! As we "feast" on the Word of God regularly, not only Sunday by Sunday as we hear it read from the pulpit, but privately as well during the week in our daily devotions as we seek for *daily strength for daily living*, let our testimony always be that of the Psalmist, *"I have hidden your word in my heart that I might not sin against you."* It is a well-known fact that prevention is better than cure. So let us remember this, a healthy heart kept strong with God's Word needs no cure!

111

Psalm 119:45 – I will walk about in freedom, for I have sought out your precepts.

One of the indictments we sometimes hear directed at us as Christians is that we are so bound by rules and regulations that we have become prisoners of our own beliefs. No doubt many of us have had it said to us on more than one occasion, "I wouldn't like to be a Christian. You can't do this, you can't do that, you can't do the other..." – whatever all that may mean! Yet nothing can be further from the truth. The Psalmist realised this and testified to it in this verse. He said, *"I will walk about in freedom, for I have sought out your precepts."* No one can be a prisoner if he is walking about in freedom.

It says elsewhere in the Bible that the truth will set us free *(John 3:32)*. No one can be bound if he is free. As true Christians we have a liberty, a sense of freedom, which even the world does not have. When we are accused of being kill-joys because we cannot do this and we cannot do that, our reply must be to the effect, as we mentioned in an earlier devotional meditation, that all these things which we supposedly cannot do we do not want to do anyway, and all those things which we are supposedly allowed to do are the things we want to do…and as we do them we have a real sense of peace, of joy, of satisfaction, because all the time we are doing them (or not doing them, as the case may be) we are walking about in freedom.

Of course, we need to understand that the freedom here referred to by the Psalmist doesn't just happen; it doesn't suddenly appear in an emotional moment during a special church service, for example; neither is it some magic formula we have miraculously discovered. True freedom comes from diligently searching out God's precepts (a word which means a rule for action or conduct); it is only in the Bible where we will find true freedom, but we have to search for it. As we said in the previous meditation, God's Word is the only real power we have available for our heart that is greater than the power of sin. It is sin that binds us and takes away our spiritual freedom. By searching for and finding *daily strength for daily living* in God's precepts – God's Word – we will be able to walk about in freedom every day of our life. Now, that certainly makes life worth living, doesn't it?

112

Psalm 119:81 – I have put my hope in your word.

We have said in recent devotional meditations that we can ensure having a strong and healthy spiritual heart and life by "feasting" on the Word of God regularly, not only Sunday by Sunday as we hear it read from the pulpit, but privately as well during the week in our daily devotions as we seek for *daily strength for daily living*, letting our testimony always be that of the Psalmist, *"I have hidden your word in my heart that I might not sin against you."* As true Christians we have a liberty, a sense of freedom, which even the world does not have. But this true freedom comes only from diligently searching out God's precepts (a word which means a rule for action or conduct); it is only in the Bible where we will find true freedom, but we have to search for it. The Psalmist realised this when he said, *"I will walk about in freedom, for I have sought out your precepts."*

So we "feast" on God's Word for a strong spiritual heart and life; we search out diligently God's Word to keep us free from sin; now the Psalmist moves on in this verse to encourage us to put our hope in God's Word for…what? The list could be endless, so we select just a few! Our hope of *salvation* is in God's Word because the way is made plain in its pages. Our hope of *eternal life* and our certainty of reaching heaven is in God's Word, for it is within its pages that we learn the truth of these things. The hope of *divine power* for living our lives as God would have us do is also outlined in God's Word, and the work of the Holy Spirit in this respect is fully described in its pages, too. It is this divine power which gives us *daily strength for daily living.*

Perhaps the greatest hope of all is what is referred to in the Bible itself as "the blessed hope" *(Titus 2:13).* There are many hundreds of references to this particular hope in God's Word – that blessed hope and absolute certainty that Jesus is coming again to take the faithful to be with Him for all eternity. Yes, the Bible is full of hope, which can't be a bad thing in this world of the twenty-first century, which seems to have little or no hope worth considering. So by all means let us go on "feasting" on God's Word, go on searching diligently in His Word, but never let us cease to go on hoping in that Word as well – really, it's our only hope, isn't it?

113

Psalm 119:103 – How sweet are your promises to my taste, sweeter than honey to my mouth!

Bearing in mind this verse, in an earlier Psalm, which we looked at in a previous devotional meditation, similar words can be found encouraging us to "taste and see that the Lord is good" *(Psalm 34:8).* This reminds us of the story some of us may have heard in our Sunday school days. It is about a little boy and his honey pot, and it went something like this!

There was a little boy who one day was sat by the road side enjoying dipping his fingers in the honey jar he was holding and licking the sweet substance. An elderly gentleman came up to him and asked, "Is that honey sweet, son?" to which the boy replied, "Yes, sir!" The gentleman asked again, "Are you sure, really sure, that it's sweet?" Again the boy replied, "Yes, sir, definitely sweet!" The gentleman persisted, "But how can I be sure that you're telling me the truth? How can I be *absolutely* certain that it's sweet?" In desperation the boy handed him the jar. *"Taste and see for yourself!"* he said.

The only way to be absolutely certain of anything in this life is to experience it for ourselves. The Word of God – both the Written Word, the Bible, and the Incarnate Word, the Lord Jesus Christ – can only benefit us by personal experience. It is very appropriate that honey should be used as an illustration in this verse. It is a natural substance often used to sweeten bitter things, especially in natural medicines. There are those who tell us of the healing properties of natural honey, and we all know the soothing effect when we have a sore throat, especially when mixed with glycerine and lemon!

There are times when we need to sweeten a bitter spirit – our own spirit, perhaps! No one can escape the spiritual as well as the physical injuries inflicted from time to time in this sinful world, and we need a healing balm. When we are troubled in our spirit it is good to know that there is a source which sooths away those things that would irritate us. Honey left in the jar benefits no one. The Word of God left on the shelf, neglected and ignored, benefits no one, either! "Taste and see for yourself," said the little boy. "Taste and see that the Lord is good," the Bible says. *"How sweet are your promises to my taste, sweeter than honey to my mouth!"* says this verse.

Whatever our particular need might be right now, that need will only be met, and we will only be able to say the words of this verse from personal experience rather than just "something we have read", if first of all we have tasted and seen for ourselves. Now, that makes sense, doesn't it?

114

Psalm 119:105 – Your word is a lamp to my feet and a light for my path.

A way that is dark becomes treacherous and dangerous. Frequent are the pitfalls waiting to trap us because we cannot see them in the dark. Many of us in the United Kingdom are old enough to remember the blackout during the war (World War II – 1939-1945). Not a street light anywhere, every window of every house thickly shrouded with black material from which not even a chink of light could escape for fear of a severe reprimand from the officials patrolling the streets – *"Put that light out!"* But what a different world it was when Victory Day arrived on the 8th May 1945 and the streetlights came on again and the blackout curtains were removed!

Once the light is on, then the way becomes easier, we can see the danger spots and avoid them. Life is like a journey; the natural way is dark; therefore we need light to be able to travel safely. How can we obtain this light? This verse enlightens us! Whether it is the written Word – the Bible – or the incarnate Word – the Lord Jesus, who described Himself as the Light of the World – if we accept and acknowledge the Word, live our lives daily according to the Word, then we will never travel through life in the dark. No matter how dark may be our surroundings, just where we are it is always light.

A father once asked his young son to fetch a tool from the shed at the end of their rather long garden, but it was dark. The boy pointed this out to his father, who gave him a lighted storm lantern, with the instruction once again to go and fetch the required tool. The boy protested that he couldn't see the shed from where he was standing, not even with the lantern. The father wisely encouraged him by assuring him that, as he moved forward so would the light; every step he took to the shed and back he would always be surrounded by light. The boy trusted his father, fetched the tool, and thrilled his father with the words, "You were right, Dad, I knew I could trust you!"

We cannot see the whole way ahead of us (we are not meant to – *"God holds the key of all unknown, and I am glad,"* the hymn writer reminds us, and so we can trust our Heavenly Father), but if we are daily armed with the Word, it will always be light just where we are. And as we move forward so the light moves with us, a lamp for our feet and a light for our pathway, and our way becomes safe for us to travel. Surely this demonstrates the need for regular prayer and Bible study, especially Bible meditation – keeping in constant touch with the Incarnate Word through prayer, and in constant touch with the Written Word through Bible study and meditation. We neglect both at our peril, because if we should get lost in the darkness we have really only ourselves to blame!

115

Psalm 119:171 – May my lips overflow with praise, for you teach me your decrees.

It is really a matter of common sense, a case of simple logic, and one that any right thinking person would very quickly recognise, that of the necessity of knowing a particular subject or person personally before they are able to teach others that subject or tell others about that person. Now let us translate that into spiritual terms, because in these devotional meditations we are seeking to obtain *daily strength for daily living.* As Christians we very quickly recognise the necessity of knowing the Lord personally before we are able to tell others about Him. We cannot witness until we have a witness within us; we cannot preach about the Saviour of the world with conviction until He has become our personal Saviour. We may preach from wrong motives, even preach the truth from wrong motives, but that is not preaching from personal conviction.

And so we recognise the need to know Jesus personally before we can witness, preach, communicate Jesus to others with conviction, in a convincing way. However, what we may not recognise quite so quickly is illustrated in this verse. It is really a matter of "about face" – from what we are doing *for* Jesus (witnessing for Him, to give one example) to what we are doing *to* or *towards* Him (praise and worship). Frequently the phrase appears in the Bible, especially in the Psalms, "Praise the Lord!" What we need to understand is, the quality of our praise and worship is measured by the quality of our experience. This is what this verse means. *"May my lips overflow with praise, for you teach me your decrees."*

Indeed, until we have learned to love Jesus, to acknowledge Jesus and recognise what He has done for us, until we have entered into a deep and lasting relationship with Him, we cannot even begin to praise Him. On the other hand, the more we learn of Him the more we are able and desire to praise Him; then we want to learn more, then praise Him more, and so it goes on. No experience, no praise! As we have said, the quality of our praise is measured by the quality of our experience. Of course, it could work the other way round, too, if we think about it!

116

Psalm 121:1 – I lift my eyes to the hills – where does my help come from?

In this and the next three devotional meditations I want to depart for a moment from the usual format of *Daily Strength for Daily Living* to share with you some very valuable lessons I learned from a holiday in the Spanish island of Majorca. Instead of the "we" and "us" format to which we have become accustomed, I am mainly going to use the first person form of speech, but with a few exceptions.

Majorca, that popular Spanish island set in the blue Mediterranean Sea, is an island of contrast. Whilst on holiday there back in the 1970's, my wife and I toured the whole island in a hired car (there was just the two of us because our son was on holiday in France with his school) and together, with a factual guidebook, we learned a tremendous amount about the place. It also taught me a few things about my own spiritual life, and served to remind me that whilst I may have been on holiday from my usual life back in the United Kingdom, I am never on holiday from God. My life must be the same in Majorca as it is in the UK – or anywhere else for that matter – because my standards and principles must not change.

Here is a valuable lesson we can learn. There may be a tendency, sometimes, when we are out of sight from our fellow Christians and our own church fellowship, to let our spiritual standards slip. We might be tempted to do things on a Sunday, for example, which we would never dream of doing "back home". We might even be tempted to go to places we would never, under any circumstances, visit "back home". This is a temptation we must resist at all costs, of course, because, although our fellow Christians, members of our church fellowship, cannot see us, *God can see us!* We are never out of His sight, as we have discovered in earlier meditations.

But back to the island! Back to the sun! Along the north-west coast of Majorca runs a chain of high mountains, very rugged, very beautiful. Our first tour out in the car took us up through these great mountains, and where they were too high for the road to go over we literally went through the mountain, through tunnels cut through the rock, where water was constantly dripping and cascading down – a perpetual "rain" storm! The tops of the mountains themselves were frequently enveloped in mist and low cloud, even on what could be described as a clear day.

On another occasion we travelled through the south-eastern parts of the island, and this is where we learned some more valuable lessons to help us obtain *daily strength for daily living.* We will return to the island and learn these lessons in our next devotional meditation.

117

Psalm 121: 2 – My help comes from the Lord, the Maker of heaven and earth.

In the previous, this, and the next two devotional meditations I am continuing to depart for a moment from the usual format of *Daily Strength for Daily Living* to share with you some very valuable lessons I learned from a holiday in the Spanish island of Majorca. Instead of the "we" and "us" format to which we have become accustomed, I am mainly going to use the first person form of speech, but with a few exceptions.

Following the tour through the high and rugged mountains along the north-west coast of Majorca, described in the previous devotional mediation, my wife and I travelled through the south-eastern parts of the island and learned some more valuable lessons. Two-thirds of the island (at least, it was back in the 1970's!) was one great fertile plain. What a contrast to the north-western area! Instead of the rugged, bleak, almost desolate mountains, here was lush, green vegetation. This was an agricultural area, with the farmers copiously spraying their crops with life-giving water. As we toured this part of the island we noticed something that had first attracted our attention as we were coming into land at Palma Airport – windmills, dozens of them dotted all around the countryside.

Here, then, in a semi-tropical island, with a hot, dry climate most of the year round and very little rainfall, yet apparently no shortage of water. My factual guidebook gave me the reason. Beneath the fertile plain is a gigantic subterranean water-table, or natural water-basin, which has never been known to run dry in the history of the island. It is fed with the water constantly flowing down from the mountains. That water, which we had seen the day before dripping down through the rock-tunnel roof (although that was not the only place, of course; there were many less obvious sources of supply often un-noticed by human eye!), may well have been part of the water-table beneath the plain the next day.

But how was it possible to keep the plain so green and fertile? How was it possible for the farmers to constantly spray their crops with copious amounts of water? We saw those great jets of water all the time as we travelled. They even sprayed the car as we passed on some occasions! Again my factual guidebook gave me the answer. Before a farmer could begin to cultivate a new farm or small holding, he had first to dig deep and tap the source of supply, construct a windmill attached to a water-pump, draw up the life-giving water, and then spray it on the land. Here is another lesson, which we will develop more fully in our next meditation, that we have to recognise from whom we obtain our supply of life-giving Water of Life to enable our spiritual life to flourish and grow – *"My help comes from the Lord."*

118

Psalm 121:1 – I will lift up mine eyes to the hills, from whence cometh my help. [KJV]

In the previous two, this, and the next devotional meditation I am continuing to depart for a moment from the usual format of *Daily Strength for Daily Living* to share with you some very valuable lessons I learned from a holiday in the Spanish island of Majorca. Instead of the "we" and "us" format to which we have become accustomed, I am mainly going to use the first person form of speech, but with a few exceptions.

In the previous devotional meditation we asked the questions, how was it possible to keep the plain that covered about two-thirds of the island of Majorca so green and fertile? How was it possible for the farmers to constantly spray their crops with copious amounts of water? We said, before a farmer could begin to cultivate a new farm or small holding, he had first to dig deep and tap the source of supply of the life-giving water, and then spray it on the land. We briefly said that here was another lesson, which we would develop more fully in this meditation, that we have to recognise from whom we obtain our supply of life-giving Water of Life to enable our spiritual life to flourish and grow – *"My help comes from the Lord."*

As Christians we, like the Psalmist, look to the hills – the spiritual mountaintop experiences of life, which feed us with vast spiritual wealth. Mountaintop experiences are necessary, for just as a flat landscape, without even a small hill to break the monotony, can be uninteresting and dull, so a spiritual life without a mountaintop experience can lose some of its dynamic character, lose its zest, may become a very humdrum affair. But introduce a mountain or two into the landscape and the picture takes up a new dimension. With every mountaintop experience that spiritual life takes on a new dimension, too; we begin to live.

Yes, there is a vast spiritual wealth in the mountaintop experiences of life, and there is no shortage of this wealth, for God's Word reminds us that, "my God will meet all your needs according to his glorious riches in Christ Jesus" *(Philippians 4:19).* Or, as the KJV translates it, "my God shall *supply* all your need according to his riches in glory by Christ Jesus." Just as the water is constantly flowing from the mountains in Majorca, a never-ending supply, so is God's richest blessings constantly flowing from Jesus in glory, a continuous supply and a copious supply, too.

But there are still two more valuable lessons to learn that will give us even more *daily strength for daily living*, and we will look at these in our next devotional meditation when we conclude our tour of the Mediterranean island of Majorca.

119

Psalm 121: 2 –My help cometh from the Lord, which made heaven and earth. [KJV]

In the previous three and this devotional meditation I am continuing to depart for a moment from the usual format of *Daily Strength for Daily Living* to share with you some very valuable lessons I learned from a holiday in the Spanish island of Majorca. Instead of the "we" and "us" format to which we have become accustomed, I am mainly going to use the first person form of speech, but with a few exceptions.

We said in the previous meditation that there are still two more valuable lessons to learn that will give us even more *daily strength for daily living*, as we conclude our tour of the Mediterranean island of Majorca, and here is the first! Like the farmers of that island, we must be prepared to "tap" the source of supply, to dig deep. As the old hymn puts it, *"Go back to the old wells where the waters are deep"* – the source of spiritual blessing. The Psalmist wrote, "I will lift up mine eyes to the hills, from whence cometh my help…" But he did not stop there! He went on to write, as this verse records for us, *"My help cometh from the Lord, which made heaven and earth."*

What a valuable lesson! The God who made heaven and earth, which includes Majorca, the United Kingdom, every other country in the world, as well as you and me, is the Source of our spiritual supply. If our lives are to be spiritually fertile, fruitful, useful to the Lord, we must know how and where to "tap" the supply of life-giving blessing; then, when the hot, dry and barren moments of life come – and come they most certainly will – we will be able to draw upon a refreshing "draft of the water of life" to see us through.

But are we going to keep it all to ourselves? If we receive a blessing from the Lord, if He has supplied us with even more *daily strength for daily living*, let us take it and share it with someone else, then they too will be blessed and receive daily strength for their daily living. The windmills and the water-pumps may have drawn up the water for the Majorcan farmer, but it was no use to the thirsty crops until he set up his sprays to feed them!

So here is the final lesson I learnt from my holiday in Majorca all those years ago. Look to the hills, the mountaintop experiences of life from the Lord, realise where we find the never-ending source of rich spiritual blessing, dig deep and "tap" that source of supply – but for us to fulfil God's purpose for our life, let us "spray" that blessing around so that other might be blessed, and themselves look to the hills…to the Lord who made heaven and earth, Majorca and the UK, all the other countries of the world, you and me!

120

Psalm 122:7 – May there be peace within your walls and security within your citadels.

What greater blessing can be bestowed upon us in this trouble-torn world of the twenty-first century than a wonderful sense of inner peace within our walls? Not only peace within the walls of our home, although that is vitally important and precious, but peace within the walls of our mind, too. We live in a world where peace is a commodity in short supply, but what do we mean by the word peace – what does the Bible mean when it says, *"May there be peace within your walls…"*? It is important for us to understand the veracity of this phrase.

Peace is not conditional upon the situation surrounding us. It comes from within. Real peace is an *inner* peace. Although there was a fierce storm raging on the lake that day, recorded in *Luke 8:22-25*, there was a great sense of peace in the boat because Jesus was there. Unfortunately, the disciples did not at first recognise the peace that was present in the Lord. The poignant section of that story is in part of *verses 24* and *25* – the disciples were begging Jesus to save them, and "He got up and rebuked the wind and the raging waters; the waters subsided, and all was calm. Where is your faith? He asked his disciples."

In that question, Jesus recognised the absence of inner peace in His the lives of His disciples. They failed to understand, as we so often do, when the storms of life beat in upon us, what a tremendous difference it makes if we have the Lord Jesus in the boat with us; when we recognise Him for who He is, our Sovereign, in full control. When Jesus reigns as King, then our home becomes a palace, as this verse continues: *"...and security within your citadels."* Or as the KJV translates this phrase, which is more majestic, "prosperity within thy palaces."

There is a richness beyond value which cannot be measured by money, by material wealth, and provides us with precious spiritual security. So in this verse we have two tremendous blessings which God wants to bestow on all who acknowledge Jesus as King of their lives – peace and prosperity, as well as security, within the walls of our home, the walls of our mind, which has become a palace fit for a King. Should we as Christians settle for anything less?

121

Psalm 133:1,3 – How good and pleasant it is when brothers live together in unity!...For there the Lord bestows his blessing, even life for evermore.

It is not God's will that we should be completely alone, that we should be separated from our family, but it can and does happen. There may be those of us feeling like this just at the moment, a little lonely and away from our family. But the Bible says, "God sets the lonely in families" *(Psalm 68:6)*. Christmas time is probably the greatest opportunity we have for coming together, when families meet as one, perhaps the only occasion in the year when there is such unity. But there are many other occasions when we can get together as a family, so this is not a Christmas devotional meditation! However, we can use the Christmas celebration as an illustration for *any* family "get together", no matter what time of the year it might be.

For the Christian, it is good and pleasant when we come together at Christmastime to celebrate our Saviour's birth – a unity of purpose, of heart and mind, living together albeit for a brief period, for the same reason. As Christians, it is more than just to make merry, although it will be a happy and joyous occasion, of course; it will be more than just to eat and drink, even though we may consume more food than at any other time in the year! Because we will have come to give thanks for Christ's birth, the Lord will bestow His blessing. But this verse is not just describing Christmas, for it applies whenever we meet together. *"How good and pleasant it is when brothers live together in unity! ... For there the Lord bestows his blessing, even for evermore."*

But perhaps there is no family, as such, and we will be on our own at Christmas, or because of our circumstances, there will be no family "get together" at any other time of the year, so no matter what day it is we are on our own. It is then when we should be encouraged and remember, as a Christian we are not really alone, for we are part of that greater family, the Body of Christ. Along with thousands of others who are alone, at Christmastime He will be there to help us celebrate His birth – united in Him! Of course, this same spirit should prevail no matter what time of the year it is, and for whatever occasion we are meeting together as a family.

In this spirit then, we cannot help but feel how good and pleasant it is to live together in such unity, and when the celebrations are over – for whatever reason those celebrations have been held – we will know that we have been richly blessed of the Lord as a result, for He has bestowed His blessing. But this verse has one more very important thing to say to us. We who are blessed with a loving family who do meet together from time to time, be it at Christmas or any other occasion in the year, would enable God's purpose to be fulfilled in setting the lonely together in families, if we were to invite a lonely person we know to come and live together in unity for an occasion, and when the Lord bestows His blessing as a result, it will not only be on that lonely person, it will be on us and our family as well.

122

Psalm 135:1 – Praise the Lord. Praise the name of the Lord; praise him, you servants of the Lord.

Three times in this one verse we are exhorted to praise the Lord, yet not just praise, but as emphasised in the KJV translation, "Praise *ye* the Lord" – or as we would say in modern English, *you* praise the Lord – it is a *personal* exhortation. And if we should read the whole of the Psalm from which this verse comes, we would find quite an extensive list of reasons as to why we should praise the Lord. Indeed, this is a *praise* Psalm in the truest sense of the word. We can even go further and say it is a Psalm encouraging *personal* praise for the Lord.

This word "praise" is used extensively in the Bible, especially in the *Psalms*. It is a word that, as the dictionary defines it, expresses warm approval of a person, a commendation of what that person has done and is doing, a glorification of the whole person; and praise for the Lord not only includes these sentiments, but adds much more to them, as expressed in this Psalm. So, what reasons do we have to praise the Lord? "Praise the Lord, for the Lord is good" *(verse 3)*, here is one reason! All goodness stems from God. Any goodness we may have is as a result of God's goodness in the first place. This applies, not only to us as Christians, but to the whole of mankind everywhere in every age.

Any standard of goodness, whereby we are able to define the difference between that which is good and that which is bad, is set by God, and was so even before the world began – and it applies equally to those who say they do not believe in God! After all, our God is the Supreme Creator, Governor, Controller and Preserver of the Universe, which leads us to another reason for personal praise for the Lord. We praise Him because we "know that the Lord is great" *(verse 5)*. The greatness of God is not so much in the fact that He is the Creator of the Universe, the Governor and Controller of all the stars and suns and planets, of nature itself, but in the fact that He, the Almighty God of the Universe, cares about us as individuals.

Because of this care, He sent His Son to die for us that we might have eternal life and a sure place in heaven, which He has gone to prepare for us, and will come again as He promised to receive us into that place. Here, then are two reasons why we should *"Praise the Lord. Praise the name of the Lord; praise him, you servants of the Lord."* But there are many more reasons for this *personal* praise – "Praise *ye* the Lord" ... *You* praise the Lord – as we will discover in our next devotional meditation.

123

Psalm 135:1 – Praise ye the Lord. Praise ye the name of the Lord; praise him, O ye servants of the Lord. [KJV]

Three times in this one verse we are exhorted to praise the Lord, yet not just praise, but because we have used the KJV translation, "Praise *ye* the Lord" – or as we would say in modern English, *you* praise the Lord – it is a *personal* exhortation. As we said in our previous devotional meditation, if we should read the whole of the Psalm from which this verse comes, we would find quite an extensive list of reasons as to why we should praise the Lord. Indeed, this is a *praise* Psalm in the truest sense of the word. We can even go further and say it is a Psalm encouraging *personal* praise for the Lord.

So we continue to glean *daily strength for daily living* as we continue to peruse this Psalm, and discover another reason for personal praise. We should praise Him because we know "that our Lord is greater than all gods" *(verse 5)* – or, as the KJV translates it, "that our Lord is above all gods." There are many religions in the world today with their long-dead prophets and founders; Christianity is not one of them. Indeed, Christianity is not so much a religion as it is a way of life, for our Lord, the Founder of our Faith, is *alive now.* No dead prophets as the founder, but a living, ever present Lord. In this truth alone He is above all gods, and worthy of our praise.

The Bible also says that we should praise Him, "for the Lord will judge his people" *(verse 14 KJV).* As Christians we can be happy and content to know that when the great Judgement Day comes – and we must be in no doubts about it, it really is coming – then it will be the living Lord who will be the Judge. And because we know that His judgement will be fair and just, we need have absolutely no fear *of* that day, or *on* that day, either! So we can go on praising the Lord, not just three times as suggested in this verse, but all the time, day by day, moment by moment, never ceasing – and all with very good reason, because the Lord is GOOD, He is GREAT, He is ABOVE ALL GODS, and He will be the JUDGE.

Whilst we are encouraged in this verse to make our praises *personal* – and in these two meditations we have looked at only four reasons, although there are many, many more, not only in *Psalm 135* but throughout the Bible – this verse has just one more thing to say to us. Certainly our praises should be *personal*, deep from within our heart, but let us not neglect our *corporate* praise as we join with like-minded brothers and sisters in the Lord, meeting for fellowship from time to time, thus obeying God's Word when it says, *"praise him, O ye servants of the Lord."*

124

Psalm 143:1 - "O Lord, hear my prayer."

The plea of the Psalmist in this verse was that the Lord would HEAR his prayer. Perhaps there may come a time, or even has come a time at this moment, when we find it difficult to pray because we wonder if God is actually *hearing* us. Although we still believe in God, and we continue to acknowledge Jesus as our Saviour and Lord, we are finding it very difficult if not impossible to communicate with our Heavenly Father. It seems as if there is a barrier between God and us, which try as we might we cannot break down. It feels as if our prayers are bouncing off the ceiling and landing straight back on top of us! *"O Lord, hear my prayer"* – yet somehow we feel that He is just not listening! But why should this be?

Sometimes there is what appears to be quite a logical explanation. It may be the result of some bitter experience. For example, it can happen with a bereavement, although there are those of us who would confirm that when we tasted our first real experience of death in our family, it brought us nearer to our Heavenly Father, not farther away from Him. But we are all different. It can be caused by someone letting us down badly, a thoughtless word, an unkind action, especially from someone from whom we least expect it. On the other hand we might not have found any reason at all—it just happened!

It is important to realise that to reach a point where we cannot seem to find God, when somehow we just cannot seem to get through to Him, when we find it impossible to pray because we feel God is not listening, is not of itself sinful. Jesus Himself passed through such an experience on the Cross, when He cried out, "My God, My God, why have you forsaken me?" *(Matthew 27:46)* But had God really forsaken Him? Of course not. The Father had turned His back on the sin Jesus bore for us. He did not turn His back on His Son. It is important to understand that.

If at this moment we feel that, where ever we look, what ever we do, how ever much we try, we cannot seem to communicate with the Lord. We feel cut off. We feel lost. We feel alone. Our prayers are bouncing off the ceiling again! We are crying out, *"O Lord, hear my prayer,"* but somehow we feel He is not listening. What, then, can we do? One thing is certain, *we must never give up!* Jesus didn't. It is important to realise that God does not cut Himself off from us. If we feel God is far away from us, let remember it is not God who has moved. He does not construct the barrier and shut out His children. He does not turn a deaf ear to us!

Because this could become very important in our life – and the message to anyone passing through such an experience at the moment is, *do not give up* – we will return to it in our next devotional meditation.

125

Psalm 143:1 - "Hear my prayer, O Lord." [KJV]

The plea of the Psalmist in this verse was that the Lord would HEAR his prayer. Perhaps there may come a time, or even has come a time at this moment, when we find it difficult to pray because we wonder if God is actually *hearing* us. Because this could become very important in our life we said at the end of the previous devotional meditation dealing with this subject, that we would return to it in this meditation. For those of us who may be passing through such an experience at the moment, it is vitally important that we *do not give up.*

When we are having problems with prayer, and we feel we cannot pray, when communication appears impossible, those prayers keep bouncing back, and God seems no longer to be there listening to us, we need to understand that *this originates from us.* What ever the reason or cause, it is we ourselves who have cut the lines of communication, erected the barriers, moved away from God, and shut God out. Not deliberately, of course, but nevertheless, the result is the same. We cry out, *"Hear my prayer, O Lord",* but we do not have the assurance that He is hearing us. It is a distressing situation in which to be.

Every experience in life can be for our profit if we let it. Even a bitter experience of spiritual loneliness can actually strengthen us if we are prepared to allow such an experience to teach us. A refiner of gold skims off the dross from the molten metal to reveal the pure gold underneath. It shines in contrast to the dull impurities on the surface. Now it is possible that there may be impurities in our spiritual lives which must be removed before we can be of use to our Heavenly Father. It may even be that those impurities produced the barrier in the first place which cut us off from God and made our prayers impossible – which caused us to feel that God was not listening when we cried out for Him to hear our prayer.

The important thing to remember is that God is always there, God always understands, God always cares, God never ceases to love us. If we feel the opposite of those things, either now or in the future, let us *just hold on and keep our faith* as we ask Him to refine us. Then, when we come forth as shining gold, and we eventually will, not only will we be blessed our self by such an experience, but we will be able to bring blessing to others also. So, for those of us who may be passing through such an experience right now, or need *daily strength for daily living* to prepare us for the possibility of such an experience in the future – because it can and does happen; none of us are immune – let us take heart, knowing there will come a time when we say, *"Hear my prayer, O Lord,"* and we will *know* He is doing just that!

126

Psalm 143:5 – I remember the days of long ago; I meditate on all your works and consider what your hands have done.

There are those who would tell us that it is not good to look back. We should always have an eye to the future. What is past is past! We can do nothing about it! To look to the past is unproductive. We would agree that it is not good to be *constantly* looking back, but there are occasions when to do so can be most helpful, and may even be very productive. In any case, if God intended that we should *never* look back, why did He give us the wonderful gift of memory?

Of course, memory can be a mixed blessing. Unless we are prepared to learn from our memories, from the past, to look back on our failures and disappointments can be most unhelpful. But if we are prepared to focus our memory, then the exercise can prove very profitable indeed. This is what the Psalmist did in this verse. *"I remember the days of long ago; I meditate on all your works and consider what your hands have done."* David, who wrote this Psalm, focused his memory on what God had done for him and his nation.

Today we have such an account to aid our memory in the records of the Bible. Apart from these detailed facts in both Old and New Testaments, of what God has done for those who have put their trust in Him, we have our own personal memories of God's goodness towards us. We who have acknowledged Jesus as our Saviour and Lord and received the assurance of the Holy Spirit that we now belong to Him as part of His Family, can look back and remember all the care and love and concern God has shown for us, because we trusted in Him.

He may be the God of the Universe, as we said in an earlier devotional meditation, but He is also our *personal* God, One who longs to be involved in every area of our life. So we can look back and remember with gratitude all that He has done for us, all the burdens He has borne for us daily, and can profit from such memories, for like the Psalmist David we will find from the past new confidence for the present and the future. History is of great value when we realise that it is His-story – the record of God's dealings with mankind – and we are part of that story. I am glad I am part of that story…aren't you? Or should that be…are you?

127

Psalm 143:8,10 – Let the morning bring me word of your unfailing love, for I have put my trust in you. Show me the way I should go, for to you I lift up my soul. Teach me to do your will, for you are my God; may your good Spirit lead me on level ground.

We are constantly reminding ourselves these days (and rightly so) of the importance of prayer, both individually as Christians and corporately as a Fellowship. A simple definition of prayer is *divine communion.* Prayer is keeping in touch with God and God keeping in touch with us, both elements being necessary if there is to be that divine communion. The Psalmist of old knew the importance of this communion, to hear God's voice, to know His will for him, and for the need to respond by doing His will. This was the experience of the Psalmist thousands of years ago, and it needs to be our experience today in the twenty-first century.

To help us in our in our prayers, we take three words from these two verses and apply them to our communion with the Almighty. The first word is **HEAR** – *"Let the morning bring me word…"*, or, as the KJV translates it more simply, "CAUSE ME TO HEAR." Our hearts and lives must be so in tune with the Infinite that when He speaks, and He does so often, we will recognise His voice and hear what He has to say to us. This not only applies to us as individuals, of course, but also corporately to us all as a Fellowship of God's people.

Only in this way will we be able to **KNOW** what is His will for us – *"Show me the way I should go…"*, or, again, as the KJV translates it more simply, "CAUSE ME TO KNOW." How important it is in this uncertain world to have some absolute certainty, to know where we are going, know where we stand before the Lord, know the truth that makes us free, to know that the future has no fear for us. Such knowledge in the twenty-first century is precious beyond belief!

Then armed with this knowledge we must put it in to practice in our daily living as we seek always to **DO** His will – "TEACH ME TO DO YOUR WILL." Jesus said that only those who do the will of His father in heaven would enter into the kingdom of heaven, and not everyone will *(Matthew 7:21).* So let us pray constantly that we might always *hear* His voice, might always *know* His will, and might always be willing to *do* that will – then we can be sure that our prayer really is keeping in touch with God and God really is keeping in touch with us, with both necessary elements being firmly in place, thus cementing that divine communion between the Father and His children, which is what we were saying in the first place!

128

Psalm 145:4 – One generation will commend your works to another; they will tell of your mighty acts.

What the Bible is saying in this verse is that each generation has a responsibility to each succeeding generation. Just as those who have gone before us have helped to make us what we are by passing on the benefits of their personal experiences of life, so we in turn have the responsibility of passing on our experiences to the next generation. This responsibility has the greater significance in the spiritual realm because it is dealing with issues that affect the whole of eternity. But, of course, unless the witnessing generation has a vital and personal experience of Almighty God, it can never pass on such experience to the next generation.

Let us consider again, as we have done in previous devotional meditations, the greatness of our God. We have said that as we look at the wonderful beauty and order of creation on our own planet, the earth, of the grandeur of the universe as a whole – not only our own small galaxy, but the cosmos way out in space many light years away – and realise that God is even greater than all this, then the mind boggles when we discover that this same God cares about us as individuals; that God is actually mindful of man *(Psalm 8:4)*.

The greatness of God is not, therefore, measured by the vastness of the universe He has created but by the fact that He is mindful of us, individual human beings. Indeed, He cares so much that daily He bears our burdens; He loves us and never leaves us alone; He longs to be involved in every area of our lives; He wants to give us *daily strength for daily living* through His precious Word. We can look back and remember with gratitude all that He has done for us, and can profit from such memories. But this verse encourages us, not to look back with gratitude, but to look forward with responsibility.

"One generation will commend your works to another; they will tell of your mighty acts." We can only pass on to the next generation what we have experienced in our own. Not everything will we want to pass on, of course, but if our experience of the great God of the universe is such as we have been considering here and elsewhere in these meditations, that the great works and the mighty acts reflect in us His consideration and care for us as individuals rather than the creation of a vast universe, then we are able to obey the injunction in this verse; we will be able to commend (or praise, as the KJV translates it) His works and tell of His mighty acts to our children.

But here is a sobering thought! If we have no such experience ourselves, then we will be failing in our responsibility, which could have serious repercussions…for the next generation!

129

Psalm 145:8 – The Lord is gracious and compassionate, slow to anger and rich in love.

If we stop to think about it seriously we will make a startling discovery! It is this, that very often all the things that God *is* His children *are not.* Yet, because we are called by His Name, we are called Christians, we really should be like Him in all things. There are four things in this verse that tell us about God. He is *kind* (which is another word for gracious), He is *compassionate* (which means He cares), He is *slow to get angry* (which means that He does not have a bad temper), and He is *rich in love* (which really means He is full of love to overflowing).

Now think of Christians in general, and us in particular, and ask the question, are we really like God? If we are honest, we are not always as kind as we ought to be, neither to each other nor to those who do not profess the Christian Faith. A little more kindness in the world would certainly improve our quality of life. It is easy to say we care, to be compassionate with words, but action speaks louder than words. To be a true Christian we need to *show* that we care about our fellow man, whether right next door or in a far distant country; we need to *show* compassion to others by the things that we do, which is really a vital development of the kindness we should be showing.

How many of us can say we never lose our temper, we never get angry? Not many! If we are really honest again, perhaps we should settle for "not *any*!" We are not talking of righteous anger and injustice as demonstrated by Jesus in the Temple *(Luke 19:45-48)*, but down right bad temper, which is totally unjustified. And what about this business of love, of being full of love, of being rich in love? We know the main theme of most pop songs is love, but if we analyse it very carefully, it is a very superficial kind of love that pop stars sing about. Very often their gyrations on stage have more significance than the words they sing. The Bible has a lot to say about genuine love – it is patient, kind, never jealous or envious, not demanding, does not hold grudges, creates trust and loyalty, and that is only very few of the things it has to say!

There is very little love shown in the world today. Hatred, revenge, bitterness, there is plenty, but when it comes to love, that is a very different story. More love and there would be less broken homes, less broken marriages, less broken relationships, less misunderstandings, less bloodshed, less lust and rape – we could go on and on. So what is this verse saying to us? Simply that we as Christians should set an example to the world by being more like the Lord whom we acknowledge and worship. What a different world we would live in if we could truthfully put our name into this verse in place of the Lord's – "We are gracious and compassionate, slow to anger and rich in love." It is worthy of serious consideration, do we not agree?

130

Psalm 145:11,13 – They will tell of the glory of your kingdom and speak of your might...Your kingdom is an everlasting kingdom, and your dominion endures through all generations.

We have considered in recent devotional meditations the vastness of the universe in which we live – so vast, in fact, that this planet earth seems but a minute speck, an insignificant dot, and man himself is even smaller! This could give us a tremendous inferiority complex, until we realise that God, who is greater even than the whole universe, cares about us as individuals, and loves us with an even greater love than a human father. Indeed, this verse tends to put the whole thing into proper perspective, and this is important.

Man is seeking to conquer space, to set up a space station on the moon, and even now is planning to take tourists out to Mars! Yet man has not yet learned to live peaceably on his own planet; he is trying to settle in space, but has yet to settle down on Earth. History reminds us that kingdoms come and kingdoms go, that the face of our planet is constantly changing so that maps quickly go out of date. Compare the school atlas of twenty-five years ago with one of today; think, only in recent years, of the number of countries that have disappeared to be replaced by others whose names are less familiar.

This verse says, *"They will tell of the glory of your kingdom and speak of your might...Your kingdom is an everlasting kingdom, and your dominion endures through all generations."* As Christians we belong to this everlasting kingdom. What does this mean? It means that, like the kingdom to which we belong, our lives are now *heavenly*, not of this world. Our lives will in no way be affected by the changing world around us. It means, too, that like the kingdom, our lives are now *everlasting*, which assures us that we need never fear the future, whatever may happen upon this planet, for together with those who have gone on before us and are now with the Lord, we have a share in eternal life, which began the moment we entered this everlasting kingdom (in other words, the moment we became Christians), and continues after death.

If we know that we belong to this everlasting kingdom, then that makes the universe a minute speck, an insignificant dot, by comparison with this everlasting kingdom, which is infinitely greater and to which we belong. Now, that certainly puts things into proper perspective, doesn't it?

131

Psalm 150:1 – Praise the Lord. Praise God in his sanctuary; praise him in his mighty heavens.

Because the book of *Psalms* is the old Jewish Hymn Book, it is natural that so many of its Psalms are given over to praising the Lord, much like our modern hymn books which generally have very large praise sections, especially in our more recent hymn books. It seems appropriate for us to consider once again the subject of praising God in this, the last devotional meditation from the *Psalms*. Whenever Christians come together to worship the Lord, whether it is in a simple Gospel Hall or a magnificent cathedral, in church buildings of various shapes and sizes, or even in a private home; whether it is on a Sunday or any other day through the week; they will include in their worship a period of singing praises unto the Lord.

But this verse reminds us that there is more to praising the Lord than just singing hymns and spiritual songs in church, or wherever Christians congregate to worship. As we have recently considered in various ways in previous devotional meditations the wonderful beauty and order of creation on our own planet, then beyond it to the perfect symmetry and order of the vast universe, of the greatness of Almighty God in such creation, and the place of mankind in the scheme of things, we have been greatly blessed. It is right, therefore, that we should sing praises to this great God, but that we should also remember that anywhere where we come together in His name we form part of the Church and where we meet becomes a sanctuary.

"Praise the Lord. Praise God in his sanctuary; praise him in his mighty heavens". But our praise must go beyond the sanctuary, because this verse requires us to include the mighty heavens, too. This doesn't mean we have to take a spacecraft and blast off into space to sing His praises – although, by the way things seem to be developing, there may be those who will do just that in years to come! In fact, it has already been done by American astronoughts! Who knows, we may have a hymn- singing programme from outer space one day. But that is in the future. What does it mean for now? It means that we should praise the Lord *for* His wonderful creation, praise Him *in* His wonderful creation, and praise Him *through* His wonderful creation.

God has created the universe and He has created us. God controls and governs the universe and He loves and cares about us. This great God is worthy of our praise, not only in a sanctuary, not only on one particular day, but *every* day in the world He has created. There is no time and no place where we should not praise the Lord.

132

Proverbs 1:7 – The fear of the Lord is the beginning of knowledge, but fools despise wisdom and discipline.

A paraphrase of this Bible verse puts it in the form of a question. *"How does a man become wise? The first step is to trust and reverence the Lord! Only fools refuse to be taught."* Great emphasis is placed these days upon education – and rightly so – but knowledge just for the sake of knowledge is really rather pointless; it must be tempered with wisdom and instruction. Or, to put it another way, just to *know* something is not enough, we must learn how to put that knowledge into action, to put it to good use.

This is really what this verse is saying. So let us answer the question, *"How does a man become wise?"* The answer is *"to trust and reverence the Lord."* The rest of the paraphrased verse speaks for itself! There are those who will tell us that to believe in God, to become a Christian, is only for the weak, the feeble, the ignorant, those with nothing better to do. How wrong they are! The fact is, the exact opposite is the truth. It takes great strength and courage to be a Christian. It is not just enough to know that there is a God somewhere – this is knowledge without wisdom. To be really wise takes strength of character, putting our knowledge into action by acknowledging Jesus Christ as our Saviour and becoming a Christian. Then we put ourselves into a position whereby we receive further instruction.

Let us always remember, *only fools refuse to be taught.* As Christians, we can sometimes become very discouraged and disheartened by the attitude of others, especially when we are accused of being weak and feeble because of our faith. Let us take encouragement from this Bible verse. *"The fear of the Lord is the beginning of knowledge: but fools despise wisdom and discipline"* – or, as the KJV translates the word "discipline", fools despise wisdom and *instruction.* Are we amongst this world's wise people, or are we amongst the fools? Each one of us must answer that question for ourselves – and so much depends upon that answer!

133

Proverbs 3:5,6 – Trust in the Lord with all your heart and lean not on your own understanding; in all your ways acknowledge him, and he will make your paths straight.

This is one of those Bible verses that is used in various ways. It seems to appear in autograph books quite frequently – or, it used to, because autograph books are not as popular these days as they used to be a few years ago! – which is an improvement on, "Roses are red, violets are blue…", we would suggest. Even more frequently it seems to be inscribed on the fly leaf of a book given as a gift, sometimes even in the Bible itself. Part of it has been used as the title of a Christian novel! Now, why should this be such a popular verse?

If we look at it more closely we may find the answer. To begin with, it is a very good piece of advice, especially as it is taken from the book of *Proverbs* written many thousands of years ago but well worth taking note of today for its wisdom. There is a lot of insecurity in the world today, and it seems to be increasing as we move further into the twenty-first century. We cannot always trust those we thought would never let us down, but do! Sadly, this can often happen *within* the Church – it shouldn't, but it does! So it is good and comforting to know that we have Someone whom we can trust with all our heart, Someone who will *never* let us down, Someone in whom we can find absolute security.

There are many things we cannot understand, which puzzle us, may even frustrate us, so perhaps it is good advice not to lean on our own understanding but to exercise more faith. As we look around us we wonder just where this world is heading – we are back to that insecurity again! – sometimes we feel disaster is just around the corner, and sometimes it is! Our nation seems to have lost direction, laws are being passed contrary to God's Word, practices once acknowledged as wrong, even sinful, have now become acceptable, so much so that we as individuals even wonder ourselves where we are going.

Once again, it is comforting to know that there is One who will direct us, guide us, show us the way, if we will let Him. It is good to have a definite direction in life, to know absolutely where we are going. So the advice given is simple and straight to the point. *"Trust in the Lord with all your heart and lean not on your own understanding; in all your ways acknowledge him, and he will make your paths straight."* The KJV translation of this last phrase is more simple and straight to the point – "and he shall direct thy paths." Like all good advice it is only of use if we take it. Here, then, is the advice, it is up to us to take it, isn't it?

134

Proverbs 3:33;14:11 – The Lord…blesses the home of the righteous…the tent of the upright will flourish.

This "verse" is actually made up of two separate verses from *Proverbs.* Basically, what it is saying is that, if a home is to flourish and be blessed by the Lord, it must have a firm foundation. As any good builder will tell us, it is impossible to build a strong house on a poor foundation, and the same applies, possibly more so, to the building of a strong home – and it is to a home rather than a house to which this verse is referring. A house is made up of bricks and mortar, wood and glass, but a home is made up of people, and people are far more important to God than material things.

It is a sad fact that the break up of homes has become a commonplace occurrence these days, a fact of life we seem to accept almost as being the norm. When this happens, it is not just a marriage that has broken down, but a home has been destroyed. We can rebuild a house that has been damaged (by a hurricane, a flood, or a fire, for example); it is not so easy to repair a broken home. It is an even more sad fact when we hear of Christian homes breaking up, for it is here more especially where this verse should apply.

The upright family is the one which makes its foundation according to God's Word, and which lives its life according to God's unchanging moral code. Faithfulness, mutual trust and respect, deep-rooted Christian love for God and each other provides much of the fabric for a home that is to flourish. The Bible is very definite in its advice with very plain and easy to understand statements. "Submit to one another out of reverence to God. Wives, submit to your husbands as to the Lord…Husbands, love your wives…husbands ought to love their wives as their own bodies. He who loves his wife loves himself…For this reason a man will leave his father and mother and be united to his wife, and the two will become one flesh…Children, obey your parents in the Lord, for this is right. Honour your father and mother…Fathers, do not exasperate your children; instead, bring them up in the training and instruction of the Lord" *(Ephesians 5:21,22,25,28,31;6:1,2,4).*

There is plenty of good sound advice here for a strong healthy home, and this is but a very small section of what can be found in the Bible. Please permit me a personal reference! Some years ago I remember staying with a Christian family in the North of England – father, mother and three teenage daughters – where Bible principles were rigidly applied. The visit impressed me so much that's its memory is still with me to this day. It was a home where the Lord certainly blessed this righteous home, and the upright there flourished – and are still flourishing today. So, we can see that these words from Scripture still work, even in this day and age, as that North Country home proved it, and are still proving it!

135

Proverb 6:16-19 – There are six things the Lord hates, seven that are detestable to him: haughty eyes, a lying tongue, hands that shed innocent blood, a heart that devises wicked schemes, feet that are quick to rush into evil, a false witness who pours out lies and a man who stirs up dissension among brothers.

This "verse" is rather long, certainly longer than usual. The reason for this, of course, is because it is four verses put together, and for a reason, as will become apparent when we start to look more closely at them. If we pick up our daily newspaper, or switch on a television newscast, we will read or see of those people today who are doing one or more of these seven things that God hates. This has become especially prevalent through the latter years of the twentieth century, and things are no better now we have come into the twenty-first century – if anything, they are steadily getting worse!

The moral laws of our country – indeed, of every civilised country in the world – are based on the Ten Commandments of the

Bible, although there would be many who would not acknowledge this, but it is still fact. Because God, who created the whole universe, of which our planet is only a small part, cares about the world He created, He gave us these commandments by which we should live to make this world a better place, a good and secure place in which to live. It is when we fail to acknowledge God, break His laws, and turn to our own ways (whether as nations or individuals) that problems arise.

So let us pick up that newspaper again, or turn on that television newscast, and see the evidence of a world gone wrong. We don't need to specify any particular incidents or practices because they are all around us. But we should remember these verses as we read the newspaper or watch the television newscast, and recognise the things God hates being practised before our eyes – *"haughty eyes, a lying tongue, hands that shed innocent blood, a heart that devises wicked schemes, feet that are quick to rush into evil, a false witness who pours out lies and a man who stirs up dissension."*

If, as Christians, we would contribute to a better world, a happier world, a safer world, a cleaner world, a more secure world, a world as God intended it to be when He first created it, then that contribution must begin with us as individuals acknowledging the things that God hates and by, not only hating them ourselves, but by encouraging others to hate them, too, by our Christian witness and example.

136

Proverbs 6:22 – When you walk, they will guide you; when you sleep, they will watch over you; when you awake, they will speak to you.

Daily Strength for Daily Living seeks to emphasise the importance of God's Word upon which to meditate daily to obtain the strength we need daily to live a life pleasing to the Lord Himself. Here is a verse which speaks to us of the importance of the Word of God itself – indeed, from time to time the Bible does say something about itself! So if we are going to gain *daily strength for daily living* from this verse, what does it say to us? It is warning us of the danger of neglecting God's Word and is encouraging us to read the Bible regularly – a word of *warning* and a word of *encouragement* in one verse.

We should understand, of course, that it is impossible for us as Christians to neglect or ignore the Word of God and expect to progress in our Christian way of life. Indeed, a true Christian cannot exist without regular reading of the Bible. We need daily guidance to be sure of God's way for us; we need *daily strength for daily living*, not "occasional strength for occasional living"! This verse is speaking about our "father's commands" *(verse 20)*, and begins with the need for daily guidance. *"When you walk, they will guide you..."* So we neglect the Word of God at our peril – the peril of becoming spiritually lost.

One of the virtues of leading a real Christian life is a divine sense of peace; undeniably, in the trouble-torn world of the twenty-first century, peace is a tremendous blessing, an invaluable gift. The inner sense of peace can only come when all fear is removed. It is fear that often prevents sleep – not only fear of the unknown, but sometimes it is fear of the known! Be assured the Word of God is far more effective than any sleeping tablets prescribed to help us forget our fears. *"When you sleep, they will watch over you..."* So we neglect the Word of God at our peril – the peril of becoming sick in body and mind through lack of sleep and constant fear.

A true Christian recognises that communication with God is two-way. Prayer is not all talking to God, for sometimes it is God talking to us – at least, it is when He can get a word in edgeways! God so many times wants to speak to His children, and a very effective way (in addition to our prayers) is through His Living Word. *"When you awake, they will speak to you."* So we neglect the Word of God at our peril – the peril of failing to hear God's voice when He desperately wants to speak to us.

So we can see that this verse, concerning our "father's commands", shows us that God's Word will guide us through life, give us a divine sense of peace, and enable God to speak to us; and it also reminds us that as Christians we neglect or ignore God's Word at our own peril! A word of *warning* and a word of *encouragement* in one verse is most helpful, isn't it?

137

Proverbs 13:7 – One man pretends to be rich, yet has nothing; another pretends to be poor, yet has great wealth.

In this day and age, when we have to be very careful about the un-Scriptural teaching of what has become known as the "prosperity gospel", it is refreshing to come across a Bible verse which is designed to not only make us think, but possibly to help us get our thinking straight! The is one such verse! If we were to conduct a survey in one of our public thoroughfares asking the question, "What makes a person rich?", we could almost guarantee one hundred percent of the answers would be, "Someone with a lot of money!" *And they would all be wrong!*

Money doesn't make a person rich, it only makes them wealthy – and there is a difference, a very big difference! Perhaps we are puzzled by this line of thinking, so let us get our thinking straight. A clue is actually in this verse. Wealth is measured by possessions, be it money, property, investments, or anything else that may generate more wealth. Riches are measured by those things of lasting value; a richness of character, a richness of spirit, the riches of love, of caring, of compassion. This verse explains, *"One man pretends to be rich, yet has nothing; another pretends to be poor, get has great wealth."*

There are those who are extremely wealthy by today's standards yet are very poor in spirit, living only for themselves and what they can gain to get more. It doesn't matter whom they push down as long as they push themselves up. On the other hand, there are those who are very poor by the world's standards, have very little money, very few possessions, yet possess a richness of spirit which is constantly bringing blessing and lasting comfort to many, a richness that will still have its effect long after their lifetime. So here is a word of comfort and encouragement to those of us who may feel insignificant, useless, ineffectual, unwanted, because we do not possess a lot of this world's wealth.

Perhaps we need to remember that, if we have these lasting qualities of life, the things that really matter, the spiritual things that are for eternity, then we are rich indeed. To put this verse into modern parlance, it is saying, "Some rich people are poor, and some poor people are very rich!" So let us take heart, we may be richer than we think!

138

Proverbs 15:3 – The eyes of the Lord are everywhere, keeping watch on the wicked and the good.

When I was a child my mother used to say to me, "Now remember, Denis, be good, because God can see you wherever you go and whatever you do." Then I used to say, "If I get under the bed He won't see me," but I was assured that there was no place where I could hide out of God's sight. There are many references to this truth in God's Word, in addition to this proverb. The Old Testament character, Job, for example, stated, "His eyes are on the ways of men; he sees their every step" *(Job 34:21).* The Old Testament king, Asa, was informed that, "the eyes of the Lord range throughout the earth" *(2 Chronicles 16:9),* and through the Old Testament prophet, Jeremiah, the Lord Himself informed His people, "My eyes are on all their ways; they are not hidden from me, nor is their sin concealed from my eyes" *(Jeremiah 16:17).*

And just in case we think this is an exclusively Old Testament idea, the writer of the *Hebrews* in the New Testament adopts the same theme. "Nothing in all creation is hidden from God's sight. Everything is uncovered and laid bare before the eyes of him to whom we must give account" *(Hebrews 4:13).* So, when I suggested to my mother that I might hide from God by getting under the bed, I was not expressing an original idea. Others have had the same idea, some a long time before me!

The Old Testament king, David, for example, wrote in one of the *Psalms*, "Where can I go from your Spirit? Where can I flee from your presence? If I go up to the heavens, you are there; if I make my bed in the depths, you are there. If I rise on the wings of the dawn, if I settle on the far side of the sea, even there your hand will guide me, your right hand will hold me fast" *(Psalm 139:7-10).*

We could almost add, "If I hide under the bed, behold You are there!" Therefore, what is this verse really saying to us? It is this, whether we believe in God or not, He really does exist and keeps His eyes upon us wherever we go; whether we do good or evil, God can see, we can hide nothing from Him, for He sees everything whether we believe it or not, we are never out of God's sight. My mother was right, wasn't she? God can see me, whatever I do – good or evil – wherever I go; there is no place where I can hide from Him, *not even under the bed!*

139

Proverbs 21:21 – He who pursues righteousness and love finds life, prosperity and honour.

Every day of our lives we are called upon to make a decision of some kind or another, to choose between one or more alternatives. Often the choice is easy and of little effect, such as what to have for breakfast, whether to go to the shops or take a walk along the seafront or in the park, what pair of shoes to put on, what colour tie to wear, or perhaps not to wear a tie at all – simple little decisions which have no real lasting effect, neither upon us personally or anyone else associated with us.

But once in a while our decision may have long-term results both for others, and ourselves. It is when we are faced with the hard choice, to choose wrongly and become popular in the eyes of the world, or to make the right choice and risk the wrath of our friends, that the Word of God can help us. Friends who would be angered by our right decision are friends better left alone anyway! The truth is, they are not really friends at all. If we are prepared to pursue righteousness, make the right choice how ever unpopular we may become as a result, find life, prosperity and honour in the sight of God.

The KJV gives a better translation of this last phrase! We will find "life, *righteousness*, and honour." This leaves no room for misunderstanding, as we mentioned in a previous devotional meditation. The alternative – making the wrong decision – is obvious, and just a little frightening when we stop to think about it, yet the choice is still ours to make. This is really what this verse is saying: *"He who pursues"* (or follows) *"after righteousness and love"* (or mercy) *"finds life, prosperity"* (or righteousness) *"and honour."* Now let us take the opposite point of view, it is certainly frightening. "He who pursues (follows) after evil and injustice finds death, evil and dishonour."

May we always make the right choice before the Lord, never sacrifice principles for popularity, maintain honour without question, and constantly follow after righteousness. It really is the only safe way!

140

Proverbs 30:5 – Every word of God is flawless; he is a shield to those who take refuge in him.

Many of us no doubt go to church regularly and will hear the Word of God preached during the service; there may be many of us who are forced to stay at home, unable to attend church, because of age or infirmity, and have to rely on audio tapes or CD's to hear the Word of God preached that way; on the other hand, there are many in our land who give no thought to attending a church, have no desire to read the Word of God or hear it preached, or want anything to do with Christianity. To put it another way, our land is populated with a vast number of people with varying attitudes, or lack of them, towards the Word of God.

But here is an indisputable fact! Whatever our attitude, or lack of it, it will not in any way alter the truth of this verse. We have already emphasised in previous devotional meditations that, if we are going to glean *daily strength for daily living* from its pages, we need to read and meditate on the Bible regularly. This verse is important because it speaks of the flawlessness of (or purity of as the KJV translates it) of God's Word and the protection it gives to those who believe it, who put their trust in it. There are too many people today, often under the guise of scholarship, who spend their time criticising the Bible, finding fault with it, trying to cast doubt on the truth of the Word.

One of the sad facts is that we find there are those *within* the Church who should know better than to try and undermine the teachings of such important truths as the resurrection of Jesus Christ, the virgin birth, and the Second Coming of Christ, to name but a few. Such people would do better to uplift and defend the truths of the Scriptures rather than try to discredit them. So what does this verse have to say to us? Two things! Firstly, we can trust God's Word fully because every word is flawless, is pure. The Bible does not contradict itself, as some claim, even though it may appear to do so sometimes until it is properly understood.

So the first thing, then, is that we can believe *every* word with absolute assurance. Secondly, if we are prepared to trust the Bible, believe it, live by its teachings, not try to cast doubt or find fault with it, then we will find protection, comfort, guidance, advice, encouragement – so many things to help us through life, so much *daily strength for daily living.* So if we have stopped reading it, or have ceased to read it regularly, because we have been tempted to doubt that *"every word of God is flawless; he is a shield to those who take refuge in him"*, stop knocking it and start reading it every day and encourage other to read it, too.

141

Ecclesiastes 1:9 – What has been will be again, what has been done will be done again.

What a strange verse to include in a book of devotional meditations with the title of *Daily Strength for Daily Living.* It doesn't seem to make any sense! But it must do if it is in the Bible! Let's read it again. *"What has been will be again, what has been done will be done again."* Strange! Or is it? Here is a verse which reminds us that life consists of a "daily round a common task", as one hymn writer described life; that which has been today will be again tomorrow, and that which we have done today we will do all over again tomorrow.

Last night we went to bed to sleep, we will do it again tonight; yesterday we ate our meals, and we will repeat the process again today; so we could go on and on naming the things we do quite naturally and without really thinking about it each day. Life can become very boring, repetitive, even humdrum, *but not for a true Christian!* That may surprise us! There is a chorus we sometimes sing, a line of which goes, *"Every day with Jesus is sweeter than the day before."* This isn't sentimental twaddle! This is a statement of fact. For a true Christian every day should present a new challenge, a fresh opportunity, to serve the Lord.

Our daily repetition, if done for Jesus, will take on new meaning, will have added incentive, will be anything but boring. As the Bible says, we "do all to the glory of God" *(1 Corinthians 10:31)*, even the mundane and menial tasks. I once knew a lady who actually looked forward to the daily chore of washing-up, after her large family had left for work and school, because she could be alone with God and pray over the sink! The pots and pans were always the same, day after day, but every new day was different. A life in daily communication with our loving Lord will never become boring and repetitive, but challenging, exciting, and full of glorious opportunities. It's up to us to try it, isn't it? After all, it's the only way to glean *daily strength for daily living.*

142

Ecclesiastes 8:4 – Since a king's word is supreme, who can say to him, What are you doing?

The KJV translation of this verse packs a more powerful punch! "Where the word of a king is, there is power." When we take upon ourselves the name "Christian", and have a right to call ourselves by that name, as a result of our personal relationship with Christ rather than membership of a church, then with the name goes the responsibility to speak and act for our King. We refer, of course, to the King of kings, God Himself; and this verse makes it quite plain – "Where the word of a king is, there is power."

An ambassador in a foreign country has no power or authority of his own other than that given him by the sovereign head of his country – be it a King, a Queen, a President, or any other Head of

State. When the ambassador speaks or acts for his country it is with the power and authority vested in him. This is a perfect example of our role as Christians – we are ambassadors. The world in which we live is our "foreign" country, because our homeland is heaven. As it says elsewhere in the Bible, we are Christ's ambassadors *(2 Corinthians 6:20)*. We have no power or authority other than that which He gives us through His Spirit.

There are those *today* who are waiting to hear the words of our King through our lips *today*. Notice the emphasis we place on the word "today". Why? Because we dare not delay. In diplomatic circles sometimes a day's delay can be disastrous. It can be in Christian circles, too! All the signs of the times suggest that the moment is fast approaching when Christ Jesus our King will come again for His own, and that our King will break off "diplomatic relations", when the authority and power of the ambassador will no longer be valid, no longer necessary, in fact.

Such, then, is our responsibility at the moment, to speak with power for our King, remembering that His words have greater power even than that of an earthly ruler, especially by virtue of the fact that they are words of love. We realise that the King of kings is not only our Sovereign Lord, not even just our Heavenly Father, He is our *Loving* Heavenly Father and so we must be His *loving* ambassadors. Quite a responsibility, isn't it?

143

Isaiah 5:2 – But it yielded only bad fruit.

What a sad phrase! What a disappointment! After all that time and effort, care and concern – he had even put in a winepress, so he was expecting good fruit to produce good wine – then nothing but bad fruit at the end. Sad though it is, just how is this relevant to us today? Let us think for a moment of what the Lord has done for us. He cared so much, loved us so deeply, that He gave His Son to die for us, to give us eternal life; and when the work of Christ was complete here on earth, and He had returned to His Father, He sent the Holy Spirit to empower us to do the work that Jesus had begun.

He has fenced us around with His love, made a way to gather out the stones of sin, planted within us the choicest of vines, the very nature of God Himself, and like "the one I love" who built a watchtower in the middle of it, so we are never out of God's sight. Jesus said of Himself that He was the true vine and we are the branches, the purpose of which is for us to bear much fruit – rich, luscious fruit that should produce good "wine that gladdens the heart of man" *(Psalm 104:15)*. How sad and disappointed Jesus must be when we fail to reach the standard He has set for us, and we produce only bad fruit.

If we could but fully appreciate what the Lord has done for us, realising His purpose for our lives, we would never fail Him. Think of "the one I love" in *Isaiah*, the work and sacrifice to try and produce good fruit, then look at the result. He did all he could! He couldn't have done more! Now think of Jesus, His work and sacrifice on our behalf, to produce in us good fruit, then look at the results in our lives. He did all He could. He couldn't have done more. Are we bringing joy to the Lord by the way we live, or are we making Him sad? What sort of fruit are we producing in our lives? Yes, it is true to say that Jesus has done all He could, He couldn't have done more … the rest is now up to us to yield only *good* fruit!

144

Isaiah 6:1 – In the year that King Uzziah died, I saw the Lord seated on a throne, high and exalted.

Many of us, if we are totally honest with ourselves and stop to think seriously about it, claim only a vague awareness of God in all His Majesty. Admittedly, we may have a sense of the presence of God in our lives as we pray and read our Bible, and although we feel He is close to us, constantly acknowledge the existence of, and direct our worship and prayers to, a Superior Being "somewhere out there" (wherever "out there" happens to be), it is not the same as recognising the full beauty and majesty of God for ourselves, or realising just how vital a vision of Him can be. What a difference it would make if we could look through the eyes of one who has experienced such a vision.

This verse gives us such an opportunity! Compared with the great men of the Bible, sometimes we are very short sighted. But God has not changed; He still wants us to "see" Him as He really is. So we will borrow the eyes of Isaiah, who wrote this verse, and see what he saw. *"In the year that King Uzziah died, I saw the Lord seated on a throne, high and exalted".* The long reign of Uzziah had ended and Isaiah wondered about the future. Would the old order of security change? Would a new king with different policies endanger the previous fifty years work under the old king? Pondering these problems in the temple, suddenly he finds their solution.

He sees the Lord, high and exalted, and realises that God is not endangered by changes in earthly conditions. God *never* changes. Such a vision of God is one we should value today. We live in a world of uncertainty and change. Is there going to be a nuclear war or a nuclear disaster? The twenty-first century has inherited the legacy of the previous one, and we are still surrounded by a world of unrest. A war here, a bomb there, a radiation leak somewhere else, nations against nations, fightings and killings, bloodshed and carnage – what a world we live in! Yet the biggest blast produced by man cannot even shake, let alone destroy, the Throne of God. He is high and exalted. As the old hymn puts it, *"Change and decay in all around I see; O Thou who changest not, Abide with me!"*

None of us knows the future – God intended it that way – but none of us need fear the future, if we are prepared to acknowledge that God is on the throne, King of our lives, high and exalted. Such a vision is precious, it gives us security in a very insecure world, and as a bonus it will enhance that sense of the presence of God in our lives as we pray and read our Bible.

145

Isaiah 40:8 – The grass withers and the flowers fall, but the word of our God stands for ever.

We hear much these days about "global warming" – it is a stock phrase which is bandied about immediately there is a dramatic change in the climate. It is true that we are experiencing some strange phenomena in the weather all over the world, but lengthy heat-waves are not a new phenomena, not even in the United Kingdom! Many years ago, before "global warming" became an "in phrase", the UK experienced one of its longest and hottest summers in living memory, and the Government even appointed a Minister of Drought! The water shortage and the drying up of reservoirs caused great concern, as did the devastating forest fires in some parts of the country.

All over the country the strong sun and lack of rain caused flowers and shrubs to wither and die. In one seaside town on the South Coast many rhododendron bushes died which were over eighty years old. This was the last thing to be expected of such well-established bushes. The local Superintendent of Parks and Gardens stated in the local press that scorched grass would have to be replaced, because even the roots were dead – grass that had existed in some cases for almost one hundred years! Who would have thought such a situation could arise in the UK! Is nothing secure? Is nothing safe? Is nothing permanent? Is there nothing that will stand the test of time?

The answer to all these questions is a resounding YES! The Bible says, *"The grass withers and the flowers fall, but the word of God stands for ever."* Thank God for His Word! Religious fashions come and go. Theological and other literary works have their sway for limited periods, then disappear. Men's ideas and fancies are introduced, often dressed up a little to give greater attraction, and have their influence for a time. The world seems constantly to be changing with never two days alike! What held good yesterday is today completely out-dated. *"Change and decay in all around I see..."* as we said in the previous devotional meditation. But, whilst like the grass and flowers these things wither and fall, God's Word stands for ever, stands secure, firm, unchanging, reliable and sure.

What can we learn from this to give us *daily strength for daily living*? We must be sure that we pattern our lives upon God's Word; that we put our complete faith and trust in God's Word; that our whole future is closely bound up in God's Word. There is no real security in this life except that found in God's Word. If we trust the grass and flowers of man-made ideas and man-inspired writings, there will come a time when they will wither and fall, and we may be lost to all eternity. On the other hand, if we trust the Word of God, the Holy Spirit-inspired writings, it will stand for ever, and our whole future is secure. After all, there isn't much other security in life, is there?

146

Isaiah 41:10 – I will strengthen you and help you; I will uphold you with my righteous right hand.

All through the Bible God has made many promises to His people, and because He is God we know that He is able and willing to keep every promise He has made. In this verse we have, not one, but *three* precious promises in quick succession. First there is the promise of STRENGTH – *"I will strengthen you..."* All Christians need spiritual strength for daily living – *daily strength for daily living*. In our own strength we will fail time and time again, and the devil will have his way. Let us not underestimate the power of the devil. We need the daily strength God has promised us to overcome evil and maintain a faithful witness.

Secondly there is the promise of HELP in time of need – *"...and help you..."* Every day has its problems and difficulties, something unexpected may arise, and in our hearts – often without fully realising it – we send up a cry to the Lord for help. There is no situation in which we may find ourselves where His promise does not apply. He has promised to help us, and His promises are sure with a sense of the presence of God in our lives as we pray and read our Bible, to those who believe. Thirdly there is the promise of

SUPPORT – *"I will uphold you..."* One of the most precious promises in the whole Bible is that God is able to keep us from falling. A line from an old hymn seems appropriate here! *"I dare not take one step without Thine aid"*, and yet so often we try to go it alone!

God has promised us His support, to uphold us, if we put our trust in Him. There is no need for us to fall because He will not let us down, He cannot let us down, since He has promised. So let us claim these precious promises as our spiritual right now (as indeed they are our spiritual right, or God would not have promised them in the first place!) Day by day we can experience His strength, His help, and His support from this moment on. He has made us these promises; it is up to us to believe them day-by-day! Then we will not only receive *daily strength for daily living*, but we will also receive daily *help* for daily living, and daily *support* for daily living – a valuable daily trinity for daily living, we might say!

147

Isaiah 43:2a – When you pass through the waters, I will be with you.

From time to time, as we read and meditate regularly on the Scriptures, occasionally a verse will appear to leap out at us from the page, its message being so powerful that it seems to be demanding attention. This verse from the book of *Isaiah* is one such verse. So powerful is the message for us that it is going to take three of these devotional meditations to embrace all that God really wants to say to us through this verse.

The first thing this verse says to us is this. Just because we are Christians, it does not mean all the cares and frustrations of life will pass us by. The verse does not say "if" but "when", and naturally assumes that at some stage in our life we will be faced with some problem, some difficulty, some anxious moment. That first word of the verse is very important – *"WHEN you pass through the waters..."* If someone should tell us that being a Christian is just one long "path of roses"; that the moment we repent of our sins and give our heart to the Lord, commit our life fully to Him, all our cares and worries will be over; we would do well not to believe them! It's just not true!

Please permit me a personal illustration. I well remember sitting in a service many years ago where the preacher took that line, and literally deluded (there is no other word for it!) his congregation into believing Christianity was the antidote to all the unhappy and unpleasant things in life. One "dose" and life would be perfect; one "dose" and you could live without a care in the world! I was on holiday at the time, and as a visitor felt constrained from standing up in the middle of his sermon and shouting "rubbish!" I did, however, tackle him at the door on my way out after the service, and his reply was, "What I have said I have said!" The sad thing was this, *that minister actually believed what he was preaching was the truth!*

We have only to look around us and we will quickly realise that Christians suffer equally as much as those who have no profession of faith – indeed, Christians sometimes seem to suffer more! Just as the storms tossed that little fishing boat around on the Sea of Galilee, so we will be tossed about on the Sea of Life. The big difference between the Christian and the non-believer, of course, is in the Person with whom we share the boat! What a difference it made to those Galilean fishermen, what a difference it makes to us, if Jesus is in the boat with us.

So the first message we receive from this verse is that *Christians are subject to the cares of life*, but although as Christians we have to pass through times of bereavement and suffering, God still cares and understands, and He will always be there to comfort, to uphold, to strengthen, in a time of need. But there is more, as we will see in our next meditation!

148

Isaiah 43:2b – When you pass through the rivers, they will not sweep over you.

So far the message from this verse has been that Christians are not immune from sorrow and distress – *"WHEN you pass through the waters...WHEN you pass through the rivers...WHEN you walk through the fire..."* That word "when" is very important. But there is more! This verse also reminds us that, whatever the tragic situation in which we find ourselves, we are only passing through it – *"When you PASS THROUGH the rivers..."* We are often told that time is a great healer in cases of sorrow and bereavement. This is really just another way of saying what the Psalmist says, "Even though I *walk through* the valley…" *(Psalm 23:4).*

There may come times in our experience when we feel life is becoming almost too unbearable to live. Every time we switch on the radio or television, or pick up a newspaper, there seems to be nothing but war, fighting, suicide bombing, killing, blood-shed somewhere in the world. Moral standards appear to be on the decline, even accelerating since we entered the twenty-first century, it seems. Whether at home or abroad the world is steadily growing worse. Where will it all end, we ask ourselves? Let us leave for a moment the national or international scene, and concentrate on our own home circle, our own social circle, even our own church circle.

No doubt there are times we can recall – or may even be passing through at this moment – when life becomes very depressing indeed. Now let us look back in our life to a time when things may have been much worse. We passed through that situation – we did not stop! On the other hand, perhaps we are saying that when we look back we can remember a time when things were much better. Take heart! The same applies. As we passed from a better situation to a worse one, so we will continue on, because the situation we are now in will not remain the same. There is a message here no matter what situation we may find ourselves at the moment.

So the second message we receive from this verse is that *we are passing through, not stopping* – a timely message to someone who may at this moment be passing through a very difficult or distressing time, or to someone for whom it may be preparing them because they might have to face such a situation sometime in the future. The Lord may be speaking through this devotional meditation, and He may be saying for us to hold on, it will not always be, because His Word declares, *"When you PASS THROUGH the rivers..."* But there is even more, as we will see in our next meditation!

149

Isaiah 43:2c – When you walk through the fire, you will not be burned.

The messages so far from this verse have been most encouraging, for they have reminded us that, although all Christians are subject to the cares of this life, whenever such a distressing situation arises, we are only passing through, we are not stopping. Encouraging indeed! But there is one more powerful message from this verse, and it comes in the form of a precious promise from our Heavenly Father. We are assured that we are never left alone in any situation and we will always have His protection – a *double* promise, which makes it even more precious.

As we have already suggested in a previous devotional meditation, Jesus will be with us in the boat when the storms of life break in upon us. We may be tossed about, but if He is with us we will not sink! No doubt we can all recall occasions in our life when, had we to face things alone without the sure knowledge that the Lord was with us, we would have "gone under". There was once a lady who witnessed to a group of Christians many years ago who confirmed this truth. In a simple and humble way this dear soul told us how she had to undergo a major operation for a very serious disease. The doctors had said that without the operation she would be dead inside six months; even with it, she might live two years, maybe even three, for there was only a slight possibility of success.

"I had to make a quick decision," she told us. "I could not face it alone. So I gave myself completely into God's hands, knowing He would be with me. I decided – or rather, God decided for me – to have the operation, although the chances of success were very slight, and the life expectancy was not very long if it was a success. Even as I went into the operating theatre, I felt God's presence with me. I honestly couldn't have faced it alone. As you see, the operation was a success. I thank God daily for not only being with me when I needed Him most in the hospital; not only for healing me so wonderfully; but I thank Him for being with me every day as I gradually got better. I can testify to the fact that He is still with me now, and has never left me ever since the operation *nine years ago.*" She looked a picture of health, a living testimony to the facts revealed by this verse.

So the third message we receive from this verse is that *God will be with us all the way.* We are all liable to be faced with a difficult or tragic situation sometime during our life. Although it may be hard to accept at the time, the situation will not remain static, for we are passing through. But the greatest message of all here is that at all times and in all circumstances God is with us and will protect us; we are never left alone, because the Bible says, *"When you pass through the waters, I WILL BE WITH YOU. When you pass through the rivers, THEY WILL NOT SWEEP OVER YOU. When you walk through the fire, YOU WILL NOT BE BURNED."* This verse certainly has three powerful messages for us; no wonder it leaps out at us!

150

Isaiah 55:6 – Seek the Lord while he may be found; call on him while he is near.

There are two very important lessons to be learned from this verse, and the first is that we should never take a verse of Scripture in isolation and try to establish a truth from it. Although the devotional meditations in *Daily Strength for Daily Living* generally centre around just one verse at a time, they are never taken in isolation. Other verses surrounding it and elsewhere in the Scriptures are always considered when preparing each meditation If we take this verse in isolation we would get the impression that it is incomplete, and it might even cause us to wonder if what it says in possible. Here, for example, we are told to *"Seek the Lord while he may be found..."*, but in isolation it doesn't say if we will be able to find Him after all our seeking. It also tells us to *"call on him while he is near"*, but in isolation it doesn't say if He is near enough or if He will hear us how ever loudly we might call. So where does that leave us?

The lesson is obvious – and encouraging! The Bible is one complete Book made up of sixty-six smaller books all in harmony with each other. Because of this completeness, we cannot take verses in isolation, nor can we take them out of their context. That is, we cannot take one verse and ignore others around it, or even in other parts of the Bible, otherwise we may end up with, at best, incomplete teaching, or at worst, false teaching. This is what some people have done through the years, with the result that false cults have arisen, which pass themselves off as Christian when they are definitely not! To safeguard against any false teaching or misunderstanding of the Bible arising in these meditations, for instance, *no verse is taken in isolation.*

"Seek the Lord while he may be found; call on him while he is near", and we take it out of isolation and look elsewhere in Scripture at the words the Lord spoke to Jeremiah – and still says to us today. "You will call upon me and come and pray to me, and I will listen to you. You will seek me and find me when you seek me with all your heart. I will be found by you, declares the Lord" *(Jeremiah 29:12-14).* It is very comforting and encouraging to know that those who seek the Lord will find Him, and those who call on Him can be assured that He will hear them – and will answer! So we who have sought the Lord and found Him can have this comforting and encouraging message to share with others who have never sought for or called on the Lord; such a message would have lacked confidence and assurance if we had kept the verse in isolation.

We said there were two very important lessons to learn from this verse, and we will look at the second in our next devotional meditation.

151

Isaiah 55:6 – Seek ye the Lord while he may be found; call ye upon him while he is near. [KJV]

We said in the previous devotional meditation that there are two very important lessons to be learned from this verse, and the first was that we should never take a verse of Scripture in isolation and try to establish a truth from it. It is a very dangerous practice. The second very important lesson, which we will look at in this meditation, may at first seem rather strange. Whilst it is wrong to take a verse in isolation, it is not wrong to take a verse occasionally and approach it *negatively*. To explain what we mean, there is a valuable lesson here for us as Christians if we approach this verse from a negative point of view.

On the positive side the Bible is here reminding us to seek the Lord while He can be found, and that we should call upon Him while He is near. By not taking the verse in isolation we have established this to be a truth which Christians are not only charged to preach and teach, but can also do so with complete confidence and assurance. Indeed, it is a command from Jesus Himself *(Mark 16:15,16)*, and a command is something to be obeyed! Now, if we look at this verse negatively it will teach us our second important lesson, because in so doing it suggests that a time is coming when we will not be able to "find" the Lord, when He will no longer be "near" as He is now; and, of course, this is true.

The time is coming when the present order of things is going to change (and the signs of the times now in the twenty-first century would suggest that this time is rapidly drawing very near); when the Holy Spirit will be taken out of this world; and as Jesus is only able to be "found" and only able to be "near" by His Spirit, this will be the occasion when this privilege and blessing will no longer be available. The important message for Christians, then, is the urgency with which we must make these truths known. "Seek ye the Lord while he may be found; call ye upon him while he is near" [KJV], because there is a time rapidly approaching when we will not be able to find Him and He will no longer be near.

The truth, which Christians are charged to preach and teach, the command of Christ that we are required to obey, takes on a greater sense of urgency when we reflect upon the *negative* aspect of this very positive statement. *Today* is the time for us to seek the Lord; *today* is the day when we should call upon Him; it is urgent, because tomorrow may be too late.

152

Isaiah 61:10 – I delight greatly in the Lord; my soul rejoices in my God. For he has clothed me with garments of salvation and arrayed me in a robe of righteousness.

Real Christians are joyful people, we are full of the joy of the Lord, and we are always praising God. Why should this be? Because day by day He blesses us so much that we cannot help but praise Him. Here is a verse that is so full of praise that one cannot help but be caught up in its enthusiasm. Not only is the writer delighting himself greatly in the Lord (the KJV translates it as "greatly rejoicing in the Lord"), but his soul is also rejoicing in his God (the KJV translates it as being joyful in his God).

One might say that Isaiah is doubly joyful because he is doubly blessed; and here is a perfect example for real Christians today. We, too, are doubly blessed, for not only can we know our sins forgiven and be clothed with the garments of salvation, but we can know also the power of the Holy Spirit in our lives as He arrays (or "covers" as the KJV translates it) us with the robe of righteousness. The wonderful truth is, our salvation experience was not the end (except in the sense that it was the end of our sinful hell-bent life) but the beginning – the moment we were clothed with the garments of salvation, and became Christians, that was the beginning of a glorious life on earth with Christ which, if we are faithful to the end, will continue on in eternity in heaven.

We have used before in these devotional meditations the analogy of likening our spiritual life to the experience of the Children of Israel as they entered the Promised Land, and for the Christian as we enter into the Land of Spiritual Experience. But it is not at that point where we are left to struggle alone. The Holy Spirit who convicted us in the beginning of our sin and drew us to Christ as we realised our need of a Saviour and repented of our sins, and baptised us with Himself as He enable Christ to enter into our heart and life, and gave us the assurance of our salvation as that same Spirit testified to our spirit that we had become a child of God

(Romans 8:16), so daily He now fills us to enable us to have the spiritual power necessary to continue possessing the Land of Spiritual Experience in the way He requires us to do.

So now we are clothed with the garments of salvation, knowing Christ as our Saviour and Lord, and as we are arrayed in robes of righteousness, knowing the daily filling of the Holy Spirit giving us *daily strength for daily living*, no wonder as real Christians we can be doubly joyful when we are doubly blessed like this, and of course, the greater the blessing the greater the joy – so why should we settle for something less!

153

Isaiah 62:6 – You who call on the Lord, give yourselves no rest.

Although this statement comes as part of Isaiah's prophecy on Zion's new name and the posting of watchmen on the walls of Jerusalem, as recorded here – *"You who call on the Lord, give yourselves no rest"*, it does not have the same impact as the same statement translated in the KJV – "Ye that make mention of the Lord, keep not silence." This version provides us with a valuable lesson! How difficult it is to keep silent about something that thrills us and gives us pleasure. Indeed, the more joy and blessing we receive the louder we want to proclaim it! Or do we?

Whilst this may well be a natural reaction, we have to confess that sometimes it does not come quite so naturally as it should for us as Christians. The joys and the blessings come, yet somehow we tend to keep silent about them. For example, what greater joy can there be in knowing Jesus as our Saviour, with a sure knowledge of our sins forgiven? What greater blessing can we have than the assurance that Jesus has given us this precious gift of eternal life? What greater thrill can there be than in receiving from Jesus the power of His Holy Spirit, enabling us to rise above those many things in life that would tend to pull us down?

If as Christians we have experienced so much joy and blessing from Jesus, then let us, as this verse reminds us, not keep silent about it. We have so much to shout about, so much to tell, that to keep silent about it is both disobedient to the Scriptures and dishonouring to the Lord. By our obedience to the words of this verse we will bring honour to the Lord, and in time we will find that to speak of God's goodness will come quite naturally. Let it come naturally to us as the Lord gives us joy and blessing day by day. Indeed, the more joy and blessing we receive the louder we will probably want to proclaim it! After all, what is more natural than to *simply mention the Lord* in our conversations… naturally!

154

Isaiah 63:7 – I will tell of the kindnesses of the Lord, the deeds for which he is to be praised, according to all the Lord has done for us.

Although this verse is taken from another chapter in *Isaiah* than the one taken for the previous devotional meditation, it nevertheless has a similar theme. We ended the previous meditation with the words, "what is more natural than to *simply mention the Lord* in our conversations… naturally!" The KJV translation of this verse begins, "I will mention the loving kindness of the Lord." When someone does us a favour, and is particularly kind to us, there is a tendency for us to quite naturally tell others. It is hard to keep such actions to ourselves – and, of course, this is the right thing to do!

Not only do we disclose what has been done, but we also want to extol their virtues, tell of their kindness, to praise them for what they are. Indeed, we want to praise them to their face, too! But supposing we deliberately reject their kindness, refuse to accept any favours from them, what then? There is nothing then for us to tell, nothing to praise, nothing for which to be grateful, for which to say thank you. What a sorry situation; what awful ingratitude, we might say. Yet this is often how we treat God. He has so many gifts and blessings He wants to bestow upon us, but we refuse them, reject them, often without really thinking about it.

How can we "mention the loving kindness of the Lord" unless we have experienced that loving kindness for ourselves first hand?

How can we praise the Lord for *"the deeds for which he is to be praised"*, when there is nothing for which to praise Him? In other words, how can we praise the Lord for nothing because we have refused to allow Him to bless us with *something* in the first place? It is not enough, incidentally, to just *say*, "Praise the Lord!" – anyone can do that out of a sense of habit! It could mean nothing! It is quite another thing, however, to praise the Lord from a full and grateful heart, and *then* say it. That *does* mean something!

The extent to which we mention, or *"tell of the kindnesses of the Lord, the deeds for which he is to be praised,* is very much governed by the extent to which we have allowed God to bestow His blessings on us – and there is no limit to that as far as God is concerned. So when He blesses us, giving us spiritual gifts, uplifting and strengthening us with the gift of salvation, the gift of peace, the gift of eternal life, and so much more besides, then let us tell others as we praise the Lord. Soon others will begin to thank and praise Him, too; but it all begins with us, *"according to all the Lord has done for us."* Let us think about it! How much has He given us lately? More to the point, how much have we let Him?

155

Jeremiah 7:2 – Hear the word of the Lord, all you people…who come through these gates to worship the Lord.

It is a well-known fact, in spite of all the doom and gloom spread about today concerning declining church attendances – in the United Kingdom, at least – that more people attend church on a Sunday than attend football matches on a Saturday! So here is a word to all those of us who are Sunday attendees! (It applies equally, of course, to those of us unable to attend church, either on a Sunday or any other day through the week, because of age or infirmity or any other legitimate reason! "Church" is people, not buildings, so our *"gates to worship"* are the front door of our home, and we have already *"come through…to worship the Lord."* This is a verse for *all* true Christians, no matter their personal circumstances.)

In every true Christian church throughout our land (whichever land it happens to be), whatever the denomination, the Bible will be read in every service on a Sunday. Many thousands of people will enter those churches where a reading will be taken from either the Old or New Testament – and in some church services there will be a reading from both Testaments. In church services during the week the Bible is usually read, so the truths in this devotional meditation are not restricted specifically to just one day! So what does this verse have to say to us? Two things, two very important things. The first, when we enter our church we do so with one purpose in mind, a singleness of purpose – to worship the Lord.

We do not go to criticise others or because our attendance will create a good impression with our neighbours. We go that we might praise and worship the God who has saved our soul and given us eternal life, who has adopted us into His Holy Family and given us the power of His Holy Spirit to enable us to live our lives according to His will and purpose for each one of us individually. Whether in a majestic cathedral with its ornate architecture or a humble home with simple furnishings, whether it is a Sunday or any other day through the week, these truths apply equally. We come to worship the Lord.

But there is a second thing this verse is saying to us – that we might *hear* the Word of the Lord. It is possible to listen without hearing! God still speaks today, and often does through His Word. Let us always be ready to hear His voice. Later in the same chapter from which this verse is taken, the Bible says, "Obey me, and I will be your God and you will be my people" *(verse 23).* Before we can obey we must hear, take note of, listen for that voice. This verse is God's word to us, good advice and well worth taking by all Sunday attendees – come to think of it, it wouldn't do the Saturday attendees any harm, would it?

156

Jeremiah 10:10 – The Lord is the true God; he is the living God, the eternal King.

Through the history of mankind, man has always worshipped many gods, but there has been only, and still is only, one true God – our

Sovereign God, Creator of the Universe. He alone has a right to our worship. It should be noted, however, (and we have said it many times through the pages of *Daily Strength for Daily* Needs) that everything which takes first place in our lives, commands the most affection and attention, involves us in the most amount of time, becomes a god. It is not always in the shape of a weird-looking idol sat on the mantelpiece (if we still have a mantelpiece in our house, that is!); it can come in the shape of a television set, a bank balance, a car, a house, or a host of other "gods" which might take first place in our lives.

Because God is our Sovereign God, the only true God, He has a right to remind us, as He does in *Exodus 20:2,3* that "I am the Lord your God … You shall have no other gods before me." Furthermore, not only has He a right to remind us thus (no, that should be *command* us) but He has a right to expect and receive our complete obedience as well. If we have ever wondered why the God of the Bible is the only true God (as this verse reminds us), and therefore the only One whom we should worship (though there have been many other "gods" available through history), and why He alone has the right to command us to have no other gods before Him (to have no other gods of any kind, in fact) then the reason is this. Our God is the only One who is a *living* God.

We do not direct worship to a dead deity. We do not pray for guidance and strength from a dead prophet (although there are many who do, we have to admit!). The sense of a Divine Presence every moment of every day is not a myth (which it would be if God were dead!), but a fact, a reality, a *living* reality. There is another very important truth contained in this word from *Jeremiah.* The God whom we worship is with us all the time; and not just for a brief period; not even just whilst we are here on earth; but for ever – because our God is also an "*eternal* King" (or as the KJV translates it, an "*everlasting* King".)

This one, true and living Sovereign God will reign for ever, and if we acknowledge Him as King of our lives, then one day we will meet Him face to face, and live with Him for ever, too. So we can have complete confidence in the truth expressed by this verse, that *"the Lord is the true God; he is the living God, the eternal King"* … and He's ours!

157

Jeremiah 21:8 – This is what the Lord says: See, I am setting before you the way of life and the way of death.

Here is a good verse for a Church Anniversary. No doubt, if we were to take it for such, we would still be tempted to dwell briefly on the past, looking back with gratitude at the number of years our Fellowship had witnessed in its particular location. But by careful application of this verse, we would be made to understand that *we cannot keep looking back!* We are reminded here, in fact, of the importance of looking FORWARD. And this applies to us as individuals as well as collectively as a Fellowship.

There are many religions in the world today – Christianity is *not* one of them. Each religion has a dead prophet as its founder – but *not* Christianity. The Faith we proclaim in our Church Fellowships (hopefully!) is not a religion, it is a Way of Life, because *our Founder is alive!* Yes, Jesus is alive today, and He is setting before us the Way of Life. *"This is what the Lord says: See, I am setting before you the way of life..."* We have already discussed this in great detail during our devotional meditations in the book of *Deuteronomy.*

What does this mean for our Fellowship, not just on our Anniversary day, but every day of the year? What does it mean for us as Christians, not just one day, but every day of the year? Simply this! Every day from now on we must be sure that we live our lives according to His will and purpose for us. As someone has said, "Only one life, it will soon be past; only what's done for Christ will last." The moment we accepted Jesus Christ as Saviour, repented of our sins, knew those sins had been forgiven, and had the assurance of the Holy Spirit that we had been adopted as a child of God, we received eternal life. Our Faith, then, is not just *a* way of life that will end with the grave, but *the* way of life that goes on into eternity.

As we look forward to the future (if the Lord tarries), not only ourselves in the immediate years ahead, but those following on after us, will realise what a difference it will make if we and them, both individually and collectively as a Fellowship, live every moment of every day in constant touch with our Living Saviour, who has not only set the way of life before us, but has promised to travel with us along this way that is never going to end – eternal life! But, we must not forget that this verse ends with the phrase, *"...and the way of death."* The choice is ours; it is implied in this verse; and we all know what the opposite to eternal *life* is, don't we?

158

Jeremiah 23:23,24 – Am I only a God nearby, declares the Lord, and not a God far away? Can anyone hide in secret places so that I cannot see him? declares the Lord.

When God was pronouncing judgement against the false prophets in Israel and Judah, and especially those in Jerusalem, He reminded them in the form of a question, as in the words of these verses, that He was a God who was always at hand, always nearby, that no one can hide his or her self in a secret place from His sight. This was certainly a challenge to those false prophets as well as a rebuke. But here is a word from God through His Holy Word to us now, for these words are as relevant for us today as they were to the people back in the days of the Old Testament.

Whilst we may accept it as a word of challenge to us, in that whatever we say or do, God knows, God hears, God sees, for nothing escapes Him, so can it also be a word of comfort and great encouragement. How? Because it reminds us that we are never out of God's sight; we are never alone. After all, we live in a world where we can do with all the comfort and encouragement we can get. So here it is! What God is saying, in effect, is something like this! *"Am I only a God nearby...and not a God far away?"* Of course I'm not far away; I am always near by. I shouldn't have any need to ask the question!

Many are our experiences through life, both as individual Christians and corporately as a Fellowship, where we have our up's and down's, our good days and our bad, but we can face them together in company with Almighty God who is always nearby and never far away. Jesus taught us that His Father is also *our* Loving Heavenly Father, and He cares about us, He is concerned about us, He looks upon us as His children, He loves us with an even greater love than our earthly father ever could, and He wants only the best for us.

So it is easy to believe, accept and understand when the Bible says He is also a God who is not far away but a caring God who is always nearby watching over us day and night. That may present some of us with a challenge, because we are also reminded in the form of another question, *"Can anyone hide in secret places so that I cannot see him? declares the Lord."* It may even serve as a rebuke. We are never out of His sight. But for many of us these verses will be a tremendous word of comfort and great encouragement. We might even say that they provide us with *daily strength for daily living.*

159

Jeremiah 23:28 – Let the one who has my word speak it faithfully.

There are two *very powerful* and important truths the Lord is waiting to share with us through this verse, and more especially because it has a direct bearing on the creation of *Daily Strength for Daily Living* as two books of devotional meditations. It was only after reading through this verse several times that realisation began to dawn! There are two imported but related truths, and that makes it all the more powerful, so we will need two devotional meditations to look at them – this one and the next! We said in a previous meditation that it can be a dangerous practice to take Bible verses in isolation, yet this appears to be what we are doing in *Daily Strength for Daily Living.* Here, then, is the first important truth, which will justify the practice as well as teach us a valuable lesson.

When reading and meditating on the Word of God we must *always, always* allow the Holy Spirit to direct that reading and meditating. Please permit a personal reference! I sincerely believe that the meditations in *Daily Strength for Daily Living* are not planned by me, but by the Holy Spirit. (I do hope I am not sounding pious!) I have found through over half a century of writing – from which these meditations have been collected and brought together into two volumes – that it is possible to take isolated verses and phrases from different parts of the Bible *under the direction of the Holy Spirit* and receive untold blessings from God.

Perhaps it sounds a little less pious to say that these devotional meditations are planned by the Holy Spirit because I have asked Him every time to direct my reading, my meditation, my thinking and my speaking. Just to string verses together under our own power spells disaster! For those who have read thus far through these meditations, a complete consistency of thought and continuity of truth will have become apparent. This has only been possible because of the direction of the Holy Spirit. *"Let the one who has my word..."* It is a humbling experience and an awesome privilege to realise that God actually entrusts us with His Word. How careful we must be when handling it!

Reading and meditating on the Word of God without the direction and guidance of the Holy Spirit could, for example, lead us to fabricate a doctrine advocating that everyone should commit suicide! This may seem very extreme, but it is reputed that this once happened to a lady who used a pin to pick out from the Bible a "thought for the day". The pin alighted on the second half of *Matthew 27:5*, but she was not happy with that verse, so tried again, this time landing the pin on the second half of *Luke 10:37*.

The pin was never used again! The Holy Spirit alone cements the verses into a truth God would have us to learn – and this is the first important truth He would teach us – always, always read the Bible *under the direction of the Holy Spirit.*

160

Jeremiah 23:28 – He that hath my word, let him speak my word faithfully. [KJV]

We said in the previous devotional meditation that it is a humbling experience and an awesome privilege to realise that God actually entrusts us with His Word. How careful we must be when handling it! This naturally leads us to the second powerful and important truth God wants to share with us from this verse. It is closely related to the first, and illustrates the continuity of thought when we are open to the leadings of the Holy Spirit. In being entrusted with the Word of God we are also given a tremendous responsibility, because, as Jesus said, "He who listens to you listens to me" *(Luke 10:16)*, which is what the second half of this verse says.

Having acquired *daily strength for daily living* from our reading and meditation of the Word of God under the guidance of the Holy Spirit – so now we "have" His Word – it is our responsibility as Christians to share that acquired daily strength with others for their daily living, so God says to us, *"let him speak my word faithfully"* – so now we "speak" His Word. But here a note of caution is necessary! In a situation like this, we hear the phrase frequently used, "I believe God wants me to share this verse with you." We have to search our soul before speaking to make sure the whole is under the guidance of the Holy Spirit (our reading and meditation in the first place, and our speaking faithfully in the second), because this phrase must never become a simple and glib catchphrase, expounding some "truth" based upon our own agenda! God often gets blamed for things that are not His fault in situations like this!

It may help us to bear in mind the words of the Lord to Jeremiah – "I am against the prophets who steal from one another words supposedly from me…I am against the prophets who wag their own tongues and yet declare, 'The Lord declares' …They tell them and lead my people astray with their reckless lies, yet I did not send or appoint them" *(Jeremiah 23:30-32).* Here, of course, is where we have the consistency of thought and continuity of truth. People will listen to us, not because of our education or so-called social position, but because they have knowledge of us that we are speaking under the guidance of the Holy Spirit in all things.

As we have said, it is a humbling experience and an awesome privilege to realise that God actually entrusts us with His Word, both to read and meditate on it and to share it with others. *"Let the one who has my word speak it faithfully."* The Holy Spirit is the Key! Just as He directs our *reading* of the Word of God, so we must ensure that at all times He is directing our *speaking* of the Word, too. And that, of course, includes "speaking" the Word through the *written* word, such as with *Daily Strength for Daily Living.*

161

Jeremiah 24:6 – My eyes will watch over them for their good.

Many times through these devotional meditations we have commented on how thrilling it is to know that never at any time are we out of God's sight; that every moment of every day His eyes are upon us. Because He is a God of love, and cares about us personally and individually, He keeps His eyes upon us personally and individually for our good. But, we may say, there are times when we cannot feel His presence. There are occasions when we feel He has turned His back on us. The truth is, of course, although there may be times when we lose sight of God, God never loses sight of us.

Because of the circumstances through which we may be passing at this present moment – or it may be an experience in the future through which we may have to pass through, so this devotional meditation may help to prepare us for such an eventuality – we may even have reached a point where we feel God no longer cares or understands. But let us be assured from His Word that this will never be the case. This verse is one of many found throughout the Scriptures that give us this assurance. *"My eyes will watch over them for their good."*

The familiar prose poem, *Footsteps*, is a good illustration. Walking along the beach of life, the individual soul looked back from time to time to see two sets of footprints in the sand, his own and the Lord's who walked beside him. Then a particular circumstance arose in his life, and the soul was troubled, more so when he looked back to see only one set of footprints in the sand. Why, when he needed the Lord most, did He leave him alone? He had reached a point where he could not feel the Lord's presence, that the Lord had turned His back on him, and that God no longer cared or understood. It was then when the Lord assured that soul of His presence; when he needed Him most, and felt all alone, seeing only one set of footprints, that was when the Lord was carrying him.

So here is a word of encouragement and blessing to help us gain *daily strength for daily living*. When we feel spiritually lost, walking along the beach of life feeling all alone, let us remember

God says to us, *"My eyes will watch over them for their good."* How ever distressing our situation might be, how ever alone or deserted we may feel, this verse will give us the assurance we need. God cares, He understands, and He loves us all the time. The moment *will* come when we will feel He is carrying us! Then we will fully realise that we have never been alone, He has never turned His back on us; indeed, we have never been lost from His sight at all – not even once!

162

Lamentations 3:22,23 – His compassions never fail. They are new every morning; great is your faithfulness.

As we open our eyes at the beginning of each new day, we are greatly encouraged that *they* are new every morning. What are? *God's compassions!* How can this help us as we look to the future? How can this help us as we seek to acquire *daily strength for daily living*? Perhaps the word "daily" should give us a clue! This verse simply reminds us that God's *"compassions never fail. They are new every morning"* – and something which occurs "every morning" occurs on a "daily" basis. So we can find the help we need from this verse.

But the word "compassion" has several meanings. One of the most beautiful is that of showing care and concern for others, of identifying oneself with another's situation, whatever that situation might be. This is what makes this verse so precious, not only at the beginning of a new year, a new month, a new week, but for every moment of our lives, at the beginning of every new day – the Lord never ceases to identify Himself with our situation, our problems, even the seemingly very insignificant things in our lives, because He cares and is concerned. As we said in our previous devotional meditation, He is a God of love, and cares about us personally and individually, and He keeps His eyes upon us personally and individually for our good.

He never fails, how ever much we may fail Him by rejecting His compassion, even sometimes resenting it! And we do, if we are honest! Even though day by day our situation may change, our problems might be different, our outlook may vary, His care and concern for us is able to meet that changing situation, because His compassions are new every morning. Because His faithfulness to us is so great, His compassions towards us never fail. So we can take encouragement and solace from this truth.

We may say, if we are faithful to God, He will be faithful to us, but that places a responsibility on us to do our part. If God is prepared to be faithful to us, then we must be prepared to be faithful to God. So as we launch out into another new day we can be absolutely sure that God loves us so much that He cares, is concerned, identifies Himself with our every situation – and it is new every day! This really is *daily strength for daily living.* But to really benefit from this tremendous truth, to fully experience His compassions personally, to really experience the greatness of His faithfulness towards us, our response and our faithfulness to Him must be renewed every day, too!

163

Lamentations 4:20 – Under his shadow we would live among the nations.

Jesus Himself realised how difficult it would be for His disciples to live in this world yet not be a part of the world, so He prayed that God our Heavenly Father would keep them faithful *(John 17:15,16)*. Jesus realises, too, how impossible it is for us as Christians in the twenty-first century to live in our own strength in an evil world without becoming part of it. But God does not leave us to struggle alone; He never leaves us alone because His eyes are upon us all the time for our good; as this verse reveals to us, we are not expected to go it alone in this evil world, for *"Under his shadow we would live among the nations."* Live *in* the world but not be a part *of* the world.

The traveller through the desert, with the sun beating so mercilessly down upon him, knows the value of, and the need for, protective shadow. Without it he would not survive. Similarly, the Christian traveller through the desert-like world of life, with the pressures and temptations of that world beating mercilessly down upon him, could never hope to survive without the protection given under the shadow of the Almighty. This was the experience of the Psalmist. "He who dwells in the shelter of the Most High will rest in the shadow of the Almighty" *(Psalm 91:1).*

We cannot live in seclusion, isolated from our fellow-man – God recognises that – so it is inevitable that we must to some degree *"live among the nations."* The KJV translates this phrase as, "live among the heathen." But we do it under His shadow, with His help and blessing and strength. Remember the experience of the Psalmist. It is a life of prayer, keeping in constant touch, dwelling in the shelter of the Most High, which makes it possible for us to be *in* the world yet not be a part *of* that world. Here, too, is the advantage and necessity of keeping close to God through reading and meditating on His Word as we glean from it *daily strength for daily living* as we "live among the nations…among the heathen."

Here, then, is tremendous encouragement and blessing. We are not alone, we are not left alone, the Lord has His eyes upon us constantly, and we do not live among the nations, the heathen, on our own, for we have protection from God through prayer and from His Word. So let us remember we live *in*, but do not become part *of* this world, *"under his shadow we would live among the nations"*, but only if we constantly "dwell in the shelter of the Most High" enjoying His protection through ceaseless prayer and Spirit inspired reading of, and meditating on, His Word.

164

Ezekiel 2:2 – As he spoke, the Spirit came into me and raised me to my feet.

Whilst it is important for us not to venerate the Holy Spirit above the Father and the Son in the Godhead (as some have a tendency to do these days), it is equally important not to underestimate the power of the Holy Spirit in our lives, either. What a difference it makes to our daily living when He enters in, in all His fullness, as Ezekiel testified in this verse. Daniel had a similar experience, recorded in *Daniel 8:18* – "While he was speaking to me, I was in a deep sleep, with my face to the ground. Then he touched me and raised me to my feet."

It is possible to let life get us down, for our spiritual life to suffer with the pressures of every-day living, to the extent that we feel we will never be able to rise above these things, to get on our feet. Instead of acquiring *daily strength for daily living*, we seem to be surrounded with daily weaknesses which tend to drag us down – something that is no help to our daily living! Try as we might, we cannot seem to be raised to our feet spiritually. Of course, in our own strength we never will! But the experience of Ezekiel and Daniel makes the impossible possible. And such an experience can be ours!

If we acknowledge the infilling power of the Spirit of God in our lives, He will set us upon our feet, He will set us upright, He will raise us to our feet in a way we never thought possible. One thing is certain, the Holy Spirit only knows one direction in the life of a seeking soul – UP! The Spirit will never push us down! Of that we can be absolutely certain. But we do need to remember that, when we are commanded to be filled with the Holy Spirit – and we find this command repeated many times in the Scriptures – it is not a one-off experience but a *daily* necessity. We are not seeking for occasional strength for daily living; we are seeking for *daily* strength.

Are there those of us who are feeling that the pressures of life are at this moment getting us down? Perhaps our prayer ought to be in the words of the chorus we sometimes sing – *"Spirit of the Living God, fall afresh on me. Break me, melt me, mould me, fill me. Spirit of the Living God, fall afresh on me."* A prayer like that, prayed sincerely, prayed daily, will certainly set us on our feet!

165

Ezekiel 3:10 – Son of man, listen carefully and take to heart all the words I speak to you.

Compared to all the sacred books of different religions throughout the world, the Bible is unique. To begin with, all the authors of those sacred books are dead! They died, some of them, many thousands of years ago! The Author of the Bible, on the other hand, is still very much *alive!* This is what makes it unique. Unlike the other books, its *living* Author makes the Bible a *living* book, and so its words are very much alive, too. So, when we read it, because it is God's Word, He speaks to us through that word. These living words have transformed the lives of countless men and women down through the ages.

If the Bible is different, therefore, from any other kind of book, then should we not read it differently, also? The answer is in our verse, which is much more powerful in the KJV – "All my words that I shall speak unto thee receive in thine heart, and hear with thine ears." It emphasises more effectively the need to receive the Word in our heart and listen to that Word with our ears. This is important, because it is possible to read without receiving and to listen without hearing. So, to make the Bible relevant to our situation and for it to fulfil its purpose in our lives, not only should we read it as we read an ordinary book, but we must receive it into our hearts, unlike an ordinary book, too.

This means putting into action what we have read. The Word of God is our Guide Book for daily living, it is our Highway Code through the journey of life, it is the place where we acquire *daily strength for daily living*, so let us live our lives daily according to that word. And the only effective way whereby we are able to follow and obey what we have read, of course, is to receive it into our heart, made possible, not just because we have listened with our ears, but because we have actually *heard* it with our ears. Head knowledge is one thing, and important, but heart knowledge is vital and more important, if we are to live our daily lives as God would have us live them.

166

Ezekiel 34:16 – I will search for the lost and bring back the strays. I will bind up the injured and strengthen the weak.

What a tender and precious promise from the Lord we have in this verse! The KJV translates this promise in such a way as to draw out more effectively the tenderness and preciousness from it. "I will seek that which was lost, and bring again that which was driven away, and bind up that which was broken, and will strengthen that which was sick." It is possible that, just at this moment, some of us may be feeling a little lonely, a little lost, a little distressed. Somehow things seem to have gone wrong – it could be a whole host of things!

Maybe we are not too happy with our church fellowship at the moment. Maybe we are feeling left out in the cold! Perhaps, worse still, we have stopped attending our church altogether, because something someone has said or done has driven us away. What a sad situation, and it is troubling us greatly. Our faith may have been shattered, our spirit has been broken, and we feel let down, depressed, maybe even a little sick at heart. It does happen, we realise. It *shouldn't* happen, but unfortunately it does! So here is a tender and precious promise from the Lord to help us in our time of need.

If we are feeling a little lonely, a little lost, just now, God has promised, *"I will seek that which was lost."* If someone has said or done something within our church fellowship, and it has driven us away, God has promised, *I will...bring again that which was driven away."* If we feel our faith has been shattered and our spirit has been broken, God has promised, *"I will...bind up that which was broken."* If we are feeling let down, depressed, sick at heart just now, God has promised, *"I will...strengthen that which was sick."* Tender and precious promises indeed! Of course, it is possible that we are not in such a situation at this moment. Then praise the Lord, and ask the Holy Spirit to recall this promise to our mind should we find ourselves in need of such comfort sometime in the future!

But we will only benefit from this promise, either now or in the future, if we take it for ourselves and do something about it. Instead of sitting at home and feeling miserable, the next opportunity we get, let us claim this promise and go to church – any church where the truth is faithfully preached – and take God at His word. This could be the best action we take!

167

Ezekiel 43:5 – Then the Spirit lifted me up and brought me into the inner court, and the glory of the Lord filled the temple.

It comes to us all! Because we are Christians we are not immune from it! We do get days when we feel a little depressed. We do get days when things seem to be getting us down. We do get days when, what is sometimes referred to as the Monday morning blues, becomes a feeling we have *every* day. Perhaps it is the world situation, or the situation in our neighbourhood, or in our church fellowship, or our family situation, or perhaps it is our own personal situation, which is causing us to feel as we do. It could be any number of things.

If we are not feeling at our best right now, and we really need some *daily strength for daily living*, then this verse is just for us. It is a verse we can take, not just for today, but for every day that we live, to lift us out of our depression and clear away the blues from our life whatever day of the week it happens to be! God has given us His Holy Spirit to help us through life. By acknowledging His power in our lives, by simply asking Him sincerely in prayer for His help, by seeking a daily infilling of His Spirit, then this verse will take on new meaning by becoming our own daily experience.

When this verse becomes more than words on a page, and becomes a personal experience in our heart and life, then we will be able to say with complete assurance, *"Then the Spirit lifted me up and brought me into the inner court, and the glory of the Lord filled the temple."* We have said in a previous devotional meditation, the Holy Spirit will never push us down. He only recognises one way – UP! Every one of us has within us the capacity to pray, an inner court where we can meet and talk with God personally. No one can come into contact with God and remain the same; when in His presence His glory will fill us in the temple of our soul.

So if we allow the Holy Spirit to lift us up and bring us into that closer relationship with the Lord, enabling His glory to fill our whole life, then there will be no room for depression or feeling blue, whatever the situation surrounding us, because we will have acquired the *daily strength for daily living* we need, and we can go on our way rejoicing. What started as one of our worst days could end up as one of the best days ever – but only if we let it!

168

Daniel 2:22 – He knows what lies in darkness, and light dwells with him.

God, in His infinite wisdom, has hidden from our view the unknown future. Just as on a dark night, with no street lights, no moon or stars, we cannot see the other side of the road, so we cannot see the future – it is as darkness to us. We know it is there, but we cannot see it. A line of a hymn so wisely puts it. *"God holds the key of all unknown, and I am glad."* How true! As Christians, we do not want to know what is going to happen to us, or our family, tomorrow, or next week, or even next year. We do not want to know what is going to happen to us today! We should be content with the knowledge that *"He knows what lies in the darkness..."* We can safely leave the future with Him.

If God wanted us to know our future He would not have hidden it from us. Can we imagine how overpowering, how absolutely unbearable, how terrifyingly frightening, it would be if we knew all that was going to happen to us each moment of each day? Even a second's contemplation of such a situation reveals the wisdom of God in hiding the future from us. But this verse says something else. *"He knows what lies in darkness, and light dwells with him."* With the unknown future before us as darkness, we need not fear, but have the assurance that as we take each step forward it will always be light where we are. How is this possible? Because the Bible says of Jesus Christ, "I am the light of the world. Whoever follows me will never walk in darkness, but will have the light of life" *(John 8:12)*.

We cannot see the whole way – we are not meant to – but God wants us to trust Him in the darkness of the future, and has given us His Son, Jesus Christ, to help us find the way. As true Christians we do not fear the future because we have the Light of the World with us. As true Christians we do not visit so-called clairvoyants seeking to know our future! This verse is a powerful message to us to give us real *daily strength for daily living.* Let us take each day as it comes, take each step in faith, realise that every moment of every day God alone knows what is in the darkness ahead of us, but that the light always dwells with Him.

If we have acknowledged Jesus Christ as our Saviour and Lord, and recognised Him as the Light of the World – *our* world – then the light will dwell with us, too. What a comforting thought! The future will never be dark!

169

Daniel 2:47 – Surely your God is the God of gods and the Lord of kings and a revealer of mysteries.

The words of this verse were actually uttered by a heathen king, not as one might suppose, by a religious leader. Now, because the actual word "trinity" does not appear in the Bible, there are those who would deny the existence of the Holy Trinity, the Triune God. Indeed, the false cults, which have arisen through the years, have based many of their erroneous doctrines on this premise. But all through the Bible there are constant references implying that God exists in three specific forms. The purpose of this devotional meditation is not to argue this point, but to see how this particular Bible verse can help us.

The amazing thing is that it took a heathen king to reveal the truth. God of gods, Lord of kings, revealer of mysteries – what an awesome truth! God our Heavenly Father is a God above every god, the Supreme Deity, our Sovereign God who knows the beginning from the end – nothing happens in the world that He is not aware of and allows – and as such has the right to command our exclusive allegiance. "You shall have no other gods before me" *(Exodus 20:3)*, the Bible also says. He really is a God, the *only* God, who has always been, and always will be above every god who has existed or ever will exist.

Then there is God the Son, the Lord Jesus Christ, who has equal right to that allegiance, because as the Saviour of the world only through Him can we have eternal life. This is one of the big issues raised by false cults who deny the existence of the Holy Trinity, but it does not alter the fact that the Bible reveals the truth, and ascribes to Jesus the Son the *exact same attributes* as are ascribed to God the Father.

And the same applies for God the Holy Spirit, the Revealer of mysteries, the true Source of spiritual power in our lives, the One who fills us daily – if we allow Him to – thus giving us *daily strength for daily living.* Our allegiance is demonstrated as we acknowledge and apply that power day by day. So what do we say? *Surely our God is Father, Son and Holy Spirit* – three in one – and each has a right to our exclusive allegiance. The question is, do they have that allegiance? Do we personally give them *our* allegiance? It really is a very important question!

170

Hosea 13:4 – I am the Lord your God…You shall acknowledge no God but me, no Saviour except me.

It is good to be reminded from time to time that the Lord is our God, not a distant Deity, but a personal and loving Heavenly Father – as He reminds us Himself in this verse, *"I am the Lord YOUR God."* Let us notice the personal emphasis in the word "your". Not just a God, either, but *the* God, the *only* God, *our* God, and as such that we should own or acknowledge no other god. The instruction is plain enough. *"You shall acknowledge no God but me, no Saviour except me."*

Impossible, we may say, for us to worship other gods in this enlightened age. Especially now we are in the twenty-first century, we would certainly not entertain the idea of little wooden idols in our homes to which we bow down in worship. Such an idea is impossible! But is it? (We have looked at this in previous devotional meditations.) Let us think about it again and learn afresh something from this verse. What is an idol? Anything that comes first in our life can become an idol; can become our god. If this is so, then what right has Almighty God to demand from us *exclusive* allegiance? Perhaps because He is *Almighty* God, that in reality there is no other god really worth considering, and because as His Word declares, there is no other Saviour except Him.

Jesus Himself said He is the Way, and that no one comes to the Father except by Him. There is no other Way. So this verse reminds us of three very important things. One, that the Lord is *our* God, personal to us, our Heavenly Father, One who cares, One who loves us collectively and individually. Two, that there must be no other god before Him. This is the first commandment, anyway! And let us remember that gods can come in all shapes and sizes! House size, television size, bank balance size, vehicle size – anything that has a greater "size" in our life than the Lord our God. Then, three, that He is the *only* Saviour of the world, that there is no other Way. He alone is the Way to the Father. "I am the way…No-one comes to the Father except through me" *(John 14:6)*.

Of course, we know all this, don't we? We have already looked at it in previous meditations. But it is good to be reminded of it just the same, from time to time, and now seems to be as good a time as any!

171

Micah 6:4 – I brought you up…redeemed you…I sent Moses to lead you.

Although in this verse it is the Lord speaking through the prophet Micah reminding the Children of Israel of their past, because we are seeking through this devotional meditation *daily strength for daily living*, here in this verse it is the Lord speaking to us right now in the twenty-first century, making His Word relevant to us today, demonstrating yet again that the Bible is a *Living* Word, and that its Author is our *Living* Lord, not a dead prophet. Here He is reminding *us* of three vital truths.

What are these truths? Firstly, He is reminding us that it was He, our Sovereign God, who has brought us up out of the degradation of sin (and let us notice that the Lord never pushes anyone down; a spiritual experience always serves to lift us UP!) As we have said in previous devotional meditations, the Holy Spirit of God only knows one direction, and that is UP! He will never ever push us down. As this verse says of the Lord, *"I brought you up..."* Then, secondly, having brought us up out of the degradation of sin, He redeemed us – *"I...redeemed you,"* the verse continues. These two actions lead us to the third vital truth God wants to reveal to us.

He who has redeemed us by the precious blood of Jesus; has lifted us up and set us on a firm foundation, as the hymn writer testifies, *"On Christ the solid Rock I stand..."*; has done so for a purpose, so that we can go and tell others of the "good news", that Jesus saves and keeps. Here, then is the third vital truth. When He who has brought us up and redeemed us calls us to go and speak to someone about their soul (and there will be no doubts in our mind concerning the prompting of the Holy Spirit in this respect) then we can be sure that He has gone before us to prepare the way, to prepare the heart of the one to whom we must speak.

Just as He sent Moses before the Children of Israel, to lead them, so today He sends His Spirit before us, to lead us. So let us not use so-called lack of power as an excuse not to go where the power of His Spirit is available preparing the way. After all, this is why He brought us up and redeemed us in the first place!

172

Micah 6:8 – What does the Lord require of you? To act justly and to love mercy and to walk humbly with your God.

The message God was trying to convey to the Children of Israel through the prophet Micah, recorded in this verse, was that He was not interested in their sacrifices and rituals as an excuse, or a means of appeasement, for their disobedience to His commands in the way they were living their lives as a nation. What God wanted was a change in their pattern of living – individually, He wanted changed lives. He wanted His people *"to act justly and to love mercy and to walk humbly with"* Him, to get their priorities right. Instead, they had forgotten their covenant with Him and the blessings that resulted from it, and turned away from Him as a nation. They became very self-centred and focused on non-essentials, eventually thinking they could appease God with burnt sacrifices and religious rituals.

But how can this incident in Israelite history help us in the twenty-first century to receive *daily strength for daily living*? It is right as Christians that we should always try to please God in everything we do, but we must be very careful to always see that we get our priorities right. If we are not very careful we can miss out on the essentials, trying to please Him in ways of secondary importance, as this verse here reminds us. It may surprise us to learn that it is possible for us to be too busy for Christ and find we have little or no time for the things that *really* please Him. We can fail to get our priorities right. So, let us turn to the question at the beginning of this verse and try to understand, what the Lord really does require of us.

What does he expect from us? For a start, He wants us to act justly in the things we do; He also wants us to love mercy in our dealings with each other; and He wants us to walk humbly with Him day by day. No amount of feverish activity "in the Lord's name" can take the place of justice and mercy in our hearts, a daily walk with the Lord in humbleness of spirit. This is not to suggest that activity in the Lord's name is not important, but if these things – justice and mercy and humbleness of spirit – are there in the first place, taking priority in our lives, then the activities of secondary importance will be pleasing to God, also. What we must always do is get our priorities right. What we must never do is to miss out on the essentials.

173

Micah 7:7 – I watch in hope for the Lord, I wait for God my Saviour, my God will hear me.

We have mentioned before in these devotional meditations that for a Christian his hymnbook is very often a companion to his Bible –

not a substitute, but a supplement. It can be very rewarding to meditate on Bible verses with the aid of the Bible itself and the hymn book side by side. We do so again here. When the person who wrote this verse penned these words he was passing through a very depressing situation, a black spot in the history of his nation. He felt he was alone, everything and everyone seemed to be against him. Yet, when everything appeared to be at its blackest, he was able to say, *"I watch in hope for the Lord."* Not only that, he was also able to say, *"I wait for God my Saviour."* And as if this was not enough, he added, *"My God will hear me."*

History has a tendency to repeat itself. Are we not living in troubled times today? Does not the world situation seem black? Is there not oppression, injustice, immorality, lying, slander, fear all around us? Very often, as Christians, we stand alone, at work, at school, at college or university, in social life. Yet we are not alone, for we can find a perfect Friend in Jesus. *"What a Friend we have in Jesus, all our sins and griefs to bear! What a privilege to carry everything to God in prayer! O what peace we often forfeit, O what needless pain we bear, all because we do not carry everything to God in prayer! Have we trials and temptations? Is there trouble anywhere? We should never be discouraged: take it to the Lord in prayer. Can we find a Friend so faithful, Who will all our sorrows share? Jesus knows our every weakness: take it to the Lord in prayer."*

No matter the situation around us, we have a true Friend in Jesus, God manifest in the flesh, and we can say the words with confidence that Micah penned, knowing that *"my God will hear me."* Here we have a Friend in the storms of life. Very often these storms test our faith. There is a story to illustrate this where Jesus is asleep in a boat in a storm. *"A little ship was on the sea, it was a pretty sight; it sailed along so pleasantly, and all was calm and bright. When, lo! a storm began to rise, the wind grew loud and strong, it blew the clouds across the skies, it blew the waves along. And all but One were sore afraid, of sinking in the deep; His head was on a pillow laid, and He was fast asleep. Master, we perish! Master, save! they cried. Their Master heard; He rose, rebuked the wind and wave, and stilled them with a word. He to the storm said: Peace be still! The raging billows ceased; the mighty winds obeyed His will, and all were hushed to peace. O well we know it was the Lord, our Saviour and our Friend, Whose care of those who trust His word will never, never end."*

Being a Christian does not exempt us from the storms of life (it would be a poor religion if it was only acceptable while the sea of life was calm). Storms come to Christians and non-Christians alike; we are *all* in the world; but it does make a very big difference if we have Jesus Christ in the boat with us when we meet the storms, and we can say with confidence, *"I watch in hope for the Lord, I wait for God my Saviour; my God will hear me"* – and we know He will!

174

Micah 7:7 – I will look unto the Lord; I will wait for the God of my salvation: My God will hear me. [KJV]

It is worth a second look at this verse, this time using the KJV translation, because there is one word which appears three times, and it is this repetition that provides us yet again with *daily strength for daily living* from God's Word. A reading of the short book of *Micah* itself will quickly reveal that the situation in which this prophet lived, and one that he describes in detail in his little book, is not unlike our own in the twenty-first century. As we said in the previous devotional meditation, history has a tendency to repeat itself.

Today we live in a world rampant with injustice, oppression, revenge, hatred, violence, wars and rumours of wars, blood-shed, and much more beside – all features of a people who have forgotten God. In the midst of all this, feeling very much alone, feeling depressed and possibly frustrated, even feeling isolated, Micah realised that he had a God who cared, who loved him, who understood him, and was always close at hand to listen to him. As Christians, it is inevitable that we will feel exactly the same from time to time in our present situation. But in the truth expressed here by Micah many thousands of years ago, we can find comfort and blessing for today.

No matter how misunderstood we may be, when even our friends may turn from us, when the situation at work or in our neighbourhood causes us to feel an outcast – and all because of our faith – let us remember that Micah's God is our God, too; a God who never changes. We can look to Him, wait for Him, knowing He will listen to our every word. We will not feel isolated because we are not alone.

This is a *positive* verse, because of the one word we mentioned earlier which appears three times. This verse has three "wills" in it, and each one helps us to feel totally secure in a very insecure world. So let us be positive in our attitude. *"I WILL look unto the Lord; I WILL wait for the God of my salvation: My God WILL hear me."* Now that can mean more than anything today, and makes our second look at this verse all the more worthwhile!

175

Nahum 1:7 – The Lord is good, a refuge in times of trouble.

We may be forgiven for asking if a verse, such as this one, written many thousands of years ago, is really relevant for us today in the twenty-first century, and our answer would naturally be a resounding yes! *All* Scripture is inspired by God and is relevant in every age *(2 Timothy 3:16).* Indeed, this verse is relevant because it speaks of the GOODNESS and the PROTECTION of God, and that really is relevant in any age.

But why did the writer of this verse say *good*? Why did he not say the Lord is *great* – we see God's greatness revealed all through the Bible in many different ways; or the Lord is *powerful* – we see His power displayed and demonstrated all through the Bible, too; or the Lord is *mighty* – we see His might recorded time and time again through the Bible? No, the only word to best describe God, to describe His essential unchanging nature, was GOOD. In everything God is good, and He is good *all the time*. When Nahum wrote, *"The Lord is good,"* he was passing through a very difficult time in his life. Now, this fact is very important.

It is easy to say God is good when things are going well; but when things are going badly for us it is not so easy. When our days seem full of sunshine, and everything around us seems to reflect beauty and colour, it is easy to say God is good. But when the day is overcast, and the colours of life seems to melt into dreary shades of grey, then it is not so easy to say God is good. Yet we must never doubt His goodness, for He knows what He is doing, He always knows best, He never makes a mistake, because God is good all the time. And there *will* come those bad times, those dreary grey days, as we have said before in these meditations. We are not promised immunity from trouble in this life, but as Christians we do have a refuge; we have Someone to whom we can go when in trouble or distress. We have Someone in whom we can hide and find PROTECTION.

"The Lord is good, a refuge in times of trouble," Nahum wrote, and he should know, because he was speaking from personal experience. The Bible has quite a lot to say about the protection of God. "The eternal God is your refuge, and underneath are the everlasting arms" *(Deuteronomy 33:27)*. "God is our refuge and strength, an ever present help in trouble" *(Psalm 46:1)*. "Call upon me in the day of trouble; I will deliver you" *(Psalm 50:15)*. "The name of the Lord is a strong tower; the righteous run into it and are safe" *(Proverbs 18:10)*. And so we could go on quoting verse after verse!

This verse relates the experience of one man – Nahum – who knew something about the *goodness* and *protection* of God, and his experience has been repeated right through the Bible and through history right down to the present day. So if we have not yet really experienced the goodness and protection of God in our life, the fault is not God's – is it?

176

Zephaniah 3:14,15 – Sing…shout aloud…Be glad and rejoice with all your heart. The Lord has taken away your punishment, he has turned back your enemy. The Lord…is with you.

This "verse" is really made up of two verses, and this is deliberate, because there are three things in the first verse – *verse 14* – that we as Christians want to do always, and in the second verse – *verse 15* – there are the three reasons why we want to do them! As Christians we seem always to be singing (or we should be!), if not from the lips then from the heart, because *"The Lord has taken away your punishment,"* or, as the KJV translates it, "The Lord hath taken away thy judgements." Our sin is taken away completely, we are justified, it is as if we have never sinned – no wonder we want to sing!

If someone has done something tremendous for us it is natural for us to shout about it, to tell others, or as we sometimes say, to shout it from the rooftops. What is more tremendous than to know that the Lord has cast our enemy out? *"He has turned back your enemies,"* or as the KJV translates it, "He hath cast out thine enemy." All those fears, all those cares, those awful frustrations that stem from the devil himself, have been cast out from us. How can we keep quite about that? And as we *"sing...shout aloud...Be glad and rejoice with all your heart,"* our praises become all the more fervent because *"The Lord...is with you,"* or as the KJV translates it, "The Lord is in the midst of thee."

This is why this "verse", to give us *daily strength for daily living*, is deliberately made up of these two verses; in a sense they form a circle. The Lord is only able to be with us, in the midst of us, because He has taken away our punishment, our judgements, and cast out our enemy, in the first place. We are only able to be glad and rejoice with all our heart because we have something to sing and shout about in the first place, too. If we think about it carefully, it is a wonderful circle, isn't it?

177

Zechariah 3:1,3,4 – He showed me Joshua the high priest standing before the angel of the Lord, and Satan standing at his right side to accuse him… Now Joshua was dressed in filthy clothes as he stood before the angel. The angel said to those who were standing before him, Take off his filthy clothes. Then he said to Joshua, See, I have taken away your sin, and I will put rich garments on you.

This may be a much longer "verse" than we have become accustomed to, but it is so full of valuable truths to provide us with *daily strength for daily living*, that it is worth breaking with custom for this devotional meditation! This "verse" – which is really three verses combined – is part of a vision Zechariah the prophet had many thousands of years ago of a former High Priest, Joshua. But ancient though it may be, it is very relevant for us today in the twenty-first century.

When each one of us professes conversion, states that we have repented of and confessed our sin, witnesses to the fact that our sins have indeed been forgiven, acknowledges Jesus as our Saviour and Lord, then testifies that we have committed our life to Christ and claims the right to call ourselves by the name of Christian, if there is no definite change evident in our lifestyle – our words and actions – as a result, then our true experience is suspect. And rightly so!

Coming to faith in Christ may be *personal*, but there is a sense in which it is also very *public*. It is one thing to *say* that we are a Christian, it is quite another to *be* a Christian! When Christ comes into our life, not only is that life dramatically changed, it must also be *seen* to be changed. This is most important, because we cannot hide such an experience if it is genuine. A perfect example of this can be found in these verses from *Zechariah*, and applies not only to Joshua, but to all true believers.

The relevant phrases are, Joshua at the beginning: *"dressed in filthy clothes"*; Joshua in the middle: *"I have taken away your sins"*; Joshua at the end: *"put rich garments on you"*. To put it another way, here we have Joshua's pre-spiritual experience, Joshua's spiritual experience, Joshua's post-spiritual experience. If we put on a new suit, everyone will naturally notice if we have always worn an old one. When we put on a new life in Christ, everyone should notice that, too. If not, then the question is, *are we still wearing the old one?*

178

Zechariah 5:1 – I turned, and lifted up mine eyes, and looked. [KJV]

When the prophet Zechariah turned, lifted up his eyes, and looked, what did he see? This twice recorded phrase in the KJV each begin the two chapters – *chapters 5* and *6* – which record part of a vision which came to the prophet. Taking but a single phrase such as this, however, does not really help us to understand the meaning of the complete vision. But, as far as we are concerned in this devotional meditation and the next two, neither the whole vision nor part of it is the message the Lord would have us share. He is directing our thoughts to the first verse of each chapter.

It is interesting to note that the words appear at the beginning of these two chapters. *"I turned, and lifted up mine eyes, and looked."* In the first instance he saw the vision of a flying scroll; in the second he saw four chariots. Once again, the objects he saw are not of vital importance to us here. The question, then, must surely be – what is the message the Lord would have us share from this repeated phrase to provide us with more *daily strength for daily living*? The answer is simple! He wants us to be like Zechariah, who saw what God wanted him to see.

If we are to see what God wants us to see concerning His will for us, then like Zechariah we must be prepared to do three things – to turn, to lift up our eyes, and to look. This may sound very simple, and, indeed, this message *is* a simple one, for God is waiting to bless those who are prepared to see what He wants them to see. The time may come in our life – indeed, it may have happened already on more than one occasion – when we must be prepared to turn from the course we are taking and possibly turn in a completely different direction. As Christians, such a turning has already taken place in our life, anyway, because there would have come a moment when we turned away from our old ways, from our sins – this is the meaning of spiritual conversion – and we were born again into a new life.

How does God call us to turn, as He did Zechariah? It may be through enlightenment that we must turn from some cherished belief to the real truth. It may be that we need to turn from a particular method of presenting the Gospel or a different approach may be required. It may even mean turning completely from our present way of life to something totally different, but nevertheless still very much within God's will for us. Please permit me once again to share a personal experience. In my case, having followed a particular avenue of Christian service for many years, I felt (together with my wife) that the Lord was leading us along a very different pathway. Like Zechariah, we needed to turn – but this will form the subject of the next meditation. In the meantime, perhaps we should ask ourselves, is God at this moment calling us to change?

179

Zechariah 6:1 – I turned, and lifted up mine eyes, and looked. [KJV]

In our previous devotional meditation we said that God wants us to be like Zechariah, who saw what God wanted him to see, and if we are to see what God wants us to see concerning His will for us, then like Zechariah we must be prepared to do three things – to turn, to lift up our eyes, and to look. We ended the meditation with me beginning to share a personal experience by way of illustration. In my case, having followed a particular avenue of Christian service for many years, I felt (together with my wife) that the Lord was leading us along a very different pathway. Like Zechariah, we needed to turn – and this will form the subject of this meditation.

In faith believing we turned in our ways, only to have the door firmly slammed in our faces! Holding on to our faith in God and His eternal purposes for our lives – it was about all we had to hold on to! – we settled down to a very comfortable existence. We \were fast becoming contented, although not completely in God's will as we should have liked, or felt we ought to be. But we remained faithful; we kept in touch with the Lord. Looking back after many years we realise just how God was preparing the way. Like a bolt out of the blue a new avenue of Christian service was opened up to us! But we were well settled in our own home and reasonably content with life as it was. If we accepted God's way we would have to up-root again – we would have to turn!

Did we want another upheaval? Not really! *But the only way to blessing is God's way.* If we were to follow that way, like Zechariah, we would have to be prepared to turn, to completely change our \way of life, to venture out into some new thing, something very different from anything we had known or experienced before. God's way must be our way, we acknowledged this fact, and so we turned and ended up launching into a totally different form of ministry, a new form of ministry, sailing in uncharted waters as far as we were concerned! But the blessings that resulted from our willingness to turn were so great, so manifold, that we are still reaping the benefit from them to this very day!

So from my own experience I share with you this thought – if we are prepared to turn, as Zechariah did, even to the extent of changing our way of life, and see what God wants us to see, He will shower us with blessings moment by moment, and go on showering us through future years. But, we may say, it is not easy in this day and age, this twenty-first century, in which we live, with its changing standards and constantly moving pattern of life. There are so many things to frustrate and discourage us. Of course it is not easy – it is not easy in any age – but there is still more to glean from this verse for *daily strength for daily living*, which we will do in the next meditation.

180

Zechariah 5:1;6:1 – I looked again…I looked up again…

We said in the previous devotional meditation that if we are prepared to turn, as Zechariah did, even to the extent of changing our way of life, and see what God wants us to see, He will shower us with blessings moment by moment, and go on showering us through future years. But, we may say, it is not easy in this day and age, this twenty-first century, in which we live, with its changing standards and constantly moving pattern of life. There are so many things to frustrate and discourage us. Of course it is not easy – it is not easy in any age – but let us remember that Zechariah did more than just turn, he also lifted up his eyes and he looked, as the KJV translates it.

There is a little chorus we sometimes sing. *"Turn your eyes upon Jesus, Look full in His wonderful face, And the things of earth will grow strangely dim In the light of His glory and grace."* Not only was it necessary for Zechariah to turn, but the Bible says he had to lift up his eyes before he saw the vision. Of course the frustrations and discouragements will come; the problems and cares of this life will always be there; whenever we feel God directing us to turn we will always be faced with seemingly insurmountable obstacles; but we must learn to look above the things of earth. When we cannot see the wood for the trees, let us look above the trees! The view may surprise us!

The third thing it was necessary for Zechariah to do was to look – *"I looked again…I looked up again…"* Now, we may say, this is obvious. If he was prepared to turn and lift up his eyes he would naturally look! But would he? As surprising it may seem, it is possible to face in a particular direction without actually noticing what is in front of us. The view has become so familiar we just don't notice it anymore. It really is possible for us to turn and lift our eyes in the right direction, yet not look. But if we are to be blessed by God by seeing what He wants us to see, then we must be prepared to look when we have turned and lifted up our eyes. Like

Zechariah we may not always like what we see, but we must be prepared to look, to look again, to look up again.

This, then, is the simple lesson the Lord may be wanting to teach us just now. He is waiting every moment of every day to shower us with His blessings, to give us *daily strength for daily living.* Wherever we are, whatever our circumstances, if we are prepared daily to turn, to lift up our eyes, and look, and look again, then those blessing-showers will continue to fall day after day after day!

181

Zechariah 8:23 – Let us go with you, because we have heard that God is with you.

Most Christians regularly attend church to worship God. We say *most* Christians, because we must recognise that there are some professing believers who are not able to physically attend church – the so-called shut-ins, for example, who are prevented because of age or infirmity; and then there are those who are serving others, such as nurses, doctors, carers, policeman, to name but a few. But the majority of Christians make their way to a building set aside for worship, not only on a Sunday but during the week as well, be it a humble hall or a stately cathedral.

The sad fact is that as we look around us on, for instance, a Sunday, we very quickly realise that there is an even greater majority who will not enter a church, neither on that day or any other. In fact, they will give no thought to God at all. Yet it is the responsibility of all Christians to invite and encourage their neighbours to "go with them". All too often, when such an invitation is given, the refusal ranges from a polite, "no, thank you", to a more aggressive, "I wouldn't be seen dead with all those hypocrites!" What a great joy it is when our neighbour accepts our invitation and comes to church with us!

But this verse takes it a stage further. *"Let us go with you, because we have heard that God is with you."* The KJV translation turns the request into a statement: "We will go with you..." How much better it would be, what even greater joy it would give, if our neighbour actually approached us and, not just *asked* if they could come to church with us, but *told* us they were coming! As Christians we often express our regrets that our neighbours have no interest or desire to come with us to church, but can we really blame those neighbours? Might not the fault be in the hands of us as Christians? Have we lived our lives in such a way as to make our Christian Faith attractive to others? Do our neighbours recognise that God is with us in such a way that they will want to come with us without even being asked?

Sadly this is not always the case. If as Christians we lived our lives according to what the Bible says, and base our thoughts and actions on God's Word, then the situation might be very different. How true are the words of the little chorus. *"I am my neighbour's Bible, he reads me when we meet; Today he reads me in my house, tomorrow in the street."* So let us remember that, when we physically go to church, and our neighbours stay at home, the situation is in our hands alone as to whether those neighbours will continue to stay at home, or will say to us, in the words of this verse, *"Let us go with you, because we have heard that God is with you."*

182

Zechariah 14:1,9 – A day of the Lord is coming…The Lord will be king over the whole earth, and his name the only name.

What comfort and encouragement we can receive, what *daily strength for daily living* we can obtain, from the fact that, *"A day of the Lord is coming."* All through the Scriptures, both in the Old Testament and the New, we find promise after promise of Christ's Second Coming. He has promised His return and we can have every confidence that He *will* return, because He has always kept His promises, and He always will. As someone once said, "The Lord promised it, the Bible said it, I believe it, and that settles it!"

But the verse continues, *"The Lord will be king over the whole earth, and his name the only name."* This, of course, is only one of the many Old Testaments references to Jesus Christ. Another one is found in *Daniel 7:13,14* – "In my vision…there before me was one like a son of man, coming with the clouds of heaven. He approached the Ancient of Days and was led into his presence. He was given authority, glory and sovereign power; all peoples, nations and men of every language worshipped him. His dominion is an everlasting dominion that will not pass away, and his kingdom is one that will never be destroyed." What awesome words!

The New Testament continues with some equally awesome words. "God exalted him to the highest place and gave him the name that is above every name, that at the name of Jesus every knee should bow, in heaven and on earth and under the earth, and every tongue confess that Jesus Christ is Lord, to the glory of God the Father" *(Philippians 2:9-11).* So how can all these verses, and many more not quoted here, give us *daily strength for daily living*? What is this verse in *Zechariah*, and others in the Old Testament, and echoed now in the New Testament, telling us? Three things!

Firstly, it confirms for us that Jesus Christ *will* return, as He has promised, although we do not know the exact day or time, only that, *"A day of the Lord is coming."* Secondly, it proclaims to us that when He comes, every knee will bow and every tongue will confess that Jesus Christ is Lord and that, *"The Lord will be king over the whole earth, and his name the only name."* Thirdly, it reveals to us the importance of being spiritually ready to meet Him when He does come by making Him King of our lives now, by receiving *daily strength for daily living* from His Word, and by living every moment of every day in the light of His return.

183

Malachi 3:17 – They will be mine, says the Lord Almighty, in the day when I make up my treasured possession.

The use of the word *Christian* really began as a nickname in a place called Antioch. A group of people lived their lives in such a way, showing the world that they not only believed in Jesus Christ but that they actually belonged to Him, that the citizens of that great city linked them to Christ by using His name – *Christ*ian. The Bible uses various names to describe people who belong to God. Down through the ages they have been referred to as saints (although some may not have always been as saintly as they might have been!) and others as servants of God. Then there are those who are referred to as disciples, a word which really means a disciplined follower, and Jesus Himself called others His friends.

All these words – Christian, saint, servant, disciple, friend – and many others beside, all describe a sense of belonging. In this verse God uses another word for those who are His, who belong to Him. He describes them as His "treasured possession" – what a delightful description, although we have to confess that we like the KJV translation of this verse, where God describes His own as "my jewels". In any case, for many, their jewels are their treasured possessions. Just as people today place great value on their jewels – some even have them insured for many thousands of pounds or dollars (or whatever currency is used in any particular country!), or have them locked away in a bank vault for safe-keeping – so God values those of us who belong to Him as jewels, as treasured possessions.

He has created us, He has fashioned us, and we are precious to Him. Man has produced simulated diamonds and pearls, sapphires and rubies, and a host of other precious gems, which sometimes only the experts can decipher from the real thing, but he has never been able to create the genuine article. No man has been able to make a Christian, either. The God of nature alone has been able to create genuine jewels; likewise, only that same God can make a Christian. The Bible also says that, "we are God's workmanship, created in Christ Jesus" *(Ephesians 2:10).* Like jewels, we are all different, even though we have all been created by the same Craftsman.

Although we are precious to Him – treasured possessions – of great value, and in a sense heavily insured by the death and resurrection of Jesus Christ (perhaps we could call it our insurance policy to eternal life, although it is really much, much more than that!), God does not expect us to be hidden away in some bank vault. He wants us to radiate His beauty in the world, to witness to all of His perfect craftsmanship in us, to reveal that we are His jewels, His treasured possessions, that we belong to Him, then one day when He comes to take us to be with Himself, as He has promised, He will recognise us as His jewels, as His treasured possessions, and we will then realise just how precious we really are to Him.

In other words, as we used to sing in Sunday school, *"When He cometh to make up His jewels, all His jewels, precious jewels, His loved and His own, like the stars of the morning, His bright crown adorning, they shall shine in their beauty, bright gems for His crown."* And that just about says it all!

A New and Living Way

Originally published in 1979, this new edition of *A New and Living Way* has been revised, up-dated and substantially expanded with the addition of several new chapters, yet retaining its original purpose of providing a devotional meditation on the need for a deeper spiritual life in the Christian Church today. Why a new and living way? Because the thing most needed in the Christian Church today, and sadly the thing I find so often lacking, as in my ministry I become involved with people from all denominational backgrounds, is a longing for a deeper spiritual experience of Almighty God. The author first wrote this in 1979, and the situation has not changed in the early years of the Twenty-First Century. If anything, it has become worse. There is a need, too, for a much more positive commitment to the Lord Jesus Christ, a going-on with Jesus in the fullness of the Holy Spirit. This book seeks to address in various ways the need for a deeper spiritual life, highlighting the importance of getting our priorities and our purposes right, the need to seek for an added meaning to our whole life in the Twenty-First Century.

ISBN: 0-7552-0259-7

Price: £5.99 [UK]
$9.95 [US]

Also published by AuthorsOnLine Ltd

Back To Basics

The Church today is in such an unholy mess—at least, in the United Kingdom it is!—so much so that unless we get back to basics and begin to believe and put into practise what the First Century Church believed and practised, then the Twenty-First Century Church will continue to decline and drive itself into oblivion. Based on the Book of the Acts, *Back To Basics* presents a thought-provoking, stimulating and challenging argument. The statement upon which this book is based is: *If we believe what the first Christians believed, we will achieve what they achieved.* The author is firmly convinced that, if we are prepared to believe what the first Christians believed, prove to God that we are serious about trying to achieve what they achieved, and get back to basics—to believe and practice what the Bible actually says—He will turn that flame into a raging prairie fire.

ISBN: 0-7552-0256-2

Price: £5.99 [UK]
$9.95 [US]

Also published by AuthorsOnLine Ltd

Grappling With Grace

Based on an original doctrinal study of God's grace, which started in the 1960's, *Grappling With Grace* is a book about the amazing grace of God and its relevance in the world today. Living as we do in an age of international uncertainty and deteriorating moral standards, the infinite and amazing grace of God needs to take on a relevance vital to every living soul in the present depressing and declining situation of the Twenty-First Century. At first glance *Grappling With Grace* may seem a rather strange title for a book seeking to understand something about the grace of God. Yet, is it? For example, do we know *exactly* what we mean by the word "grace", apart from the fact that it means "favour"? Even if we add the word "infinite" – *infinite grace*, which more accurately describes the grace of *God* – we could still be struggling to fully comprehend all that grace has to offer to enrich our spiritual experience. So to try and bring some understanding into our lives our *struggling* may have to translated into *grappling!* If the relevance of God's grace is to have any meaning for us at all, then we need to understand what we mean when we talk about it. Because of the vastness of the subject, to help our understanding of grace, its concept and its context, we have to grapple with it – which the reader is invited to do in this book.

ISBN: 0-7552-0257-0

Price: £5.50 [UK]
$9.95 [US]

Also published by AuthorsOnLine Ltd

In All Thy Ways
A Christian Novel

By acknowledging the Lord in all her ways, as Proverbs 3:6 exhorted her to do, May Eddington found He directed her paths from the ancestral home and an aristocratic lifestyle in Yorkshire to the slums of Liverpool, where she started a children's mission work, which was brought to an abrupt end by the May blitz of 1941 with disastrous consequences, yet dramatically demonstrating to May that the Lord was still directing her paths and there was still a work for her to do for Him as long as she continued to acknowledge Him in all her ways. Set in the years just prior to the Second World War, and the early years of the war itself, the story traces the loves and hates, the joys and fears, the triumphs and tragedies, affecting several Liverpool families, as well as May herself, through which the love of God is shown to be at work in every situation. Although a work of fiction, the story is based on fact – *the Bible* – and seeks to use this literary form to preach the Gospel of Jesus Christ, who Himself said, "I am the Way" (John 14:6).

ISBN: 0-7552-0258-9

Price: £8.99 [UK]
$13.95 [US]

Also published by AuthorsOnLine Ltd

Printed in the United Kingdom
by Lightning Source UK Ltd.
125255UK00001B/67/A

9 780755 202799